Othello 4 is a work of fiction. Names, characters, places, and incidents are the products of the author's imagination or are used fictitiously. Any rsemblance to actual events, locales, or persons, living or dead, is entirely coincidential.

2005 Del Rey® Books Trade Paperback Edition

Published in the United States by Del Rey® Books, an imprint of Random House Publishing Group, a division of Random House, Inc., New York.

Del Rey is a registered trademark and the Del Rey colophon is a trademark of Random House, Inc.

Originally published in Japan by Kodansha Ltd., Tokyo in 2003. North American publication rights arranged through Kodansha Ltd.

Library of Congress Control Number: 2004096774

ISBN 0-345-48000-7

Printed in the United States of America

www.delreymanga.com

9 8 7 6 5 4 3 2

First Edition

Translator and adapter—William Flanagan
Lettering—Michaelis/Carpelis Design

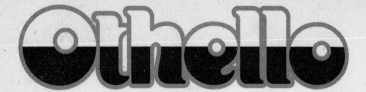

4

Satomi Ikezawa

TRANSLATED AND ADAPTED BY
William Flanagan

LETTERED BY
Michaelis/Carpelis Design

BALLANTINE BOOKS • NEW YORK

Contents

Honorifics

Throughout the Del Rey Manga books, you will find Japanese honorifics left intact in the translations. For those not familiar with how the Japanese use honorifics and, more importantly, how they differ from American honorifics, we present this brief overview.

Politeness has always been a critical facet of Japanese culture. Ever since the feudal era, when Japan was a highly stratified society, use of honorifics—which can be defined as polite speech that indicates relationship or status—has played an essential role in the Japanese language. When addressing someone in Japanese, an honorific usually takes the form of a suffix attached to one's name (example: "Asuna-san"), or as a title at the end of one's name or in place of the name itself (example: "Negi-sensei," or simply "Sensei!").

Honorifics can be expressions of respect or endearment. In the context of manga and anime, honorifics give insight into the nature of the relationship between characters. Many translations into English leave out these important honorifics, and therefore distort the "feel" of the original Japanese. Because Japanese honorifics contain nuances that English honorifics lack, it is our policy at Del Rey not to translate them. Here, instead, is a guide to some of the honorifics you may encounter in Del Rey Manga.

-san: This is the most common honorific and is equivalent to Mr., Miss, Ms., or Mrs. It is the all-purpose honorific and can be used in any situation where politeness is required.

-sama: This is one level higher than "-san" It is used to confer great respect.

-dono: This comes from the word "tono," which means "lord." It is an even higher level than "-sama" and confers utmost respect.

-kun: This suffix is used at the end of boys' names to express familiarity or endearment. It is also sometimes used by men among friends, or when addressing someone younger or of a lower station.

-chan: This is used to express endearment, mostly toward girls. It is also used for little boys, pets, and even among lovers. It gives a sense of childish cuteness.

Bozu: This is an informal way to refer to a boy, similar to the English term "kid" or "squirt."

Sempai: This title suggests that the addressee is one's senior in a group or organization. It is most often used in a school setting, where underclassmen refer to their upperclassmen as "sempai." It can also be used in the workplace, such as when a newer employee addresses an employee who has seniority in the company.

Kohai: This is the opposite of "sempai" and is used toward underclassmen in school or newcomers in the workplace. It connotes that the addressee is of a lower station.

Sensei: Literally meaning "one who has come before," this title is used for teachers, doctors, or masters of any profession or art.

[blank]: Usually forgotten in these lists, but perhaps the most significant difference between Japanese and English. The lack of honorific means that the speaker has permission to address the person in a very intimate way. Usually, only family, spouses, or very close friends have this kind of permission. Known as *yobisute,* it can be gratifying when someone who has earned the intimacy starts to call one by one's name without an honorific. But when that intimacy hasn't been earned, it can also be very insulting.

A Note from the Author

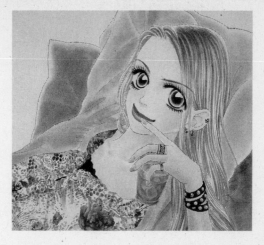

My father once said to me, "You're an
analog girl." But for the past severel years,
I've lived my life relying heavily on my
personal computer. At work, I use it for
checking my facts and doing image process-
ing for my manga pages. In my personal life,
I use it for e-mail and the net (shopping,
almost exclusively). Recently, I've developed a
hobby—to upgrade and improve my
computer! It's sooo fun!

OTHELLO
オセロ。

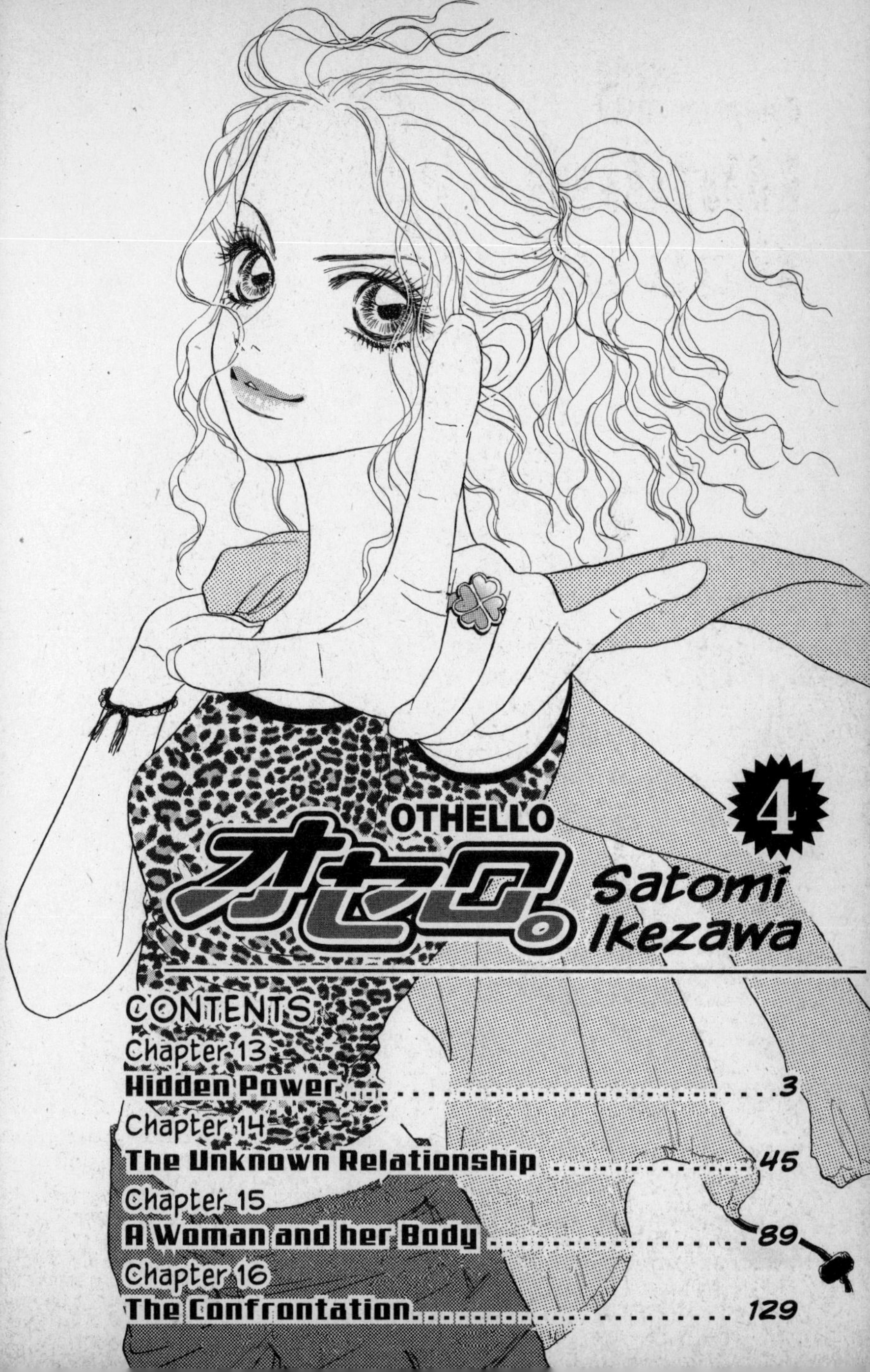

OTHELLO
オセロ。

4

Satomi Ikezawa

CONTENTS

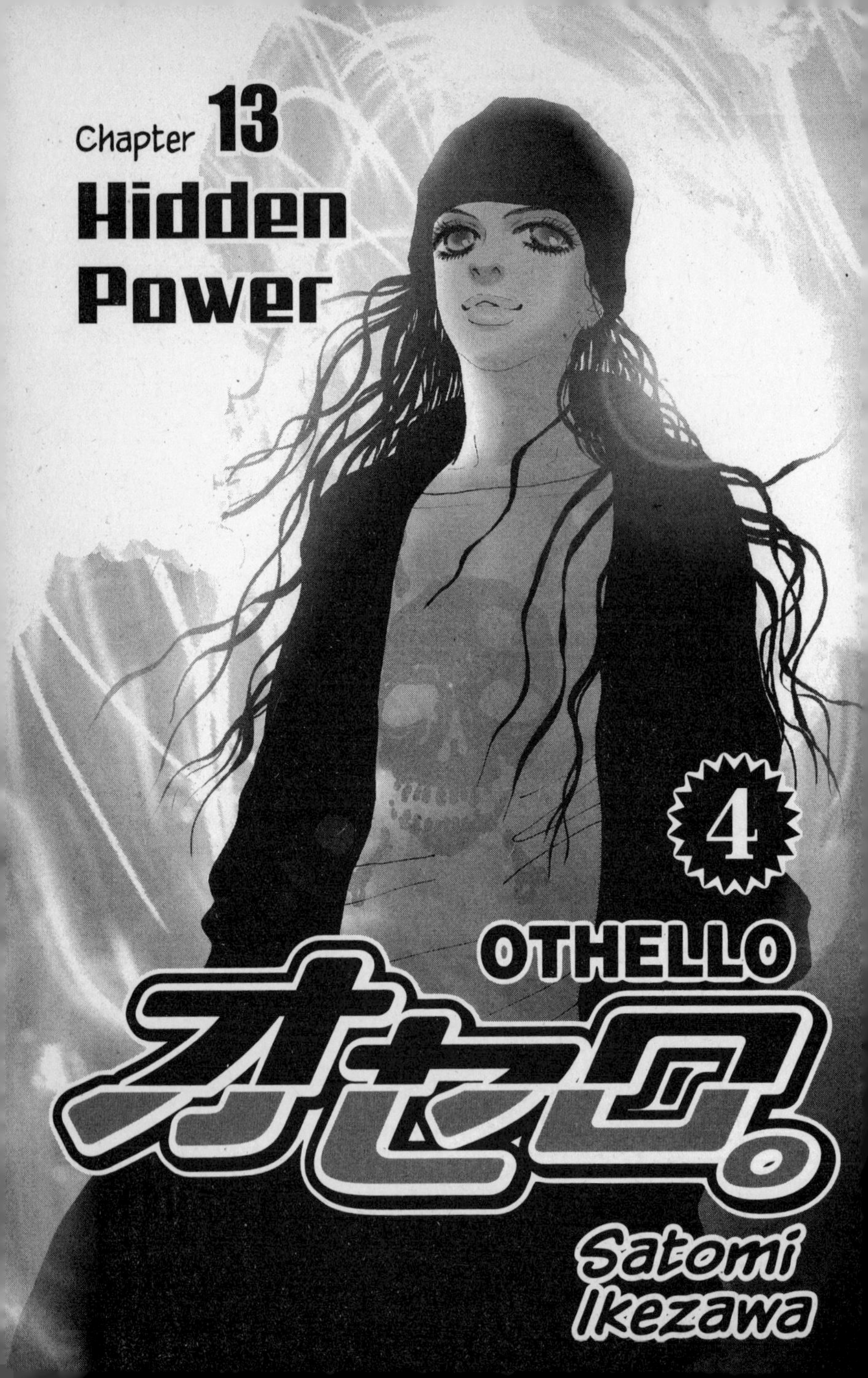
Chapter 13
Hidden Power
4
OTHELLO
オセロ。
Satomi Ikezawa

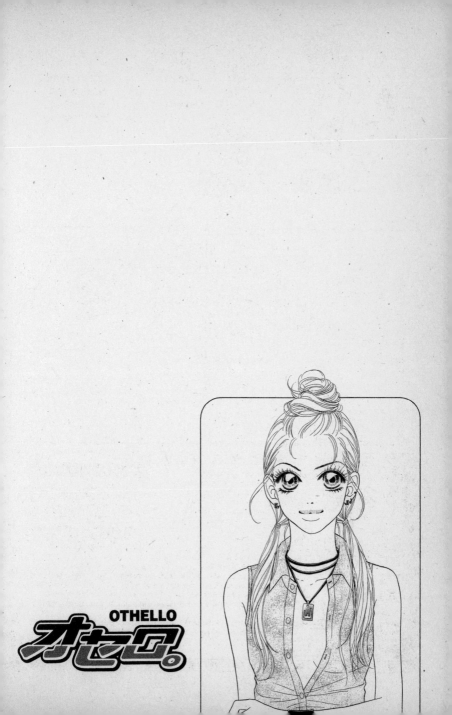

OTHELLO

オセロ。

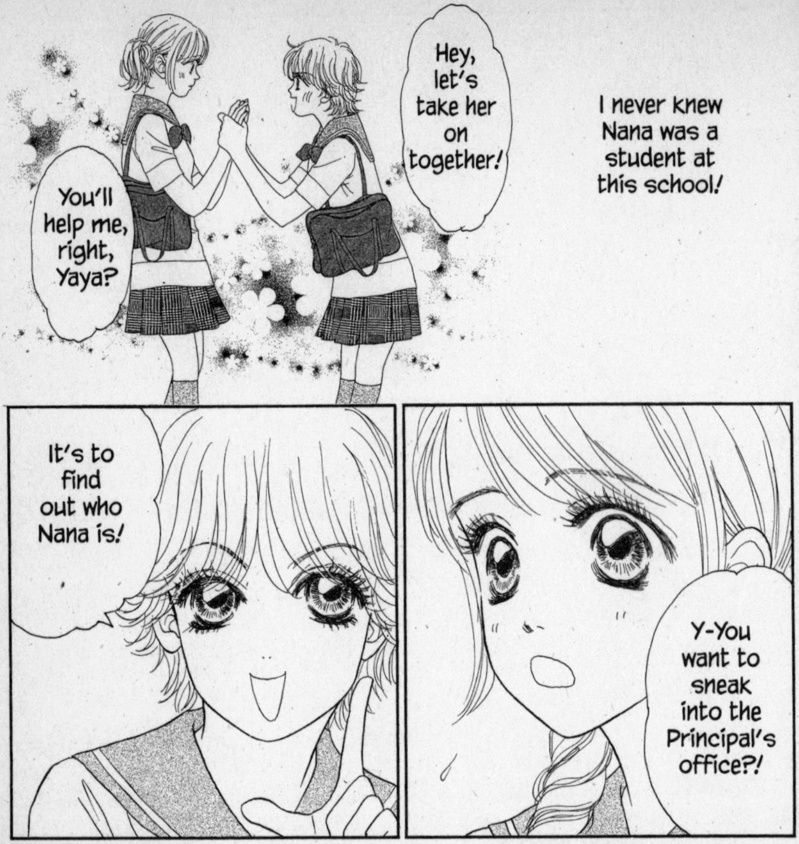
I never knew Nana was a student at this school!
Hey, let's take her on together!
You'll help me, right, Yaya?
Y-You want to sneak into the Principal's office?!
It's to find out who Nana is!

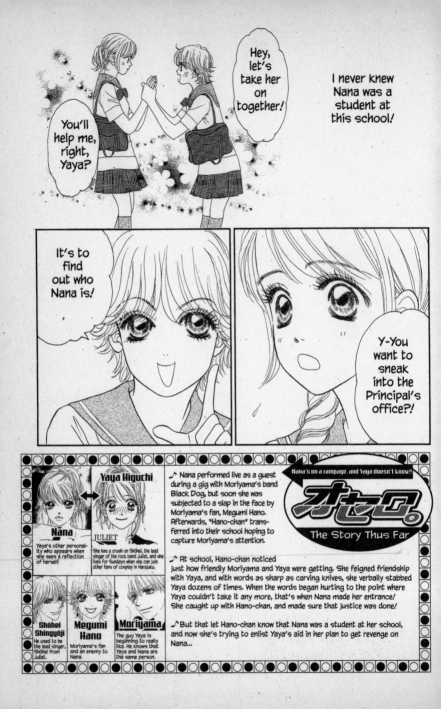

Nana's on a rampage, and Yaya doesn't know!!

オセロ。

The Story Thus Far

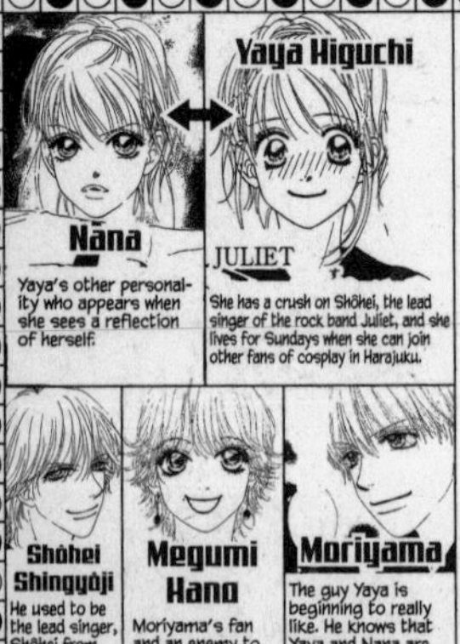
Yaya Higuchi
JULIET
She has a crush on Shôhei, the lead singer of the rock band Juliet, and she lives for Sundays when she can join other fans of cosplay in Harajuku.
Nana
Yaya's other personality who appears when she sees a reflection of herself.
Moriyama
The guy Yaya is beginning to really like. He knows that Yaya and Nana are the same person.
Megumi Hano
Moriyama's fan and an enemy to Nana.
Shôhei Shingyôji
He used to be the lead singer, Shôhei from Juliet.

♪ Nana performed live as a guest during a gig with Moriyama's band Black Dog, but soon she was subjected to a slap in the face by Moriyama's fan, Megumi Hano. Afterwards, "Hano-chan" transferred into their school hoping to capture Moriyama's attention.

♪ At school, Hano-chan noticed just how friendly Moriyama and Yaya were getting. She feigned friendship with Yaya, and with words as sharp as carving knives, she verbally stabbed Yaya dozens of times. When the words began hurting to the point where Yaya couldn't take it any more, that's when Nana made her entrance! She caught up with Hano-chan, and made sure that justice was done!

♪ But that let Hano-chan know that Nana was a student at her school, and now she's trying to enlist Yaya's aid in her plan to get revenge on Nana...

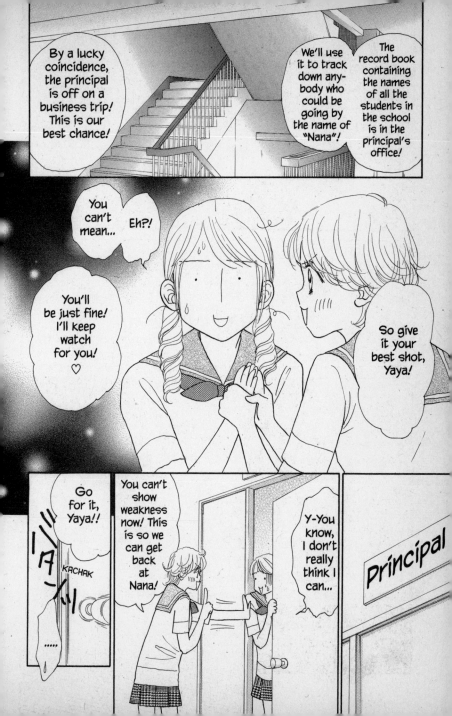

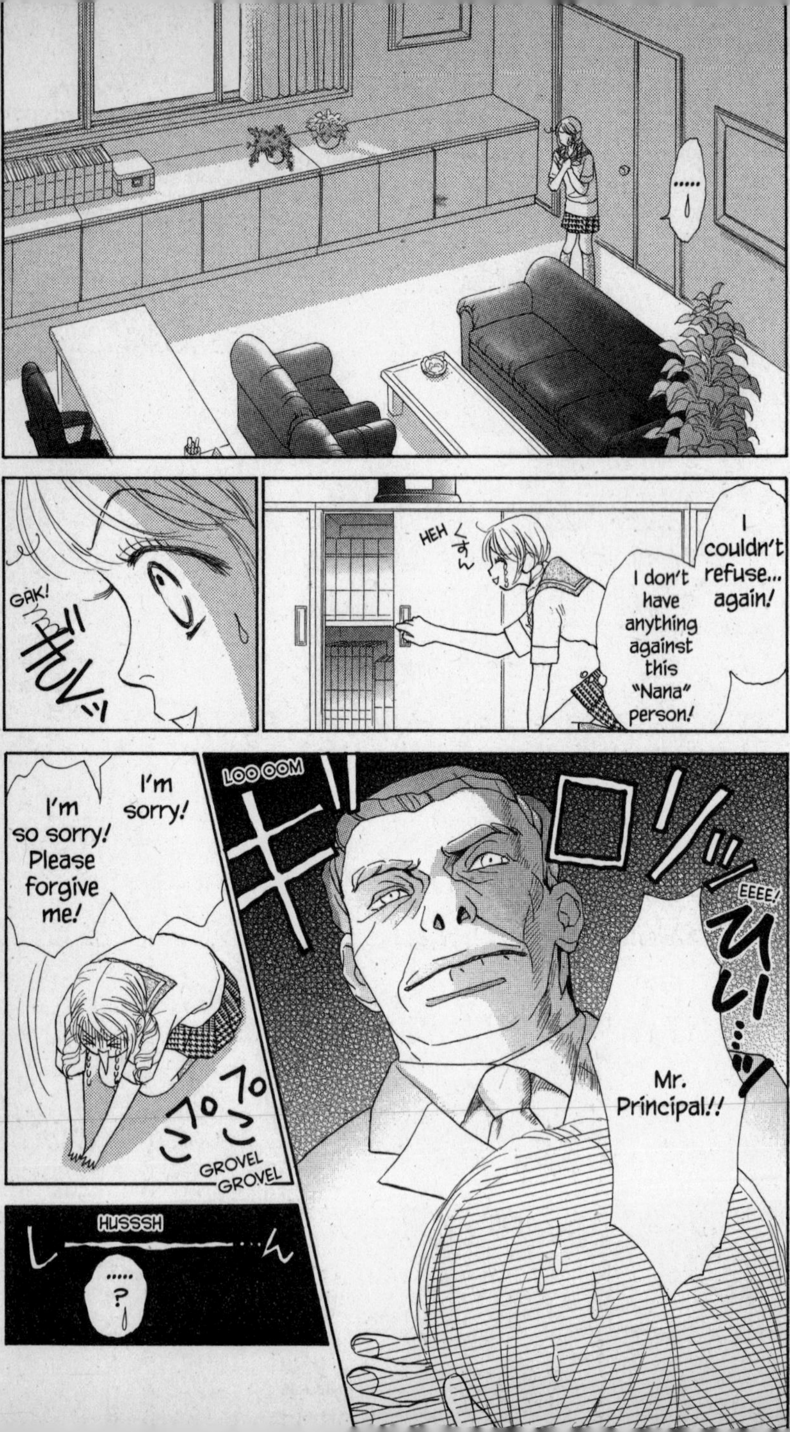

.....!
I couldn't refuse... again!
I don't have anything against this "Nana" person!
HEH くすん
GAK!
LOO OOM
ギロッ
EEEE!
Mr. Principal!!
I'm sorry!
I'm so sorry! Please forgive me!
ぺこぺこ
GROVEL GROVEL
HUSSSH
.....?

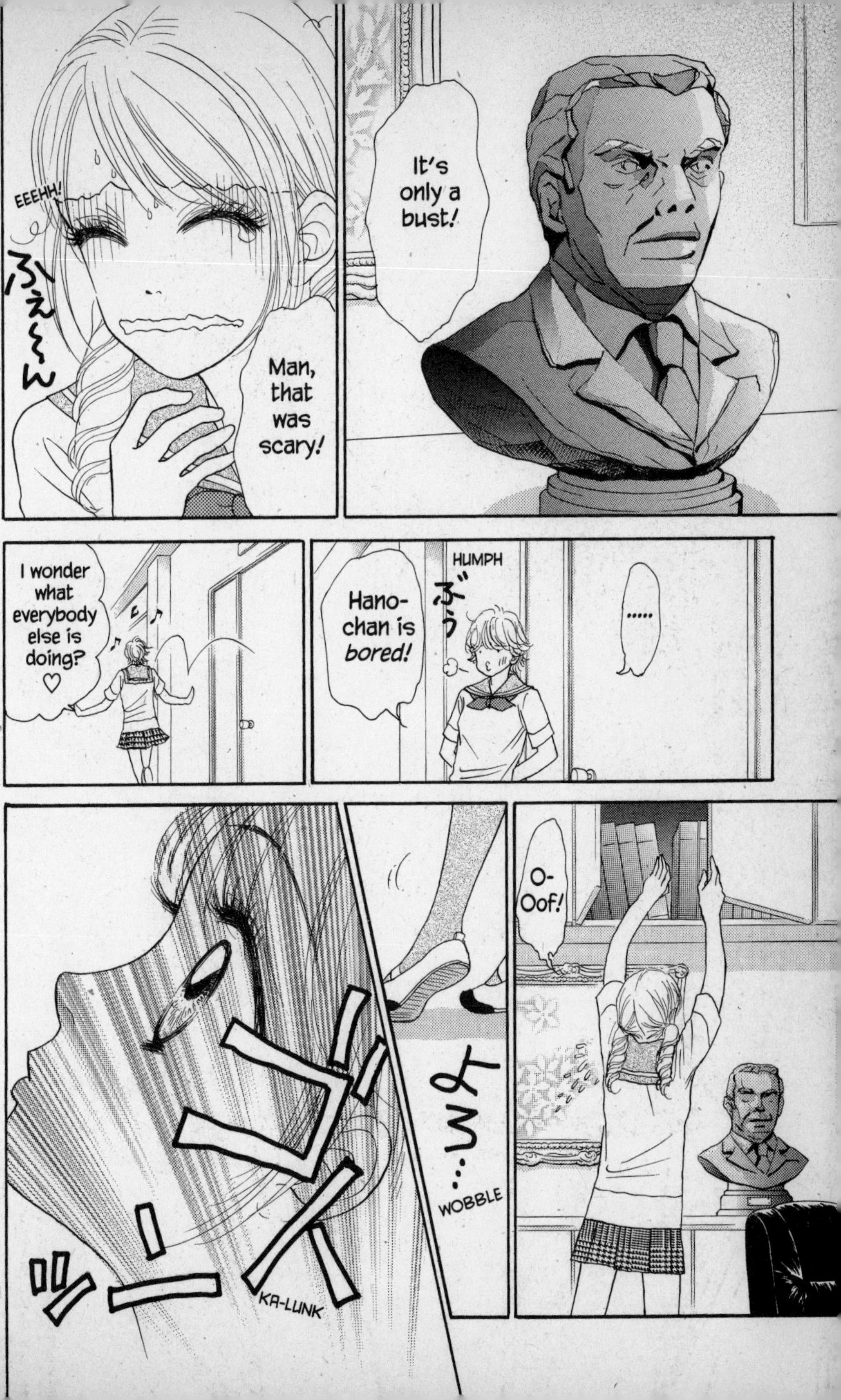
It's only a bust!
EEEHH!
ふえ〜〜ん
Man, that was scary!
.....
HUMPH
ぶう
Hano-chan is *bored!*
I wonder what everybody else is doing? ♡
O-Oof!
よろ…
WOBBLE
KA-LUNK

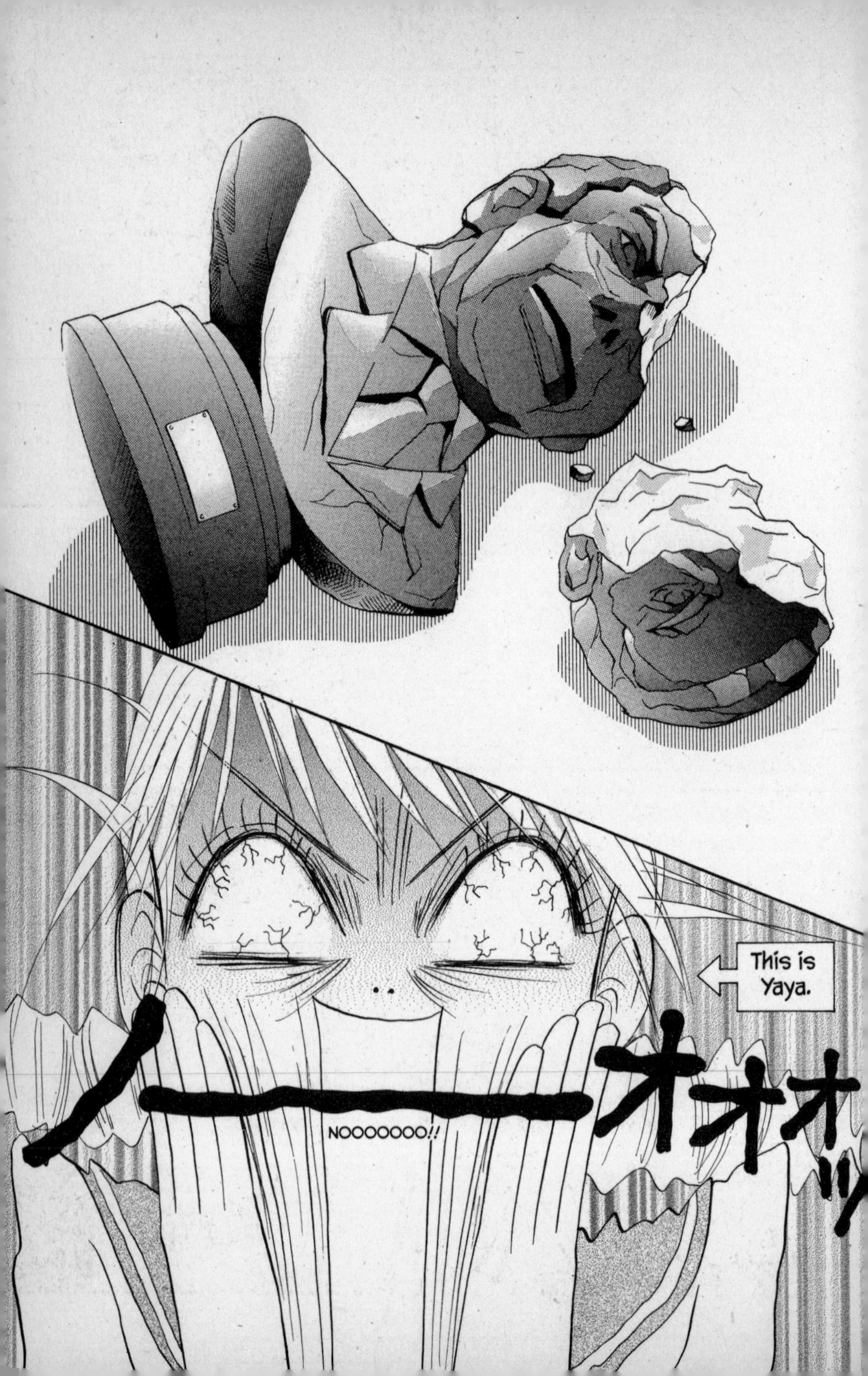
This is Yaya.
ノーーオオオッ
NOOOOOOO!!

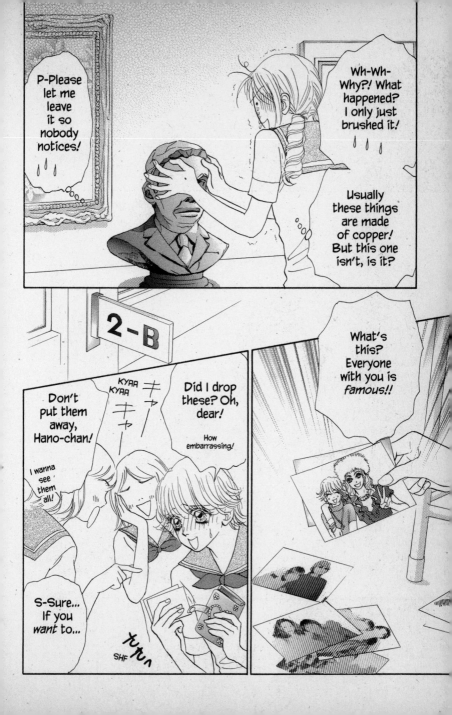

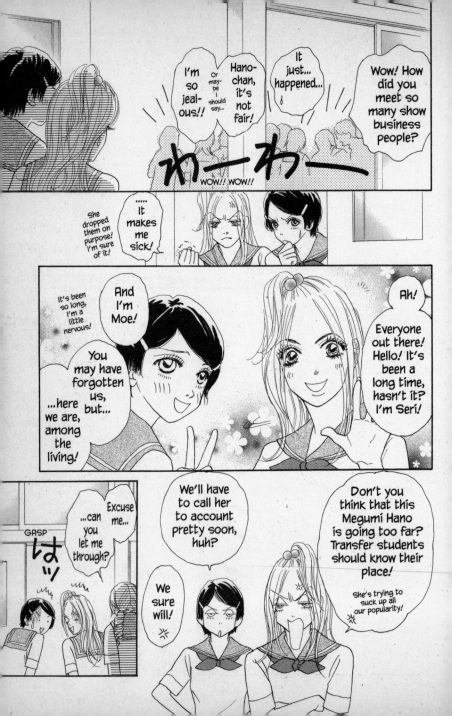

I'm so jeal-ous!! Or may-be I should say... Hano-chan, it's not fair!

It just... happened...

Wow! How did you meet so many show business people?

わーわー
WOW!! WOW!!

.....It makes me sick!

She dropped them on purpose! I'm sure of it!

And I'm Moe!

It's been so long, I'm a little nervous!

You may have forgotten us, but...

...here we are, among the living!

Ah!

Everyone out there! Hello! It's been a long time, hasn't it? I'm Seri!

...can you let me through?

Excuse me...

GASP
はッ

We'll have to call her to account pretty soon, huh?

We sure will!

Don't you think that this Megumi Hano is going too far? Transfer students should know their place!

She's trying to suck up all our popularity!

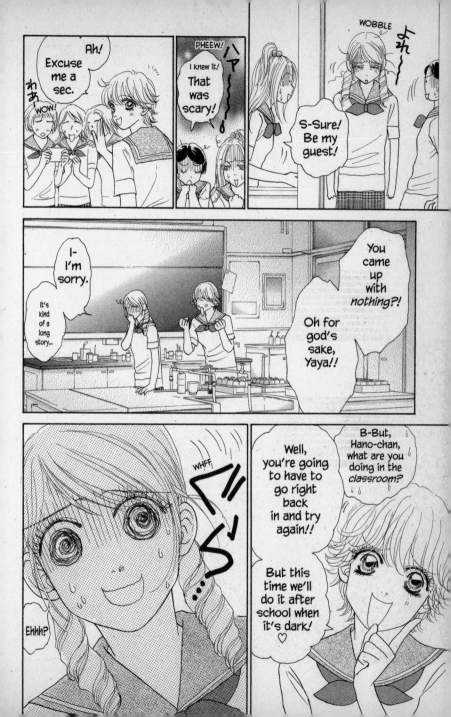

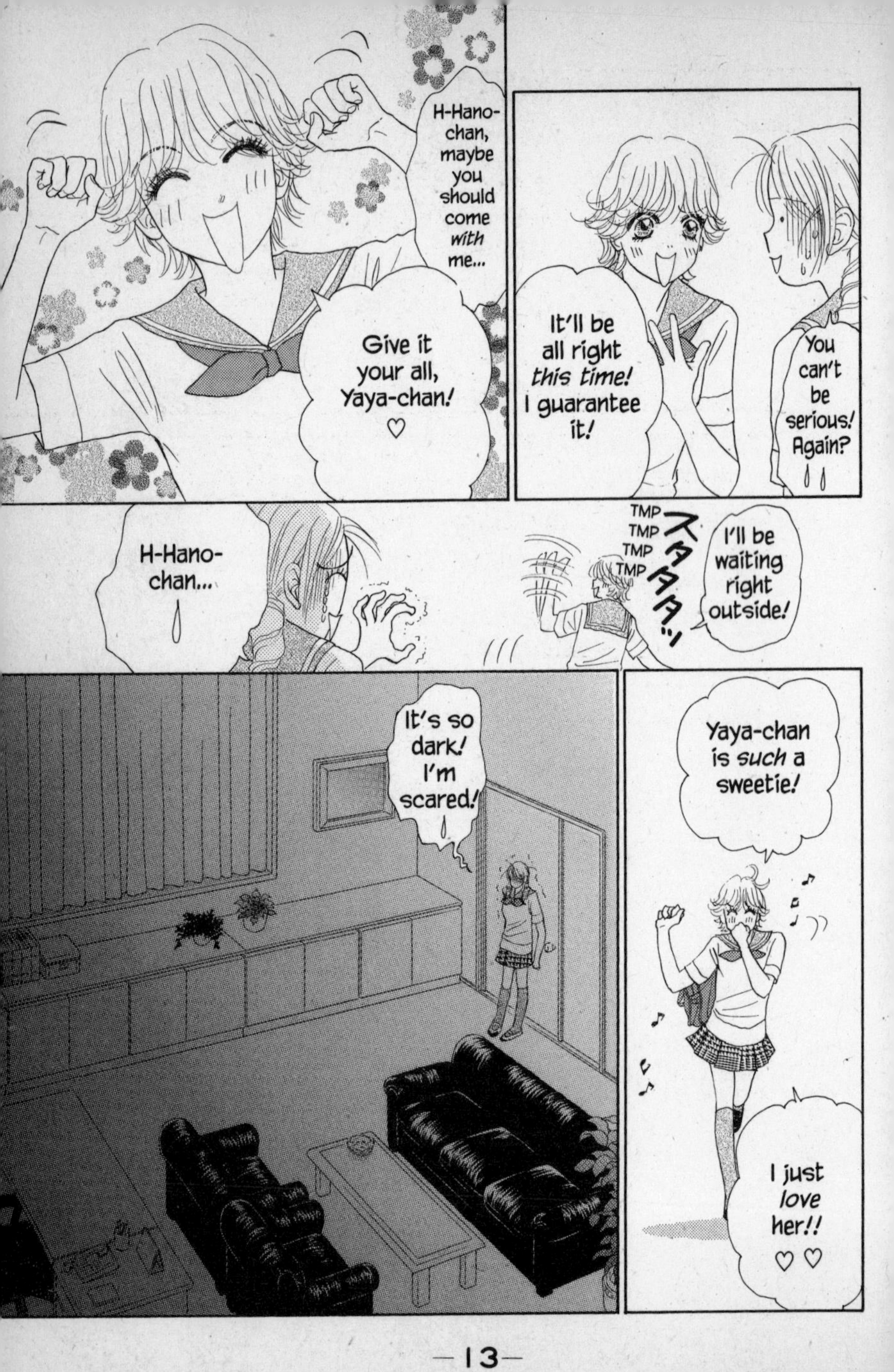
You can't be serious! Again?
It'll be all right *this time!* I guarantee it!
H-Hano-chan, maybe you should come *with* me...
Give it your all, Yaya-chan! ♡
I'll be waiting right outside!
TMP TMP TMP TMP
スタタタッ
H-Hano-chan...
Yaya-chan is *such* a sweetie!
I just *love* her!! ♡ ♡
It's so dark! I'm scared!

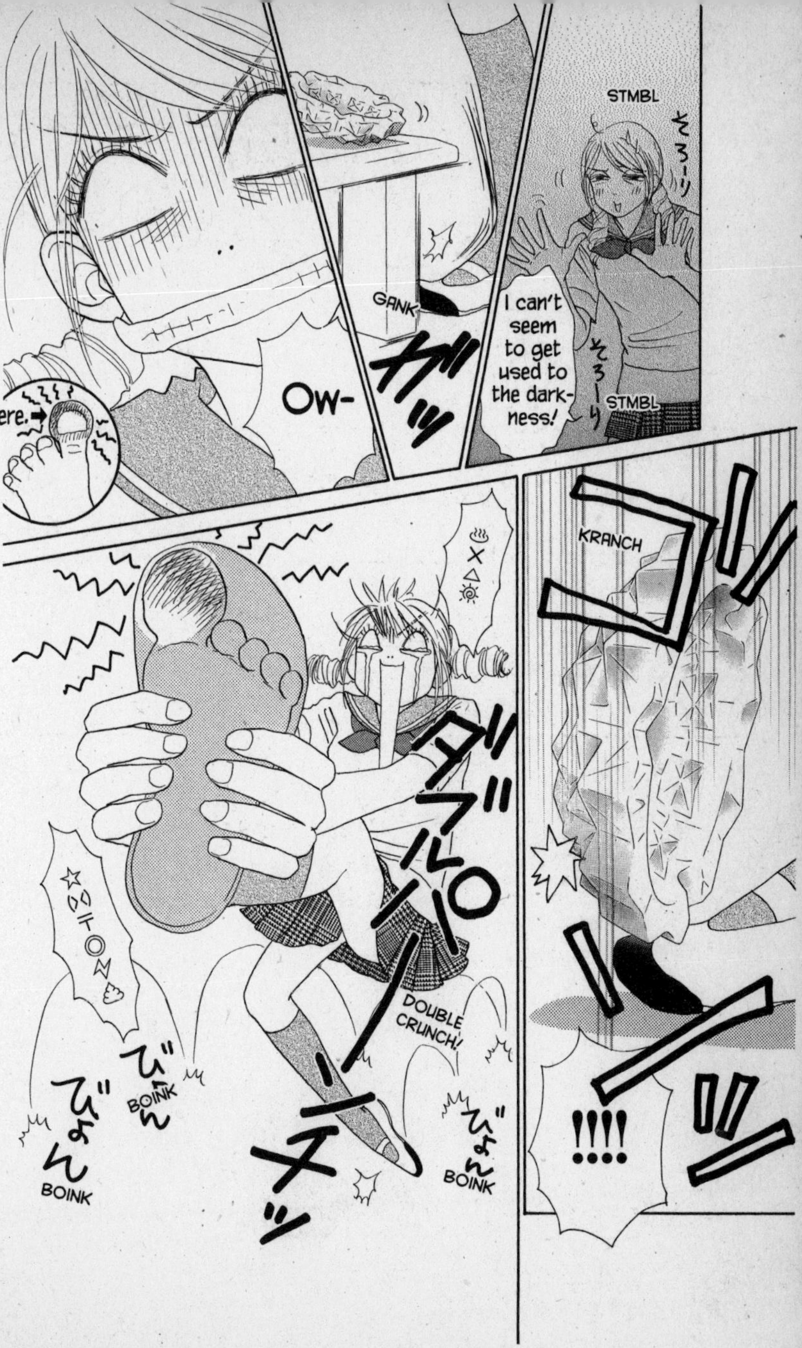
STMBL
そろーり
I can't seem to get used to the darkness!
そろーり
STMBL
GANK
OW-
Here.
KRANCH
!!!!
DOUBLE CRUNCH!
びょん
BOINK
びょん
BOINK
びょん
BOINK

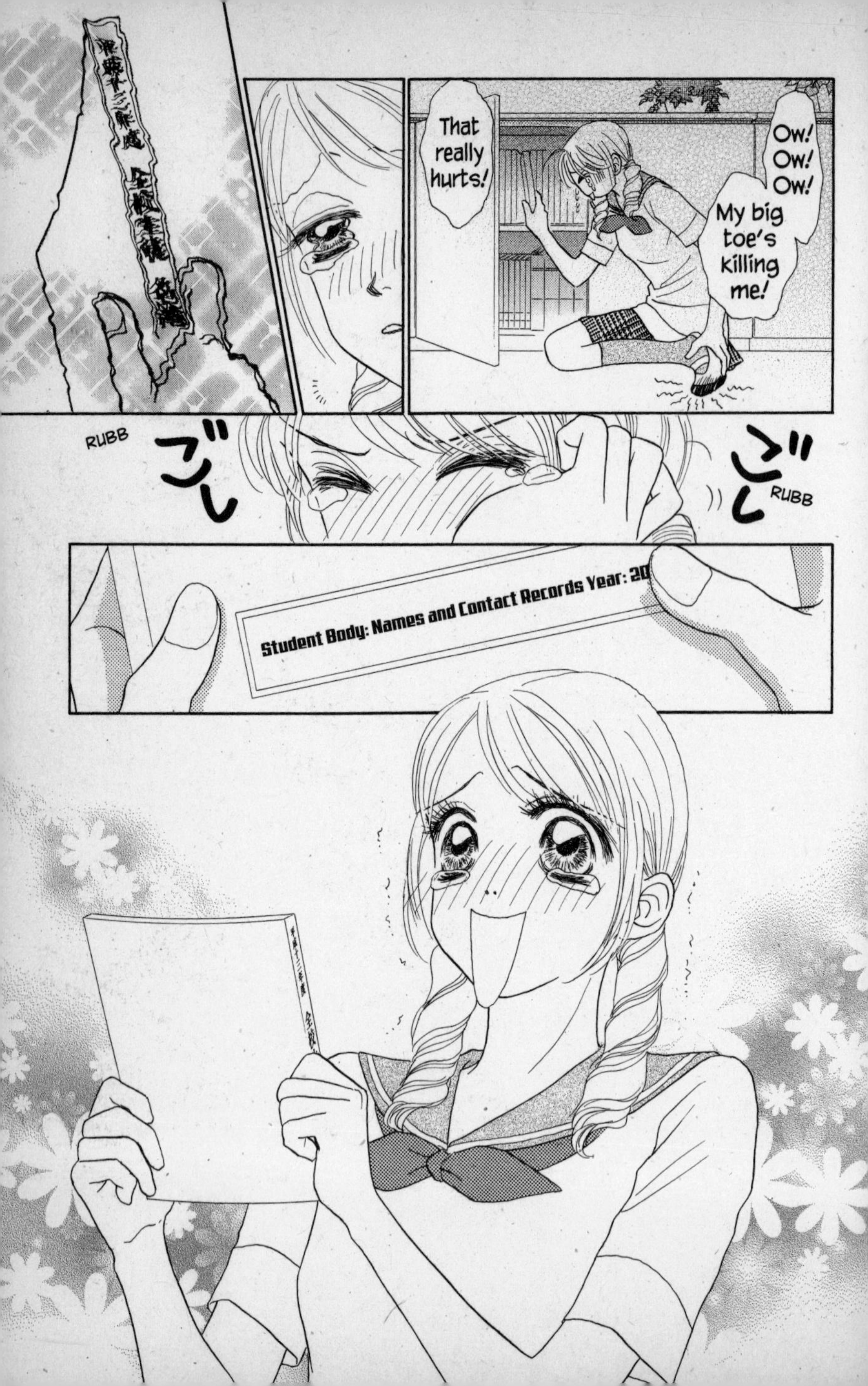
Ow! Ow! Ow!
My big toe's killing me!
That really hurts!
ごし
RUBB
ごし
RUBB
Student Body: Names and Contact Records Year: 20

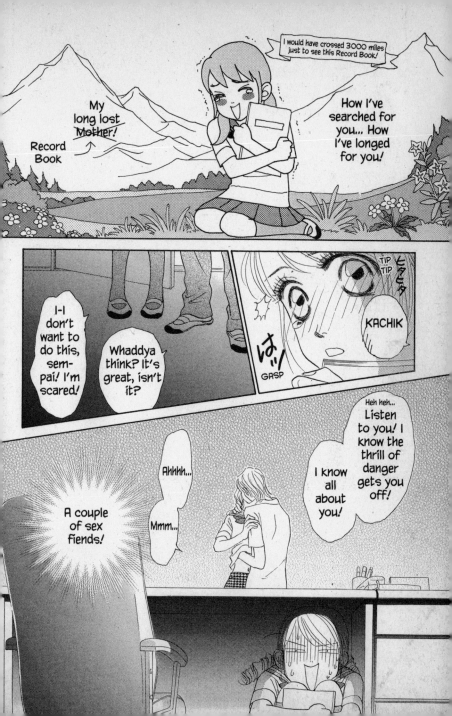

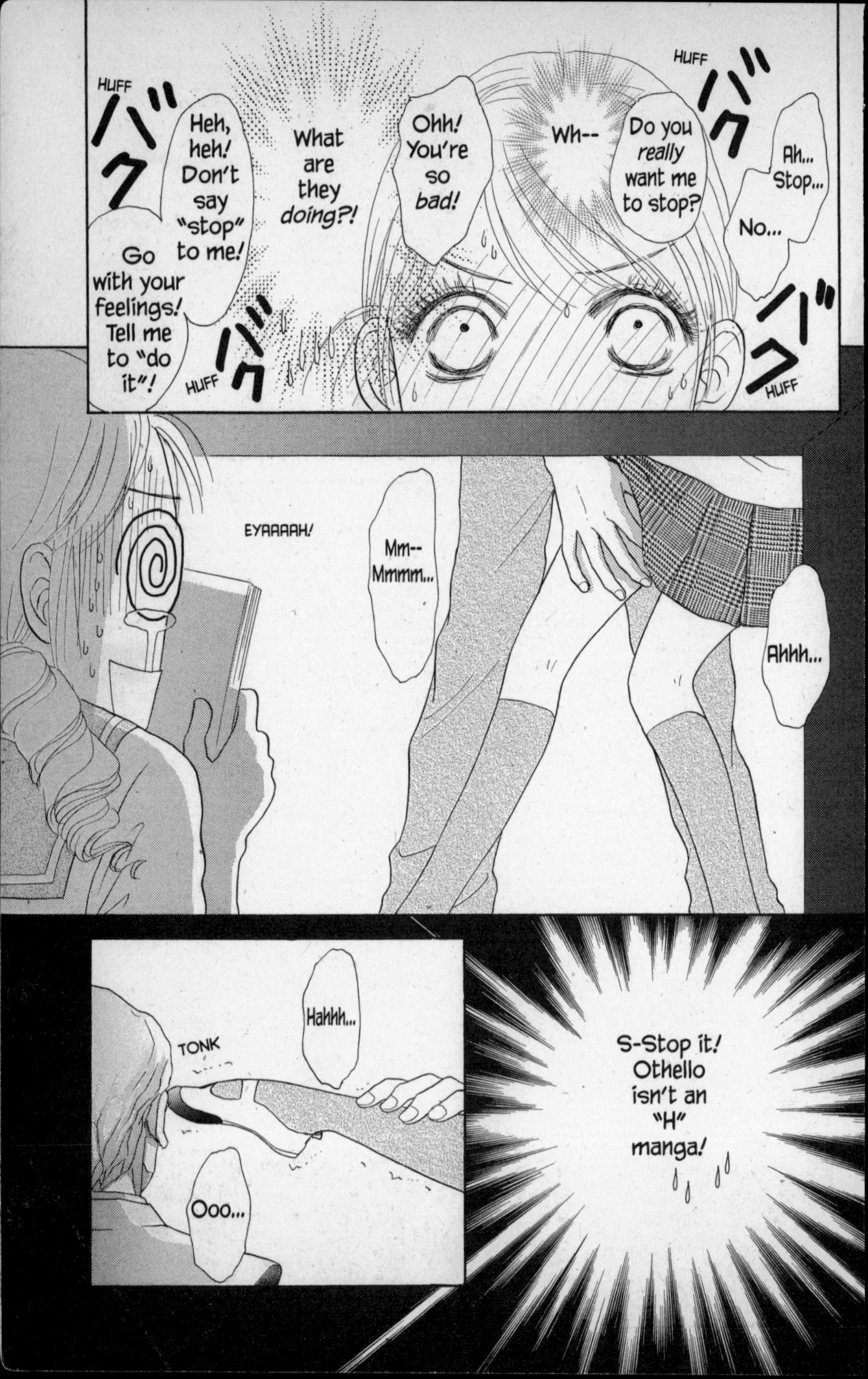
HUFF
バク
Ah... Stop...
No...
バク
HUFF
Do you really want me to stop?
Wh--
Ohh! You're so bad!
What are they doing?!
Heh, heh! Don't say "stop" to me!
Go with your feelings! Tell me to "do it"!
バク
HUFF
HUFF
バク
Ahhh...
Mm-- Mmmm...
EYAAAAH!
S-Stop it! Othello isn't an "H" manga!
Hahhh...
TONK
Ooo...

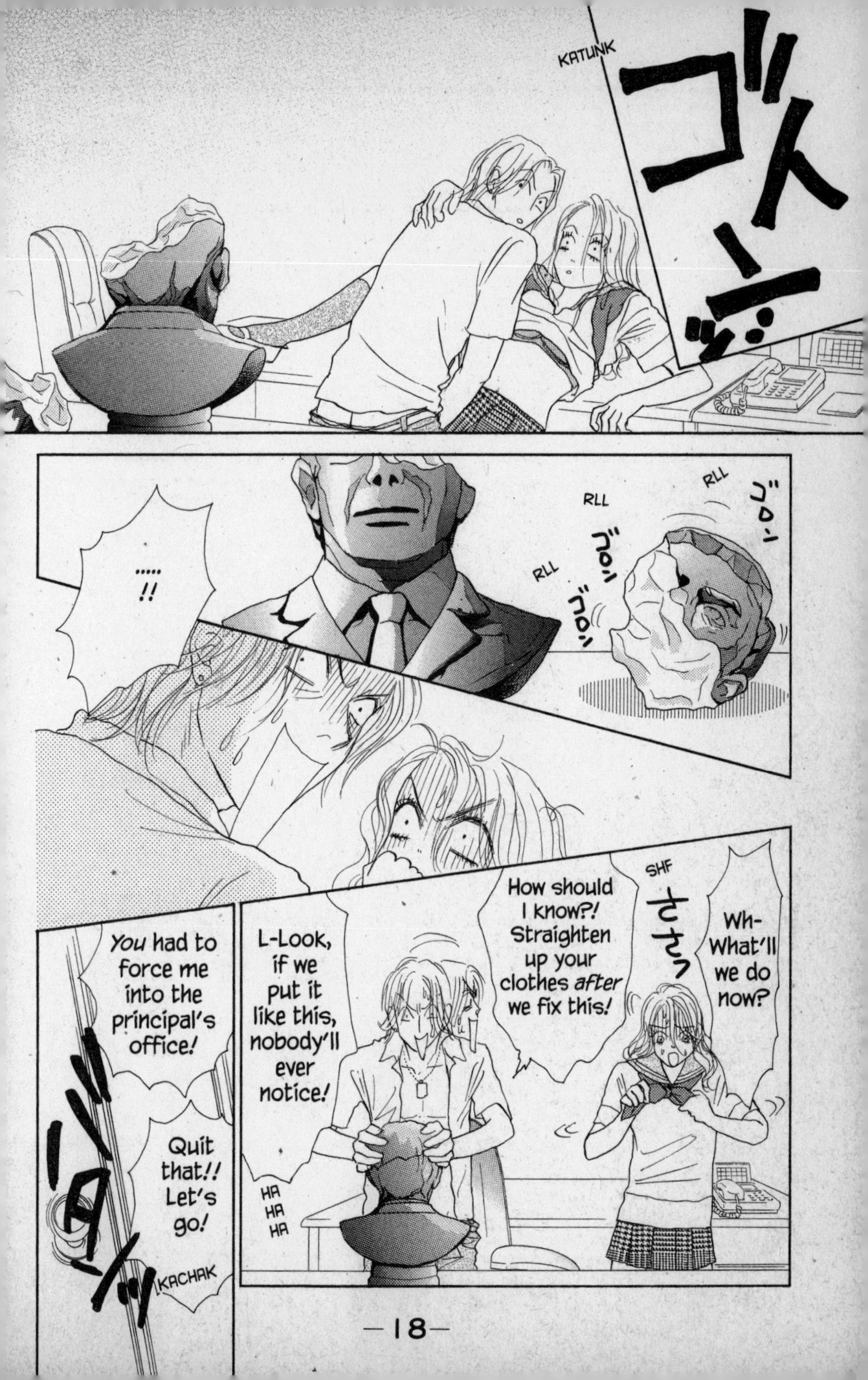
KATUNK
ゴトーンッ
RLL
ゴロン
RLL
ゴロン
RLL
ゴロン
.....
!!
Wh- What'll we do now?
SHF
さっ
How should I know?! Straighten up your clothes *after* we fix this!
L-Look, if we put it like this, nobody'll ever notice!
HA HA HA
You had to force me into the principal's office!
Quit that!! Let's go!
KACHAK

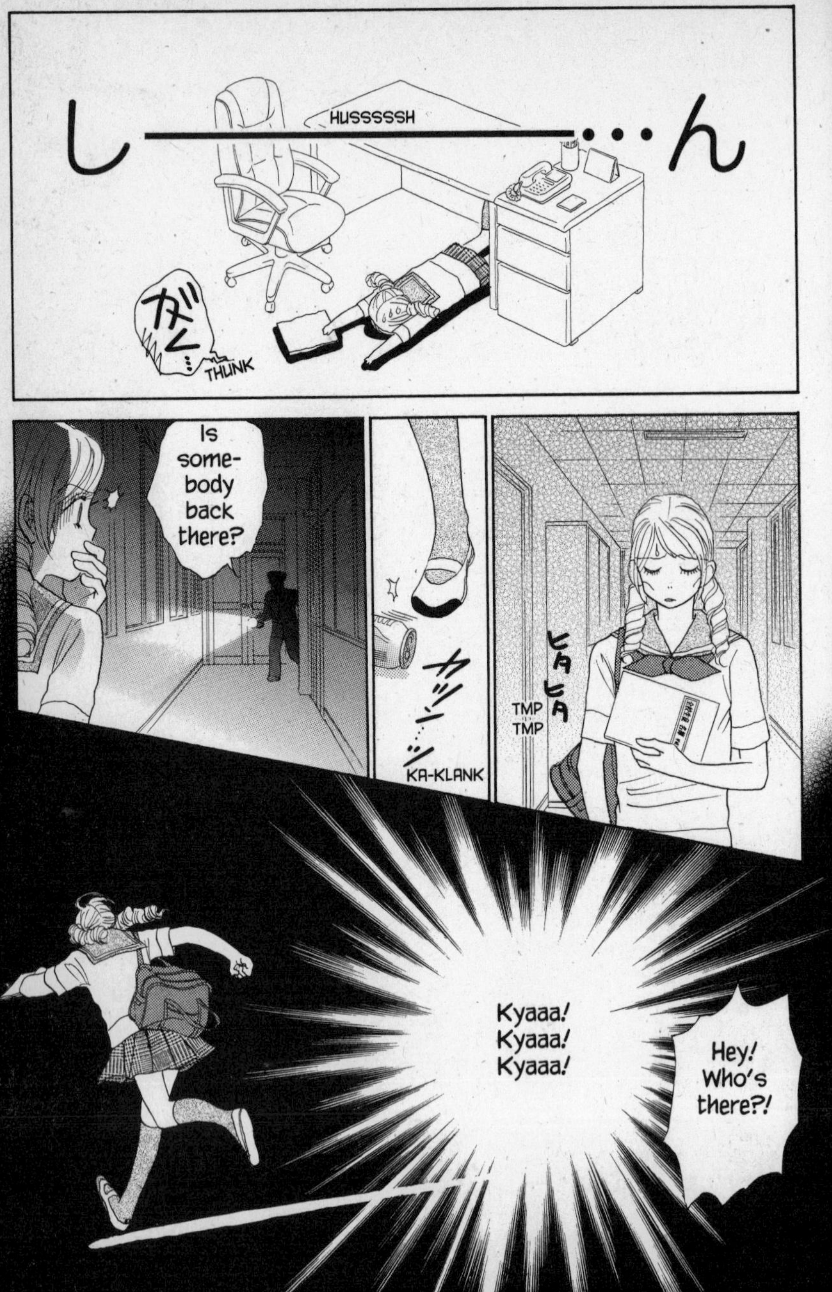

し———…ん
HUSSSSSH
がく…
THUNK
ヒタヒタ
TMP TMP
カッン…ッ
KA-KLANK
Is some-body back there?
Hey! Who's there?!
Kyaaa! Kyaaa! Kyaaa!

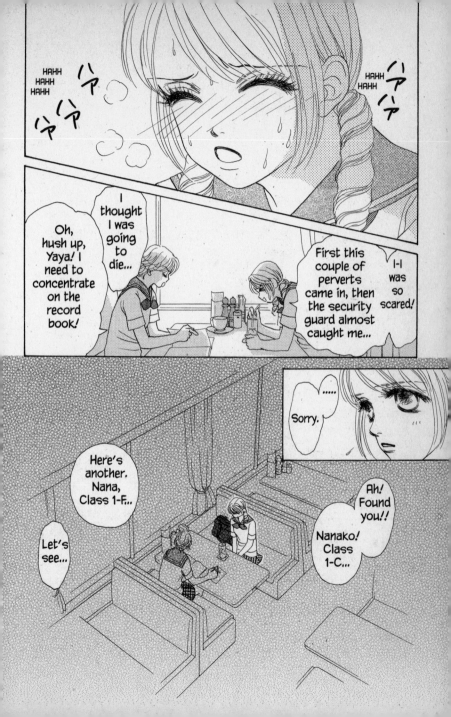

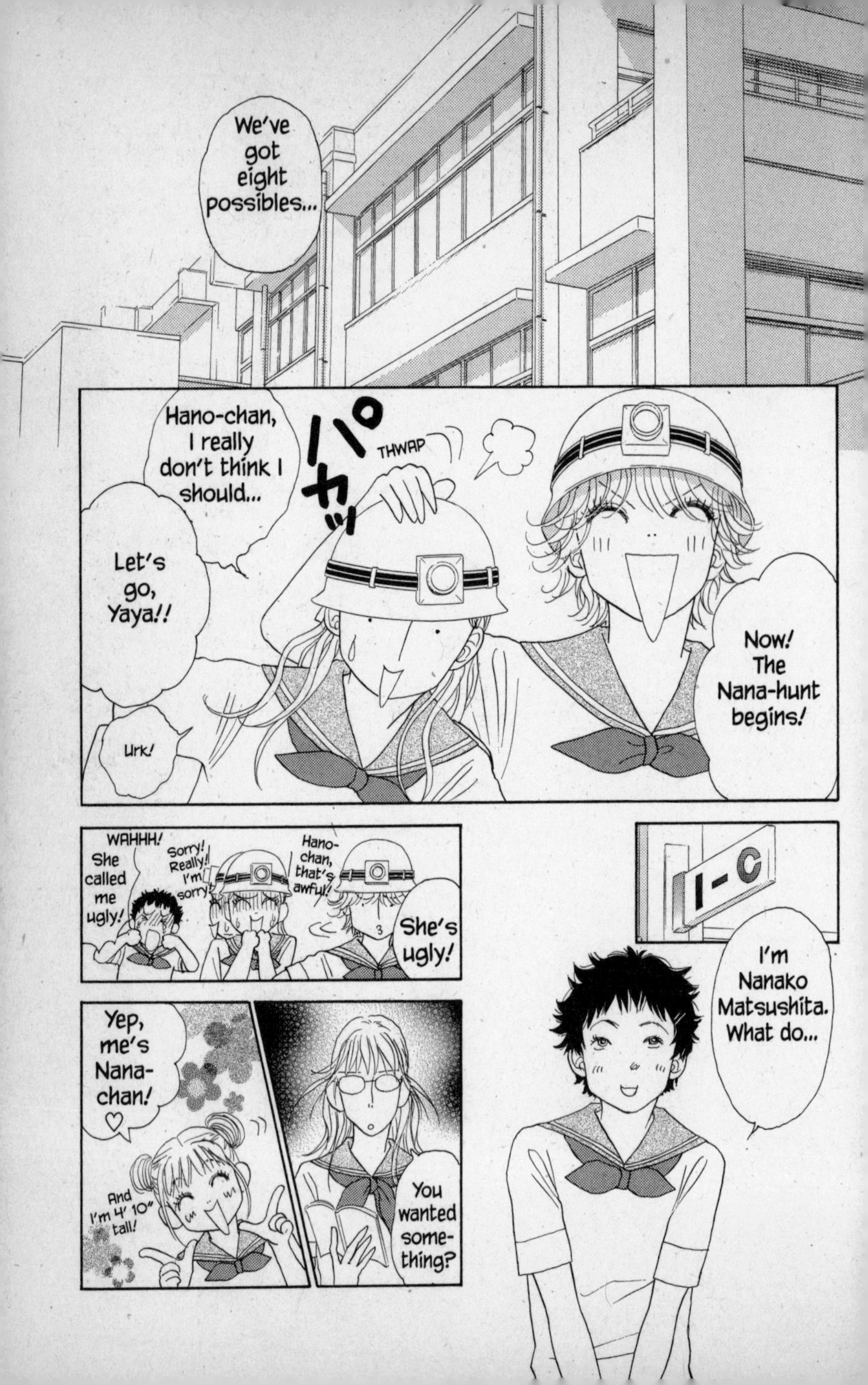

We've got eight possibles...
パカッ
THWAP
Hano-chan, I really don't think I should...
Now! The Nana-hunt begins!
Let's go, Yaya!!
Urk!
I-C
I'm Nanako Matsushita. What do...
She's ugly!
Hano-chan, that's awful!
Sorry! Really! I'm sorry!
WAHHH! She called me ugly!
You wanted something?
Yep, me's Nana-chan! ♡
And I'm 4' 10" tall!

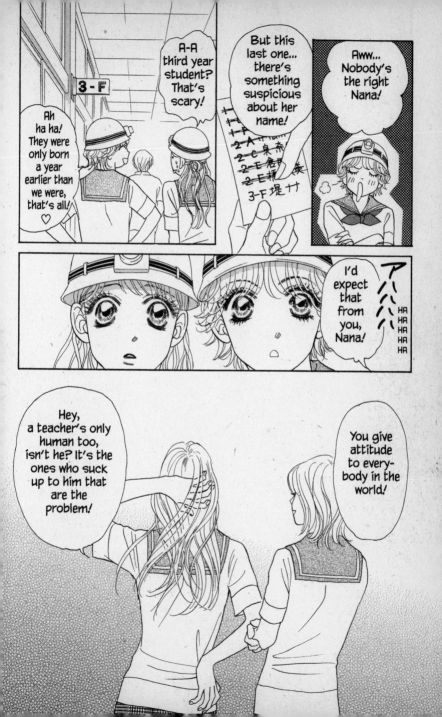

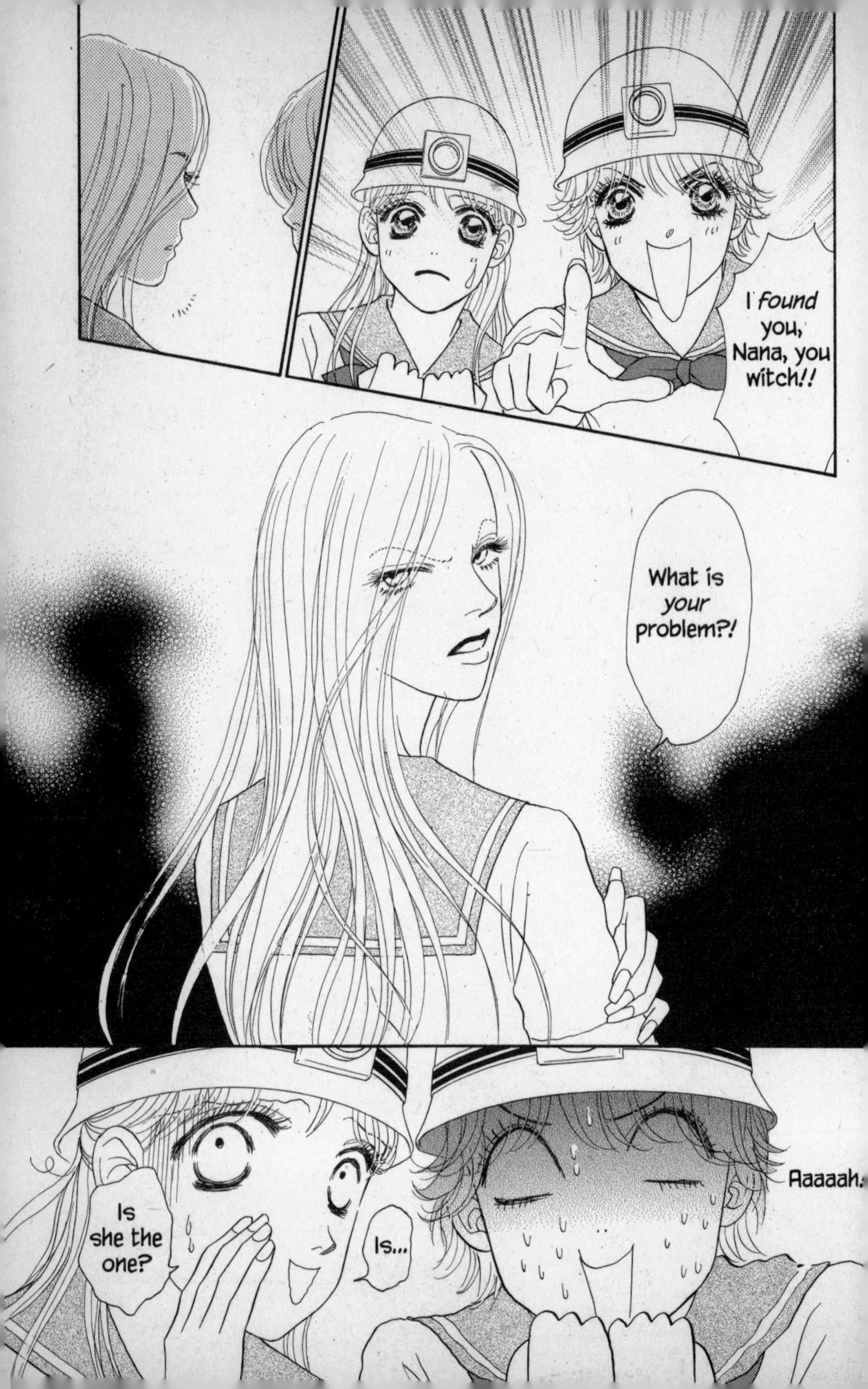
I found you, Nana, you witch!!
What is *your* problem?!
Aaaaah.
Is...
Is she the one?

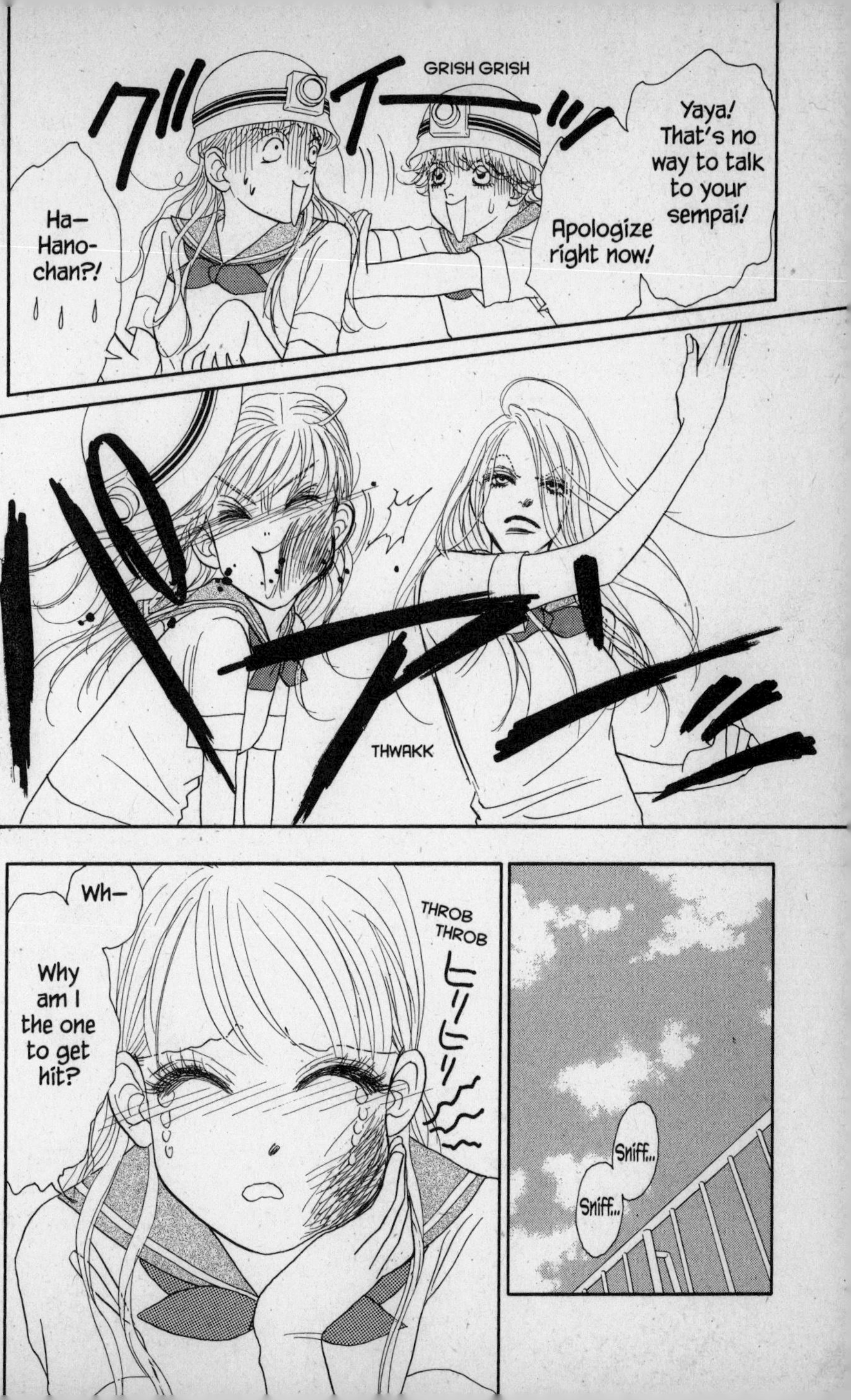
Yaya! That's no way to talk to your sempai!
Apologize right now!
GRISH GRISH
Ha— Hano-chan?!
THWAKK
Sniff...
Sniff...
THROB THROB
Wh-
Why am I the one to get hit?

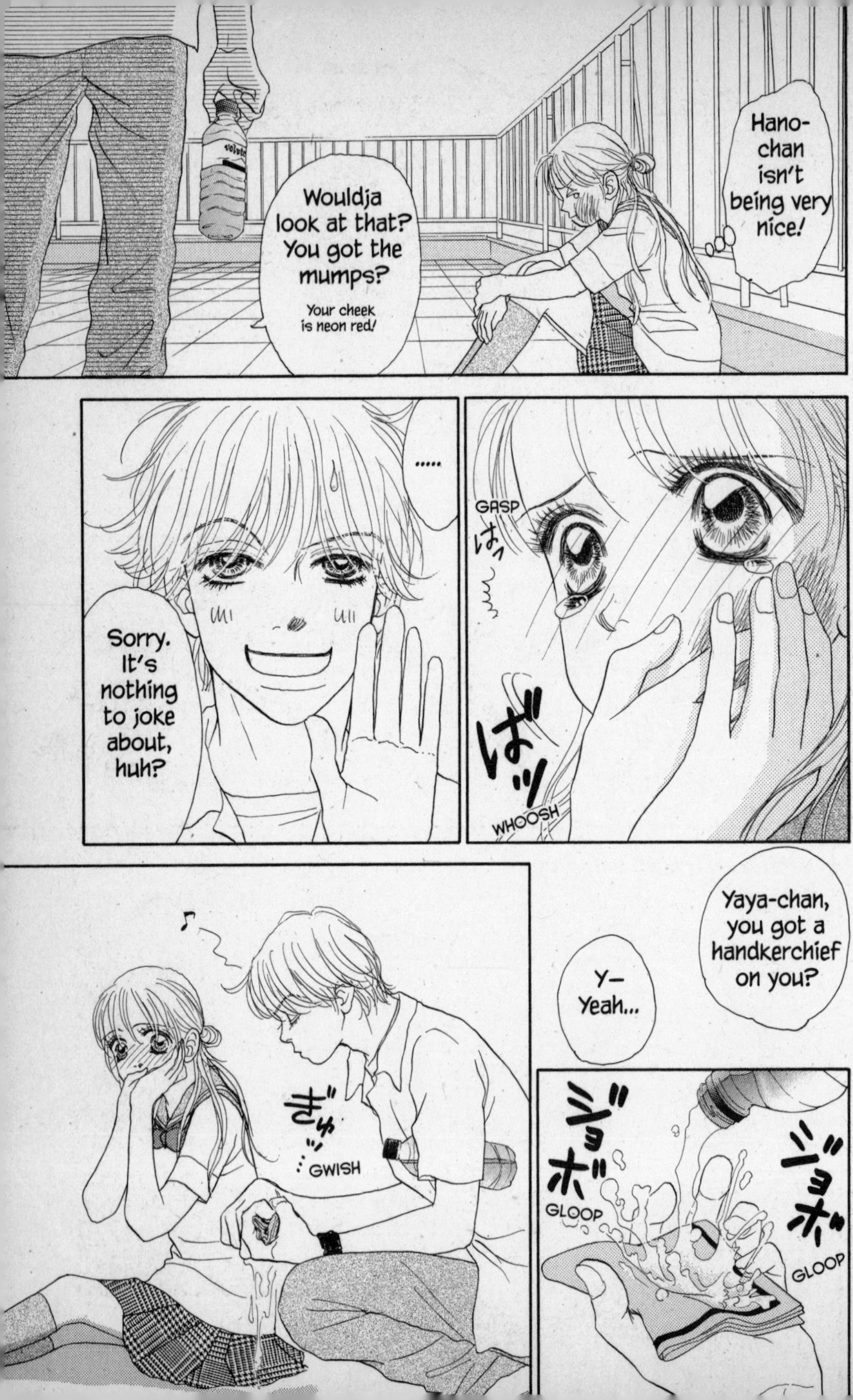
Hano-chan isn't being very nice!
Wouldja look at that? You got the mumps?
Your cheek is neon red!
GASP
は
ばッ
WHOOSH
......
Sorry. It's nothing to joke about, huh?
Yaya-chan, you got a handkerchief on you?
Y— Yeah...
ジョボ
GLOOP
ジョボ
GLOOP
ぎゅッ
GWISH

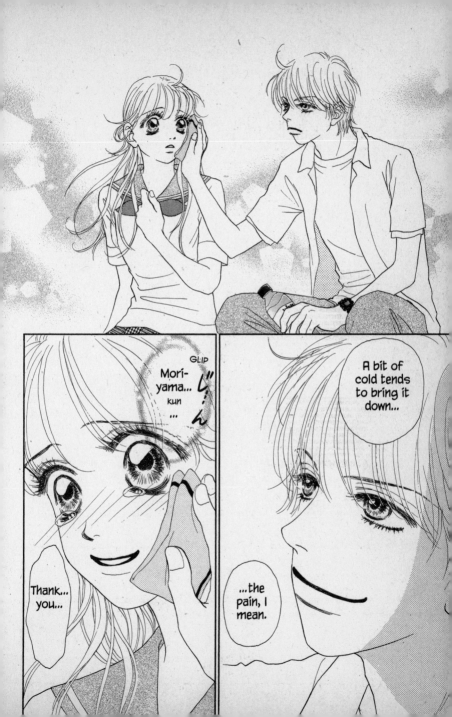

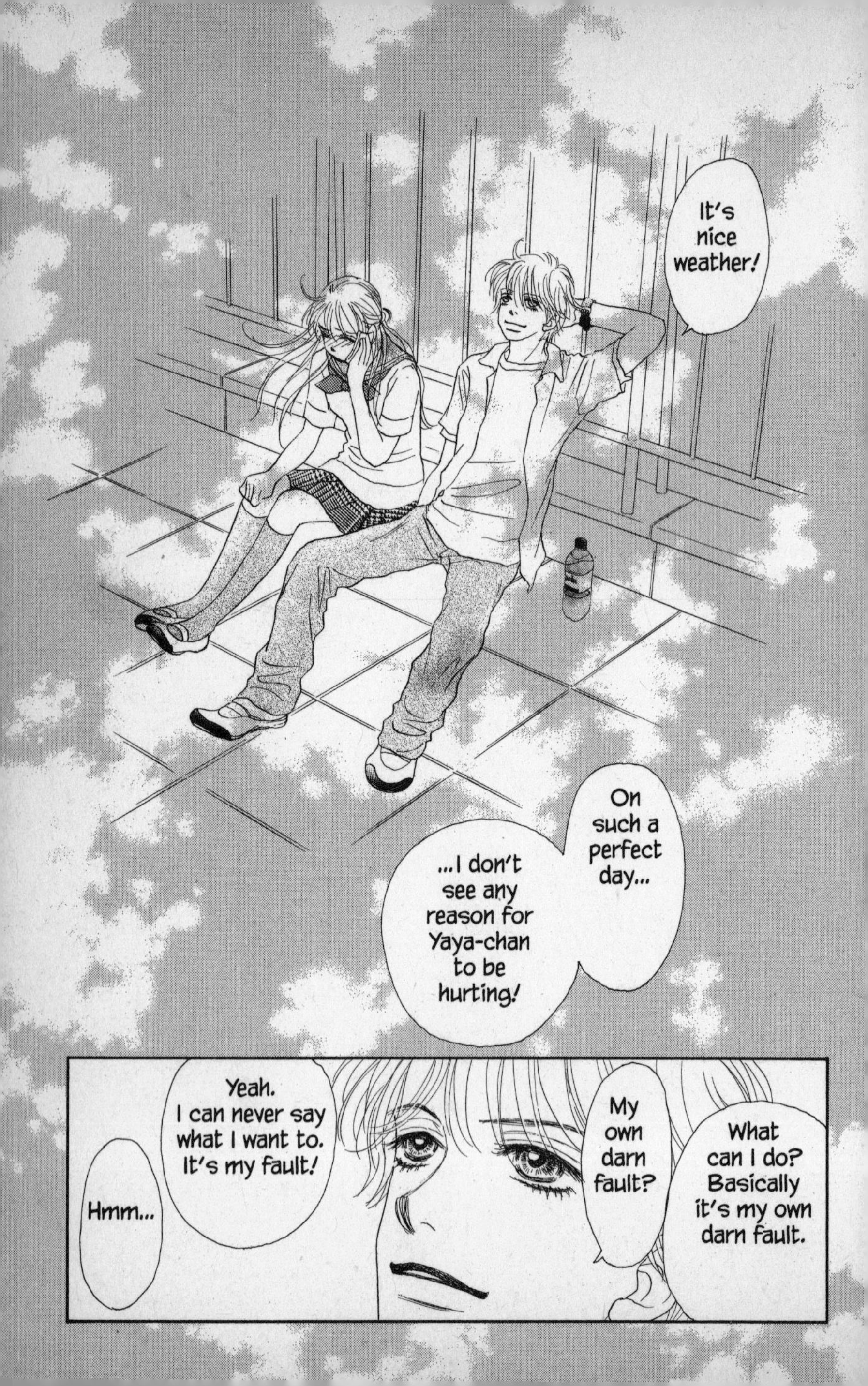
It's nice weather!
On such a perfect day...
...I don't see any reason for Yaya-chan to be hurting!
What can I do? Basically it's my own darn fault.
My own darn fault?
Yeah. I can never say what I want to. It's my fault!
Hmm...

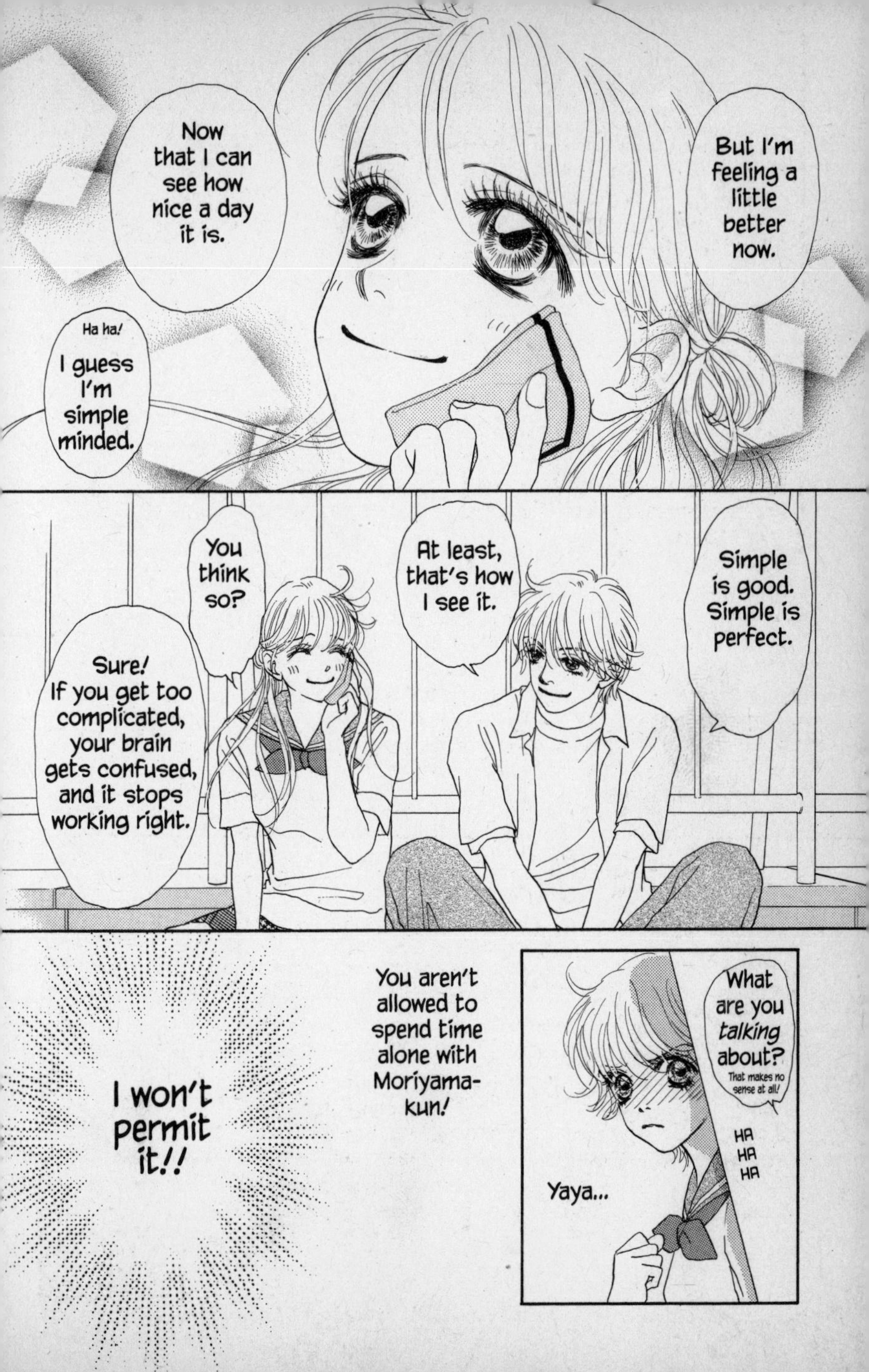
But I'm feeling a little better now.
Now that I can see how nice a day it is.
Ha ha!
I guess I'm simple minded.
Simple is good. Simple is perfect.
At least, that's how I see it.
You think so?
Sure! If you get too complicated, your brain gets confused, and it stops working right.
What are you *talking* about?
That makes no sense at all!
HA HA HA
Yaya...
You aren't allowed to spend time alone with Moriyama-kun!
I won't permit it!!

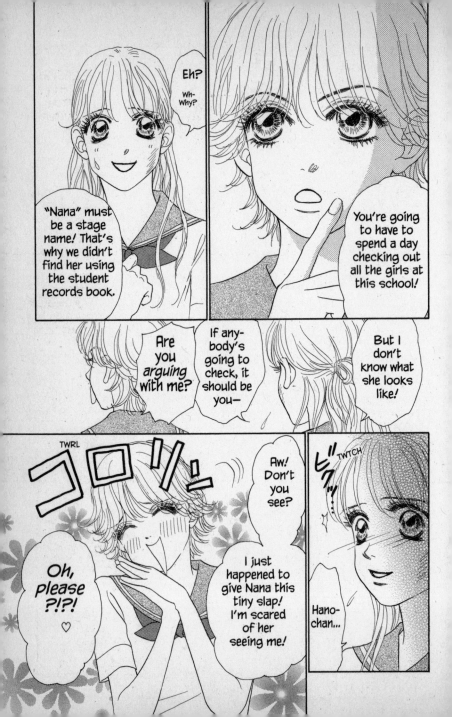

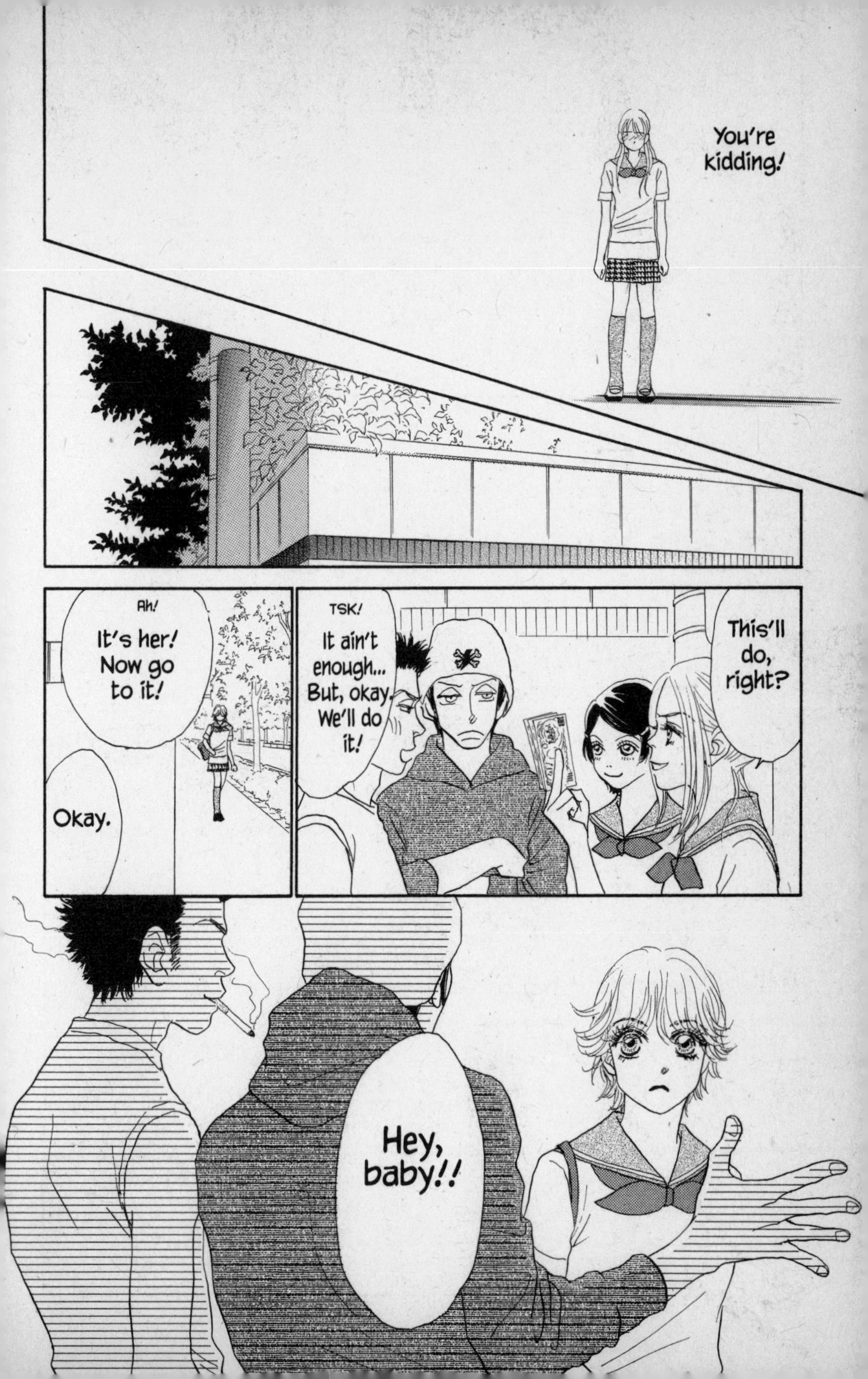
You're kidding!
This'll do, right?
TSK!
It ain't enough... But, okay. We'll do it!
Ah!
It's her! Now go to it!
Okay.
Hey, baby!!

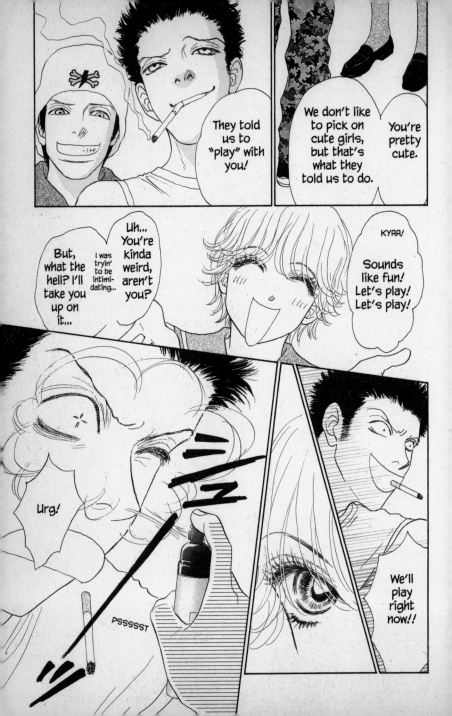

His real name is Teruo.

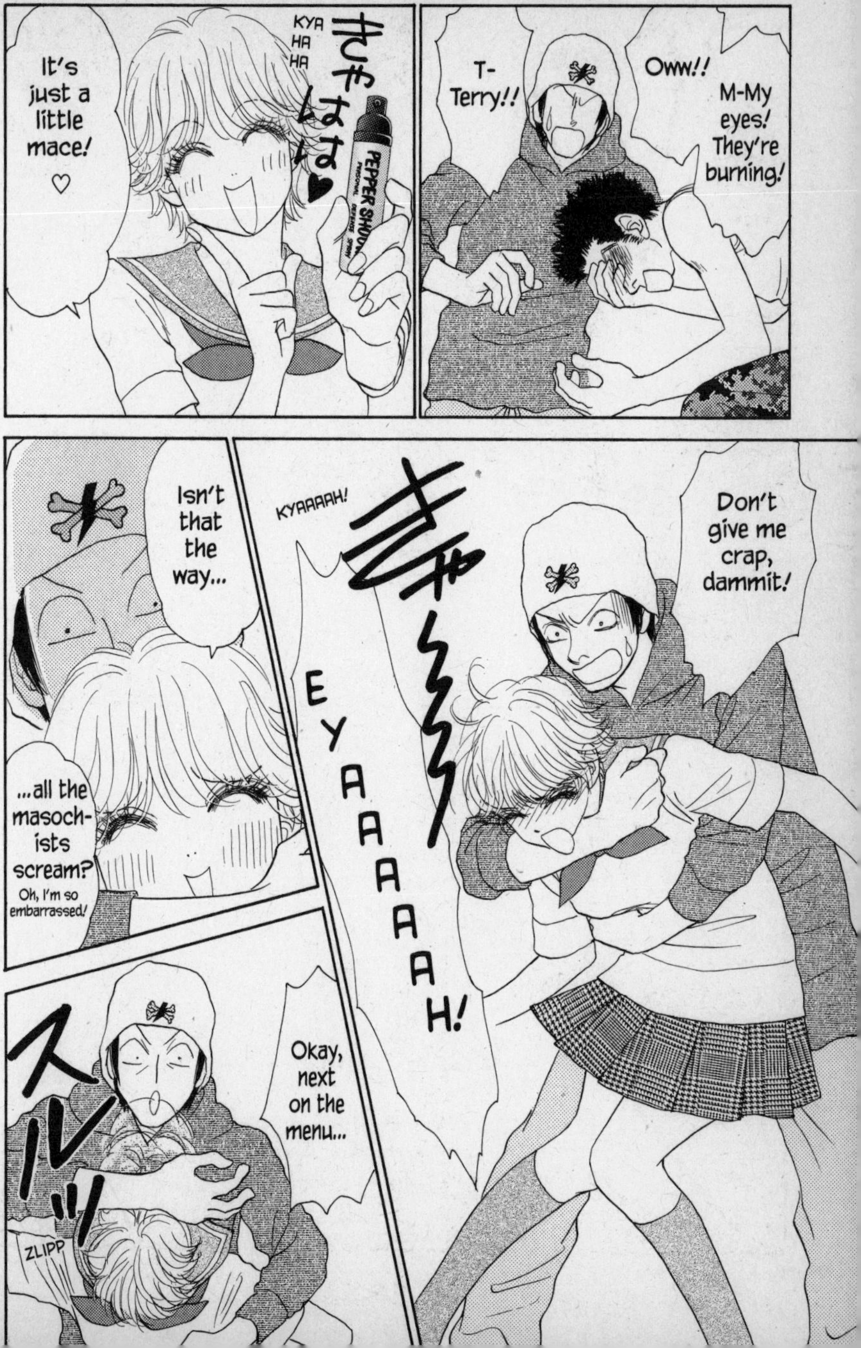

T-Terry!!
Oww!!
M-My eyes! They're burning!
きゃはは♥
KYA HA HA
It's just a little mace! ♡
Don't give me crap, dammit!
KYAAAAH!
EYAAAAAAH!
Isn't that the way...
...all the masochists scream?
Oh, I'm so embarrassed!
Okay, next on the menu...
スルッ
ZLIPP

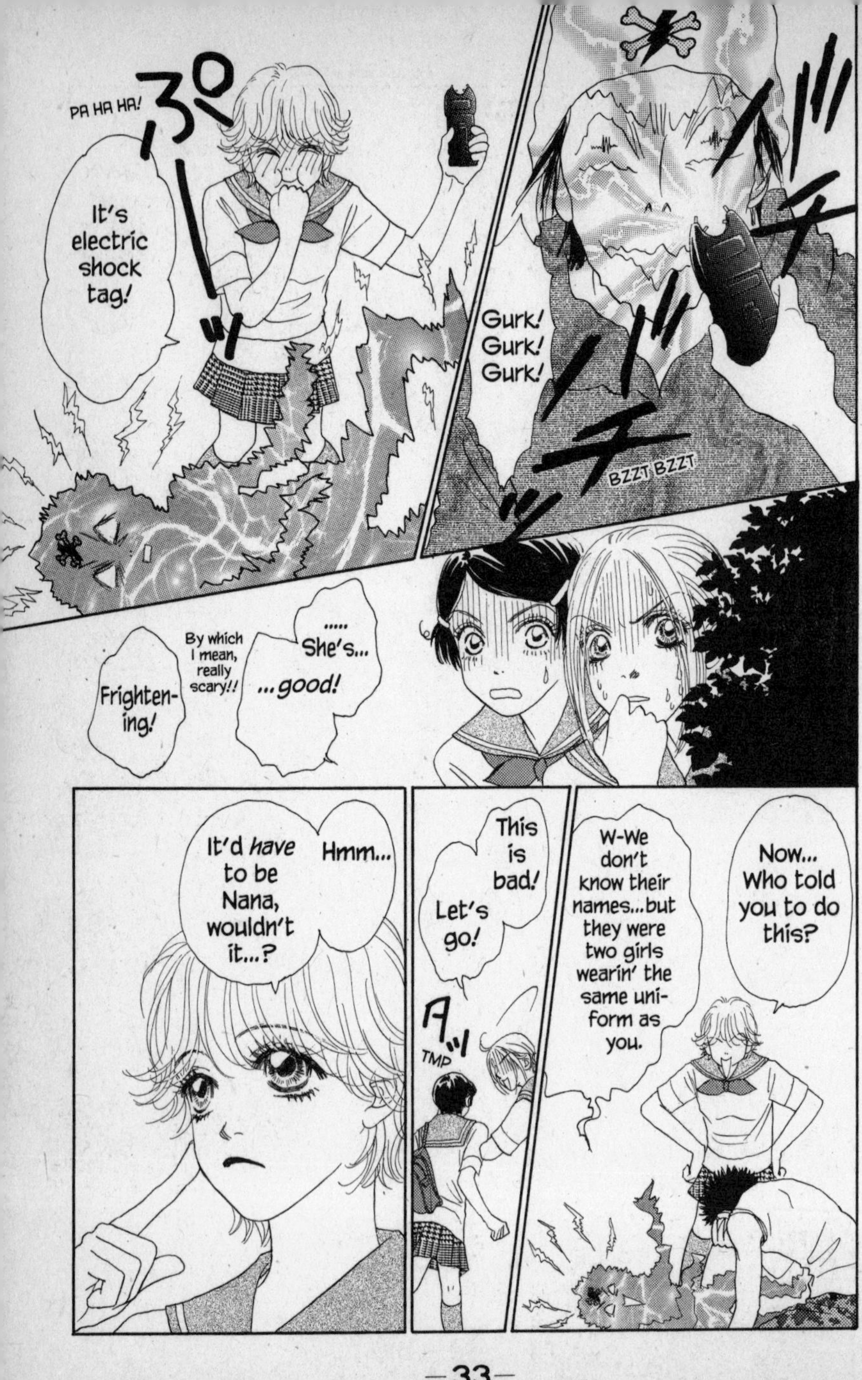
Gurk! Gurk! Gurk!
BZZT BZZT
PA HA HA!
It's electric shock tag!
..... She's... ...good!
By which I mean, really scary!!
Frighten-ing!
Now... Who told you to do this?
W-We don't know their names...but they were two girls wearin' the same uni-form as you.
This is bad!
Let's go!
TMP
Hmm...
It'd *have* to be Nana, wouldn't it...?

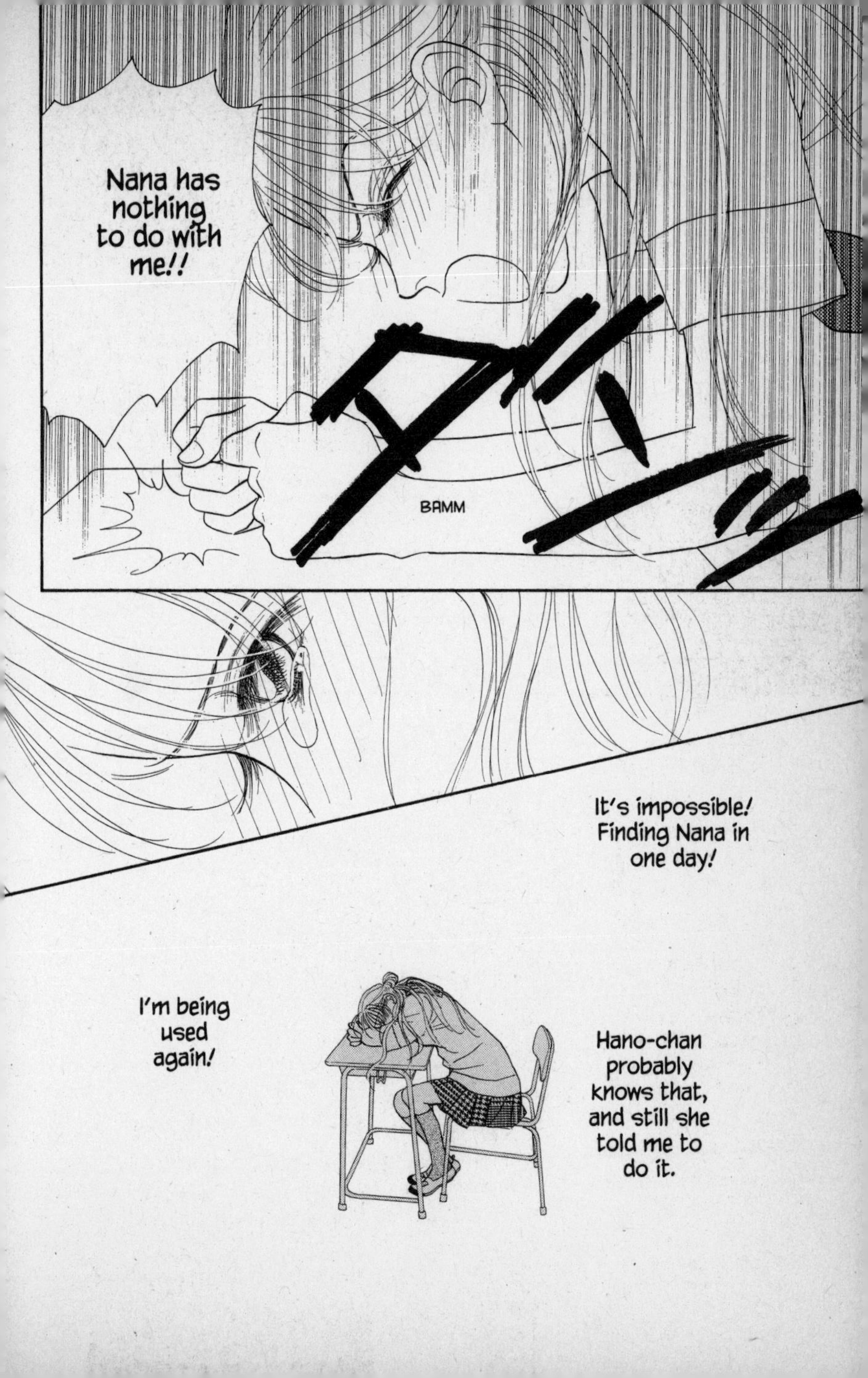
Nana has nothing to do with me!!
BAMM
It's impossible! Finding Nana in one day!
Hano-chan probably knows that, and still she told me to do it.
I'm being used again!

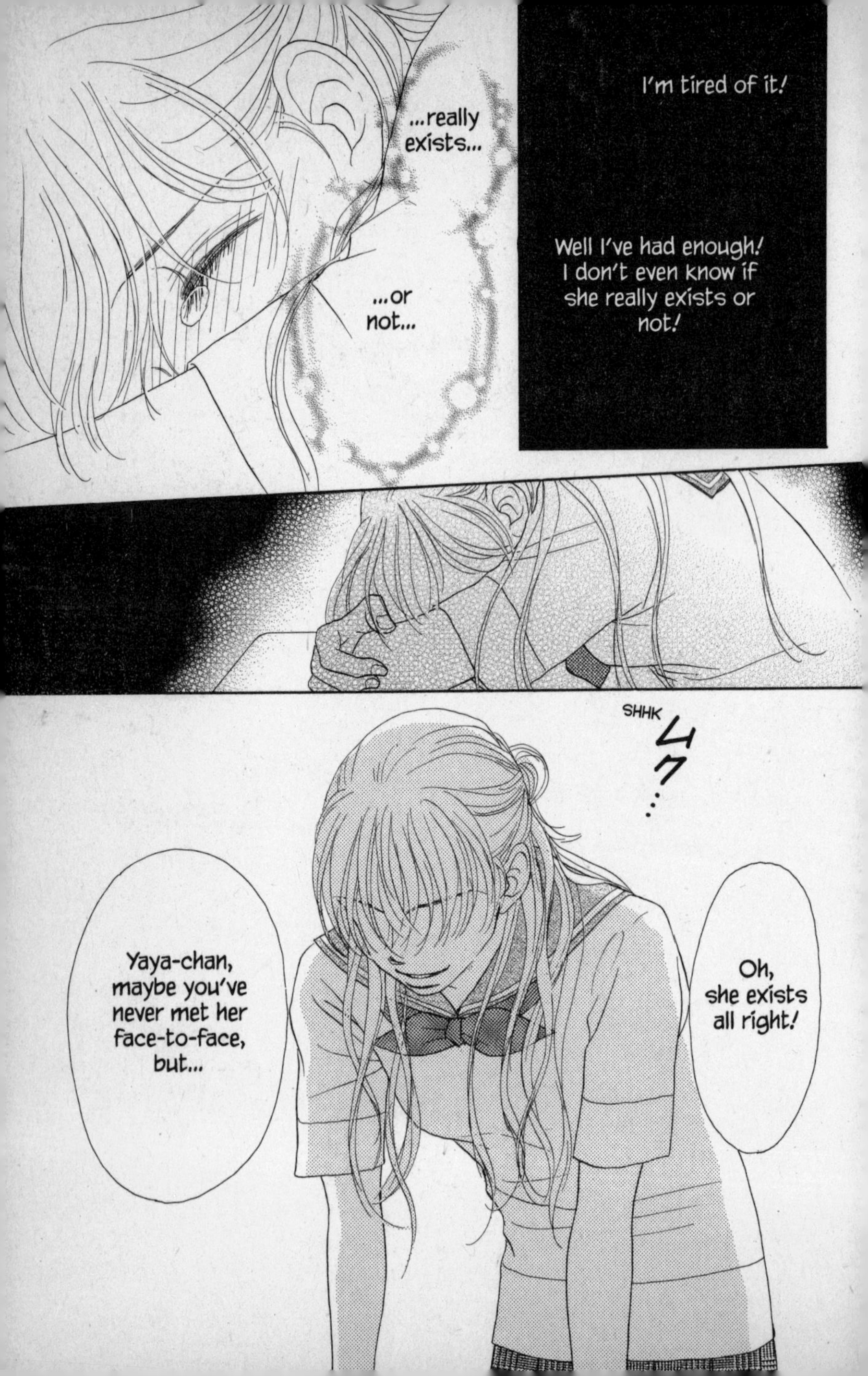

I'm tired of it!
Well I've had enough! I don't even know if she really exists or not!
...really exists...
...or not...
SHHK
Oh, she exists all right!
Yaya-chan, maybe you've never met her face-to-face, but...

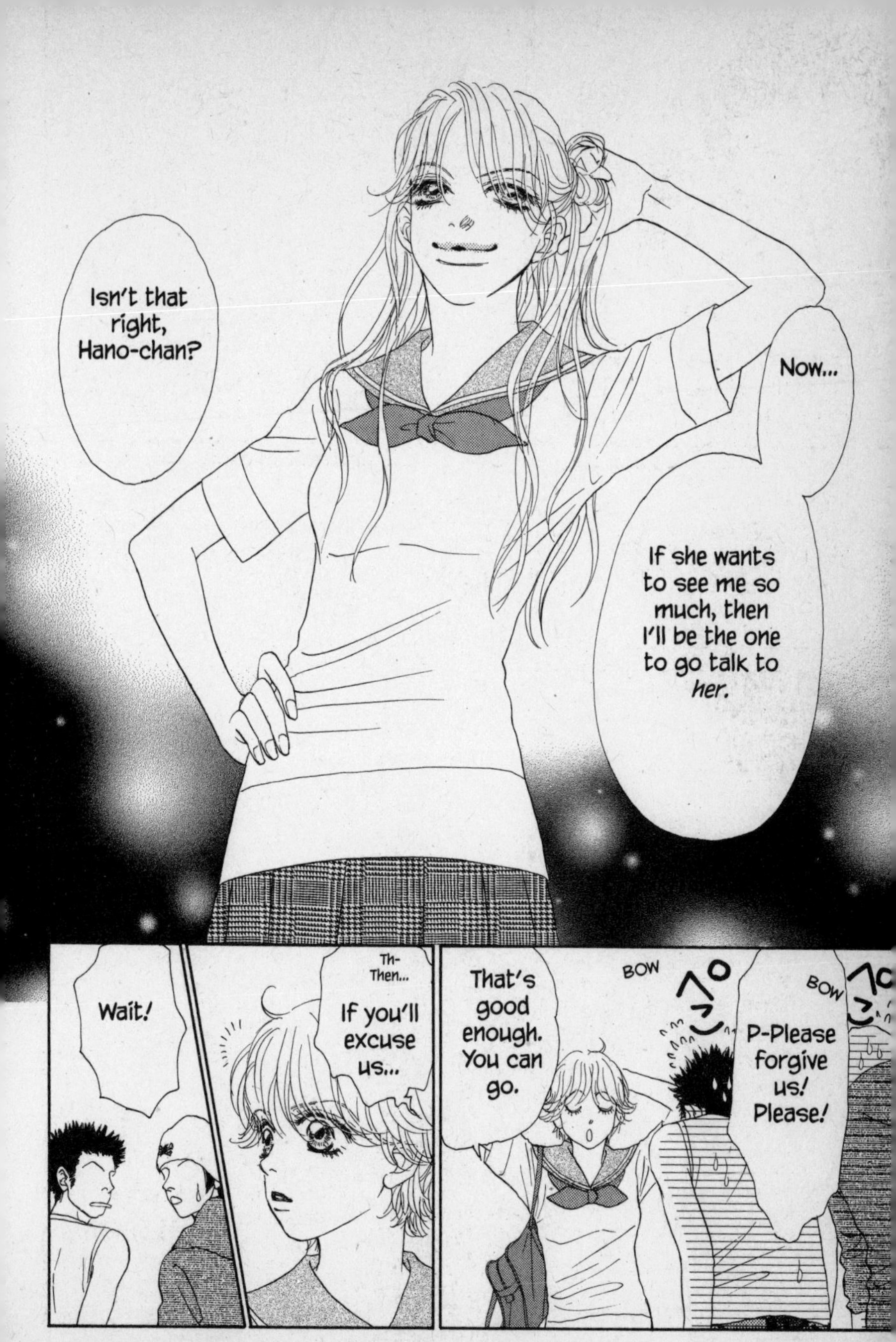
Now...
If she wants to see me so much, then I'll be the one to go talk to *her*.
Isn't that right, Hano-chan?
BOW
BOW
P-Please forgive us! Please!
That's good enough. You can go.
Th-Then...
If you'll excuse us...
Wait!

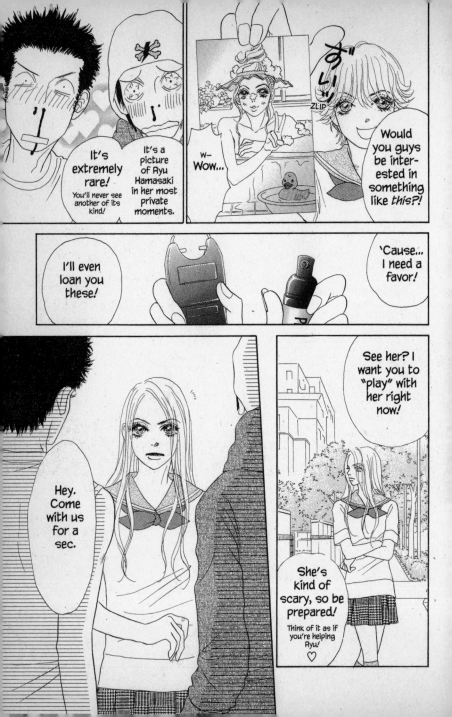

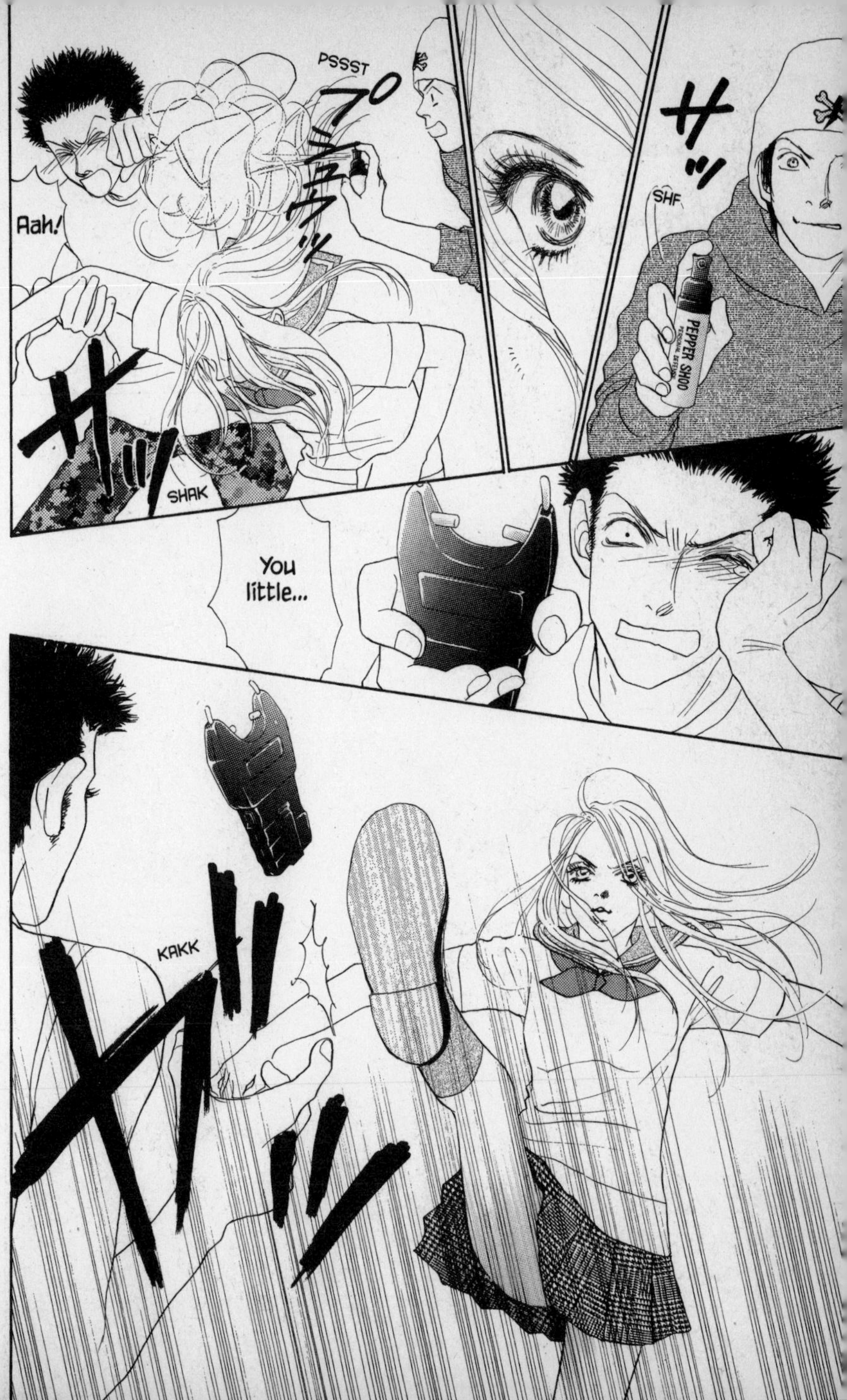
サッ
SHF
PEPPER SHOO
PSSST
プシュウッ
Aah!
ザッ
SHAK
You little...
KAKK
ガッ

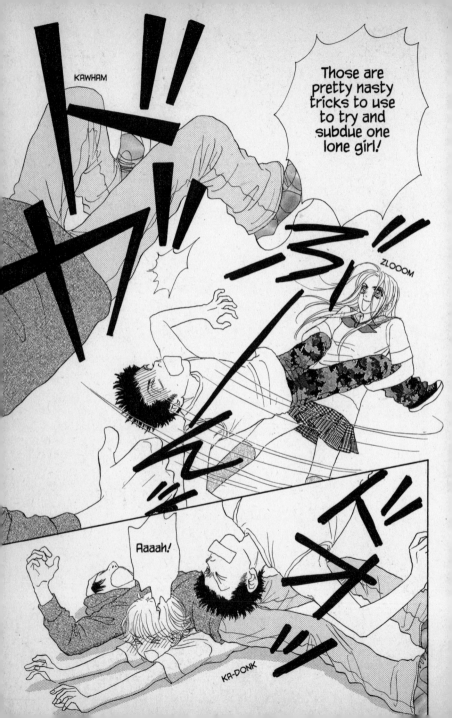

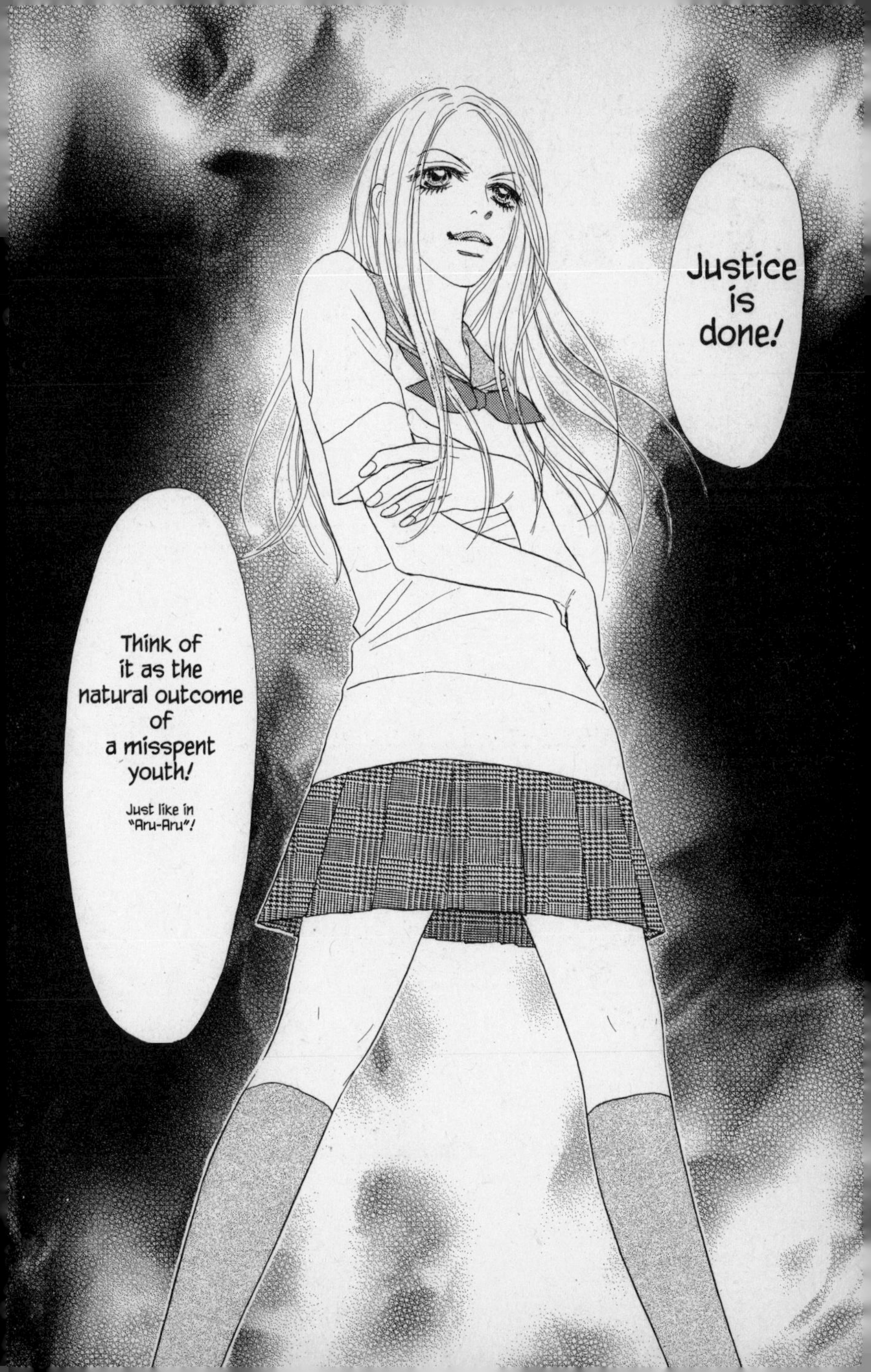
Justice is done!
Think of it as the natural outcome of a misspent youth!
Just like in "Aru-Aru"!

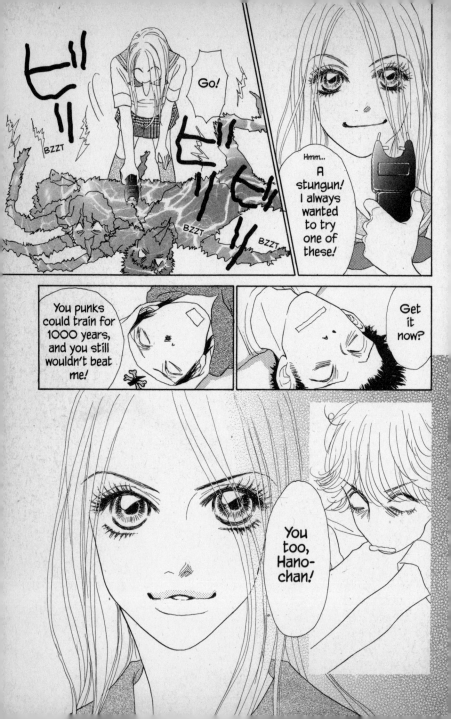

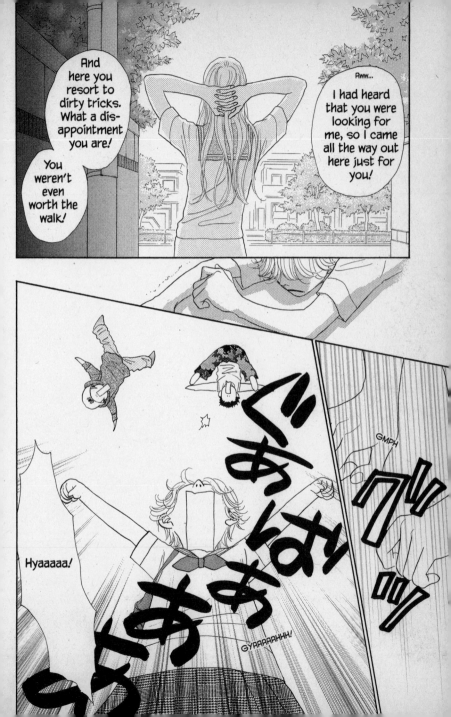

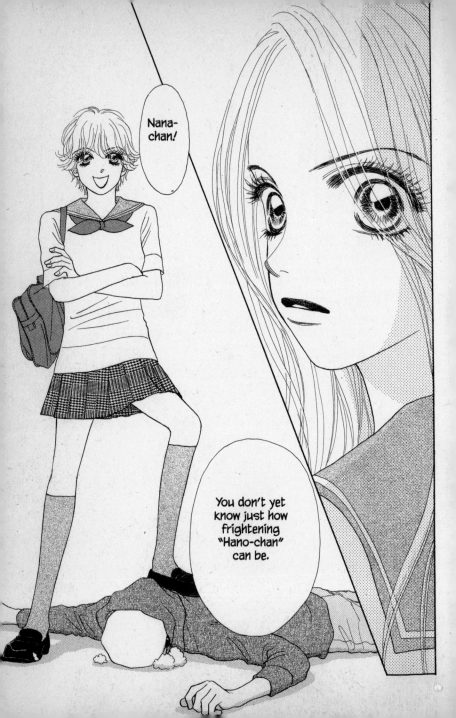

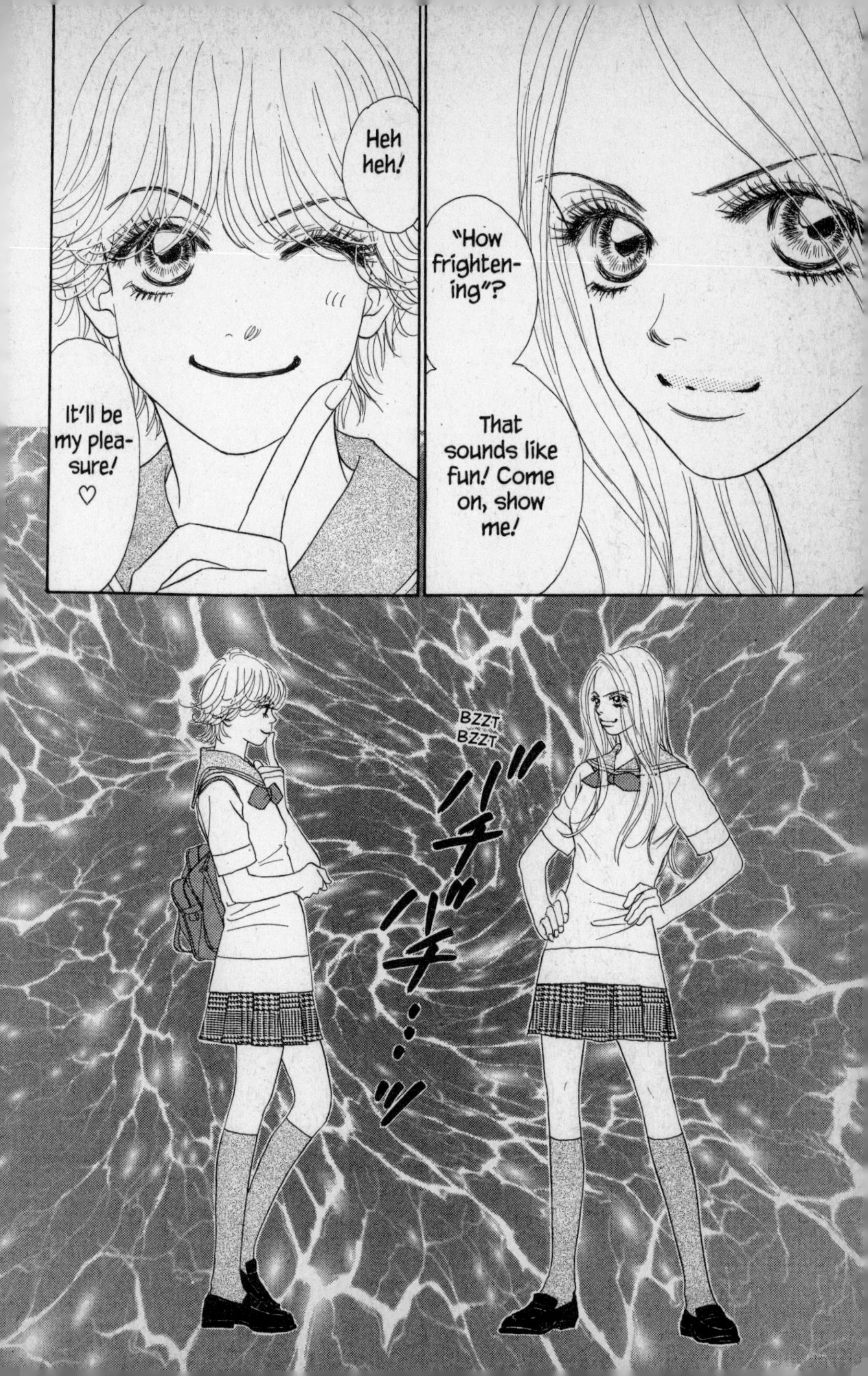
"How frightening"?
That sounds like fun! Come on, show me!
Heh heh!
It'll be my pleasure! ♡
BZZT BZZT
バチバチ…ッ

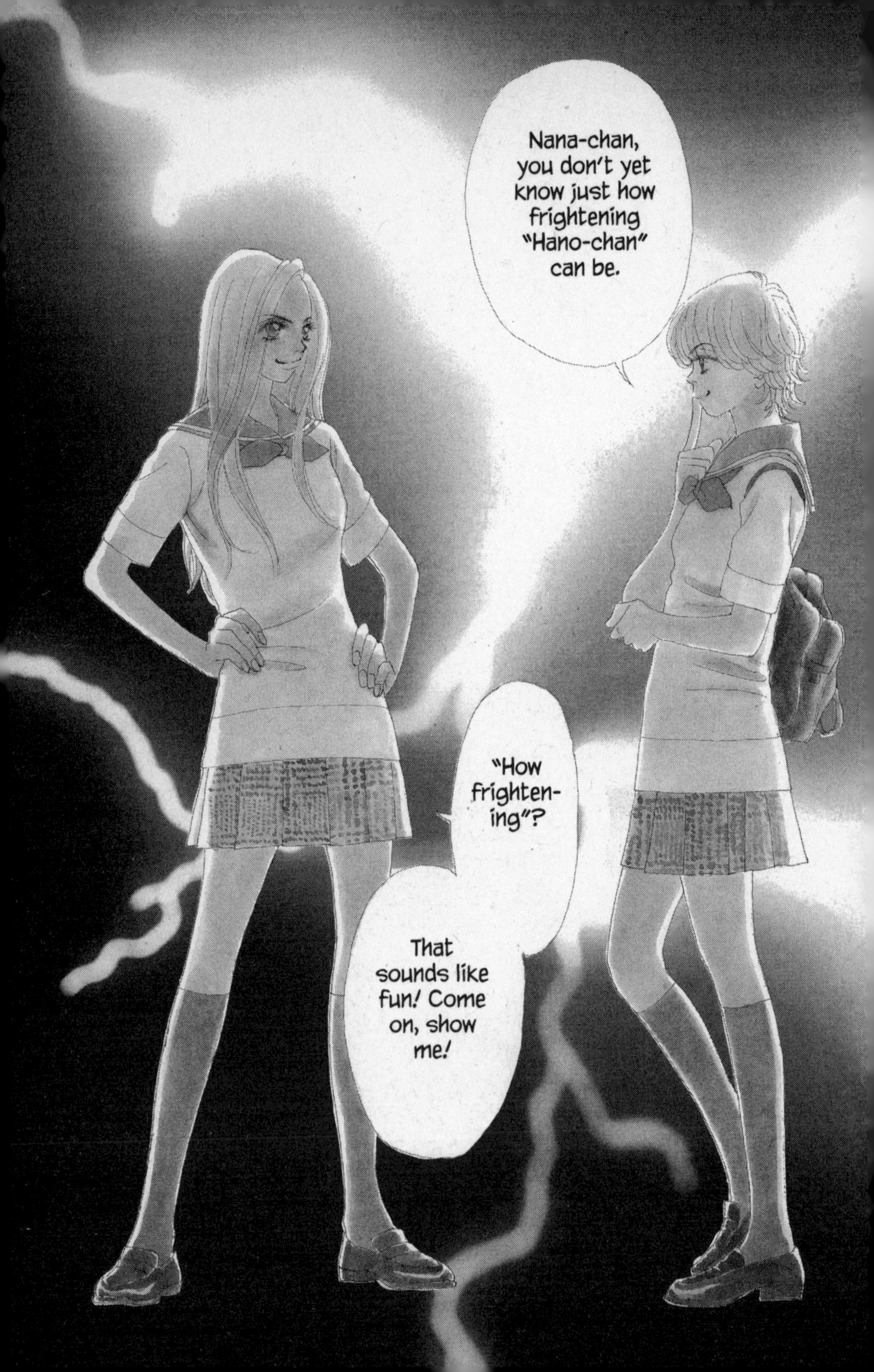
Nana-chan, you don't yet know just how frightening "Hano-chan" can be.
"How frighten-ing"?
That sounds like fun! Come on, show me!

Chapter 14

The Unknown Relationship

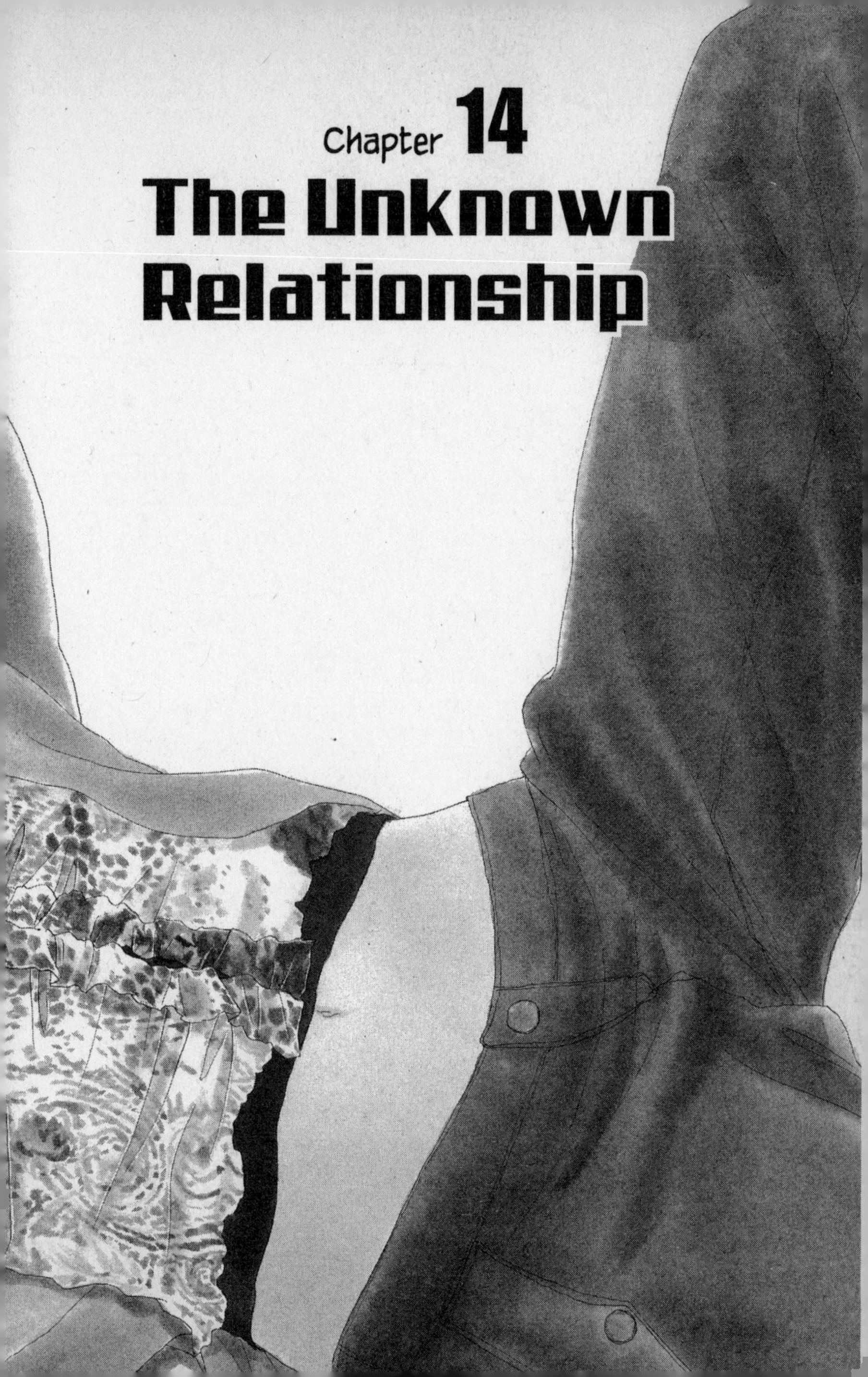

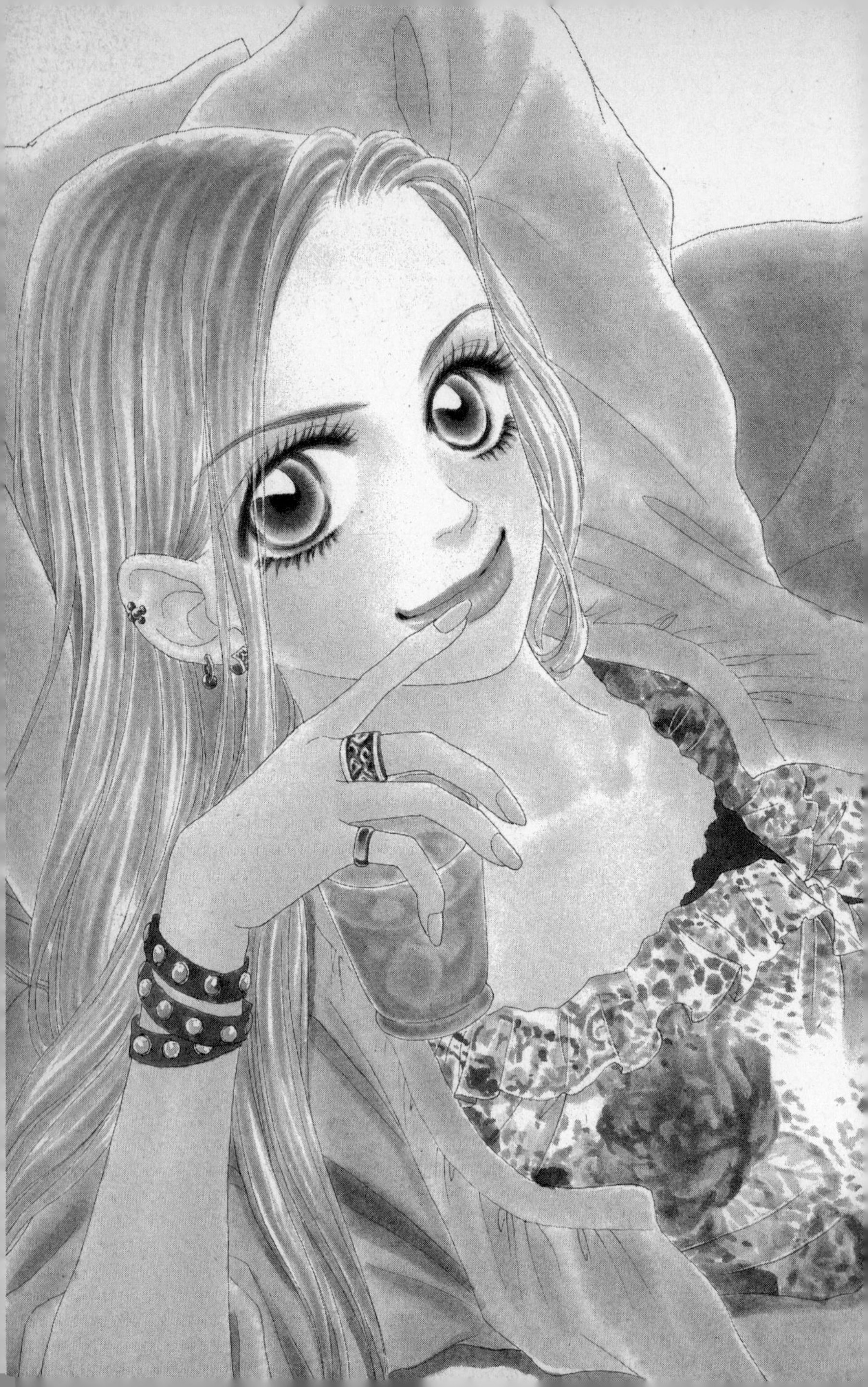

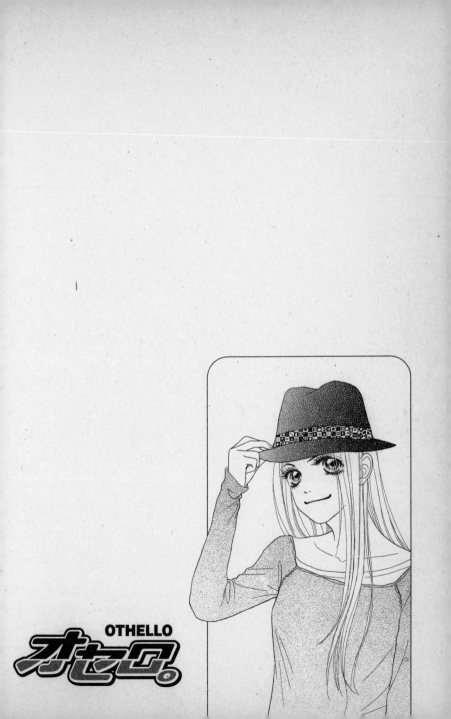

OTHELLO
オセロ。

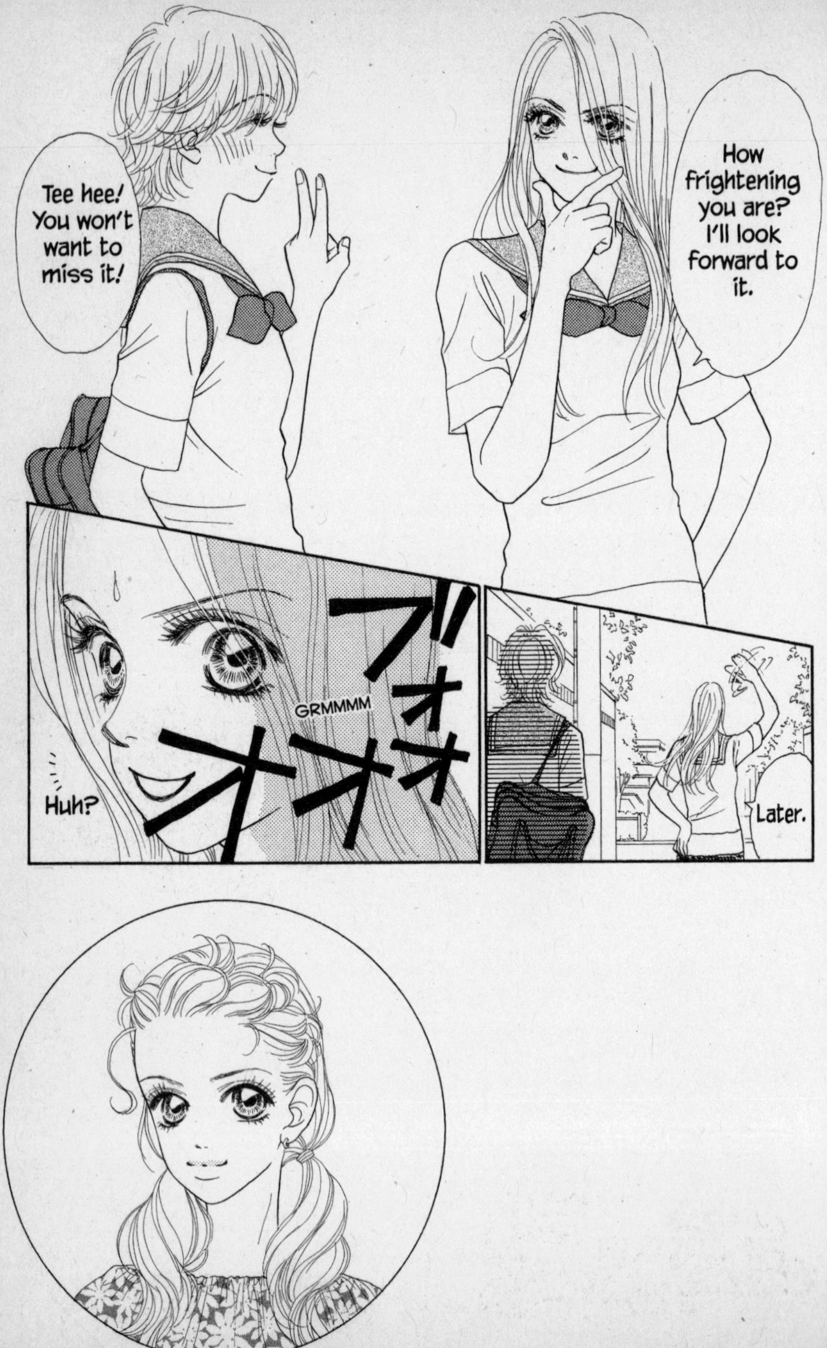
How frightening you are? I'll look forward to it.
Tee hee! You won't want to miss it!
Later.
ブオオオ
GRMMMM
Huh?

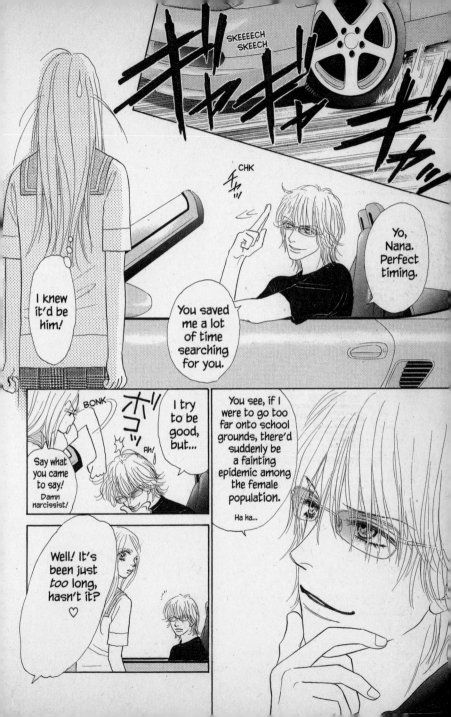

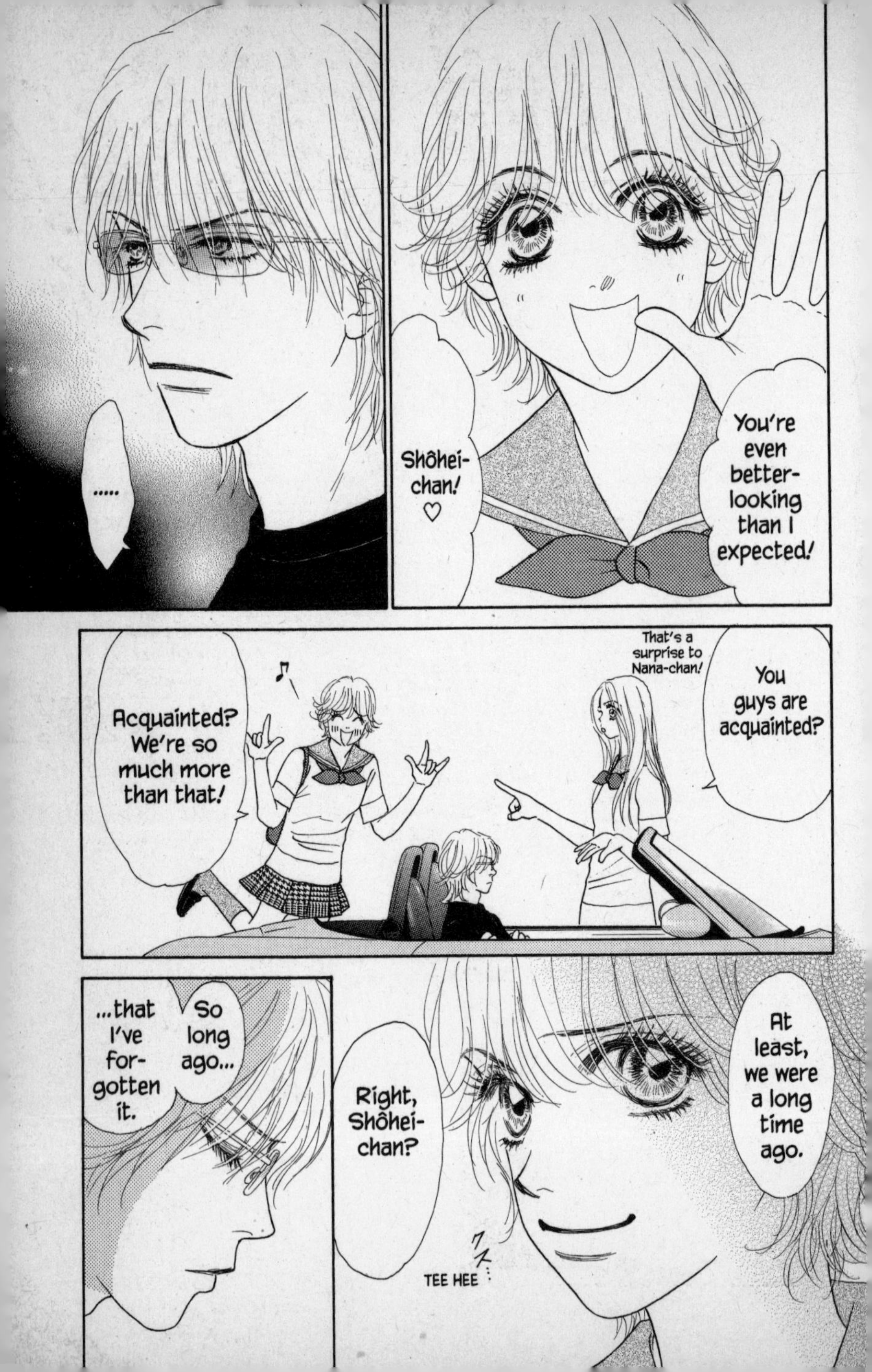
You're even better-looking than I expected!
Shôhei-chan! ♡
.....
That's a surprise to Nana-chan!
You guys are acquainted?
Acquainted? We're so much more than that!
At least, we were a long time ago.
Right, Shôhei-chan?
TEE HEE
So long ago...
...that I've forgotten it.

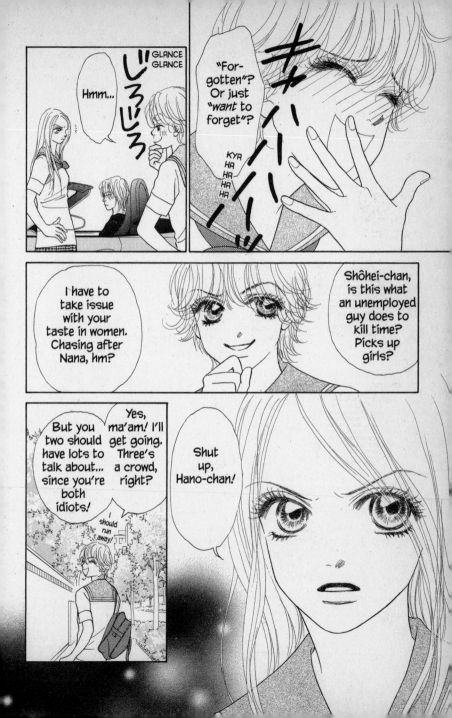

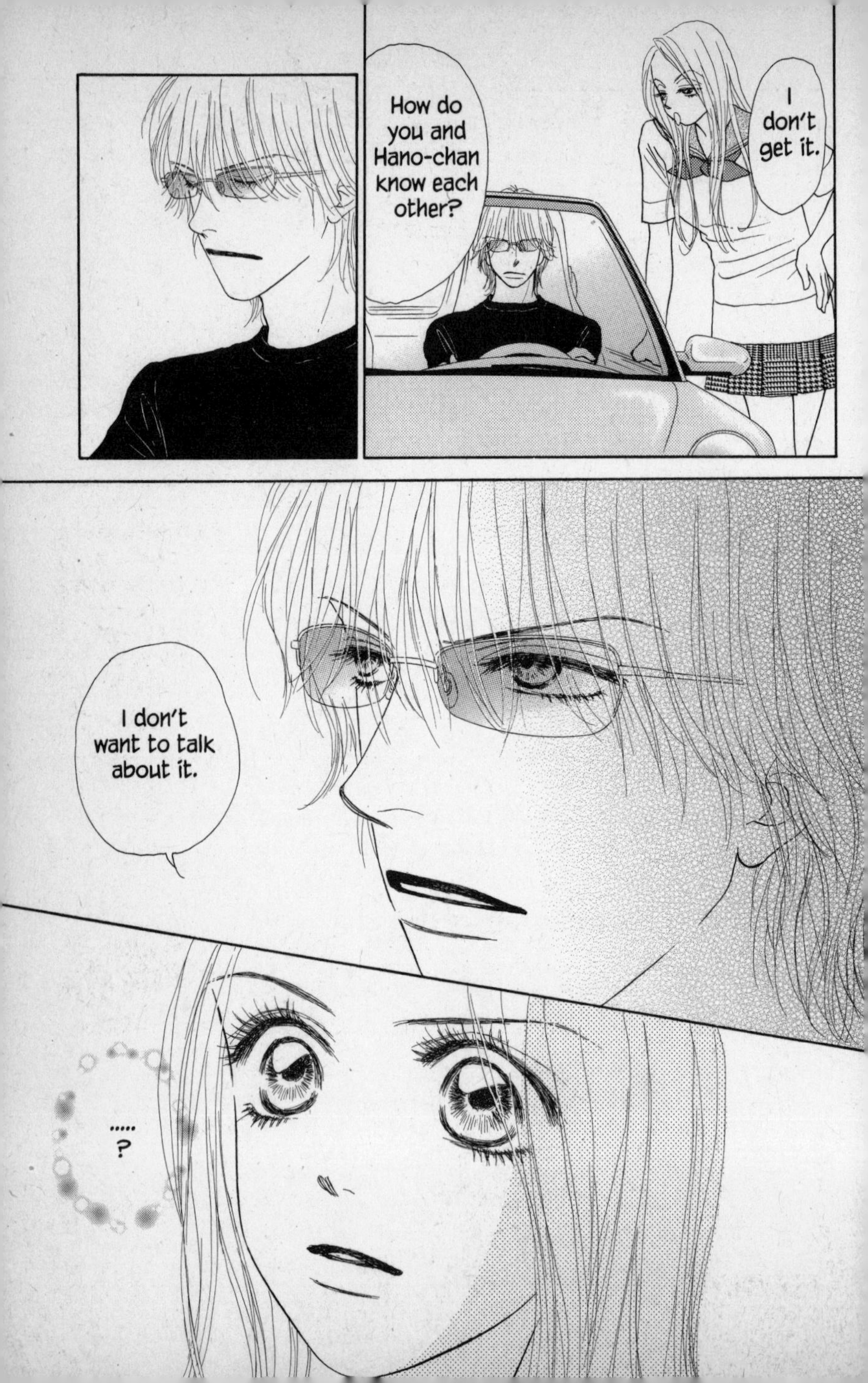
I don't get it.
How do you and Hano-chan know each other?
I don't want to talk about it.
.....?

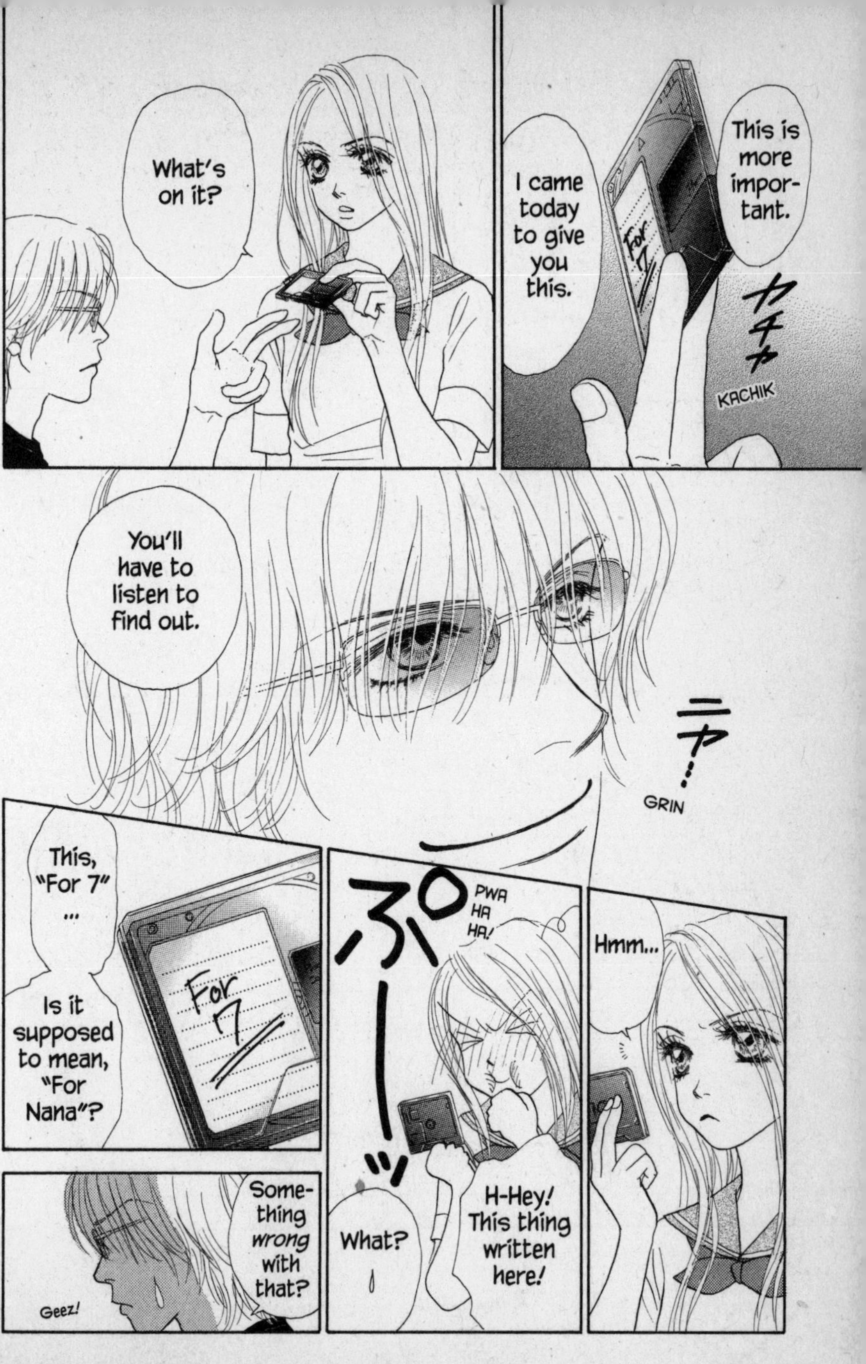
This is more important.
I came today to give you this.
カチャ
KACHIK
What's on it?
You'll have to listen to find out.
ニヤ…
GRIN
Hmm...
PWA HA HA!
ぷーッ
H-Hey! This thing written here!
What?
This, "For 7" ...
Is it supposed to mean, "For Nana"?
Something wrong with that?
Geez!

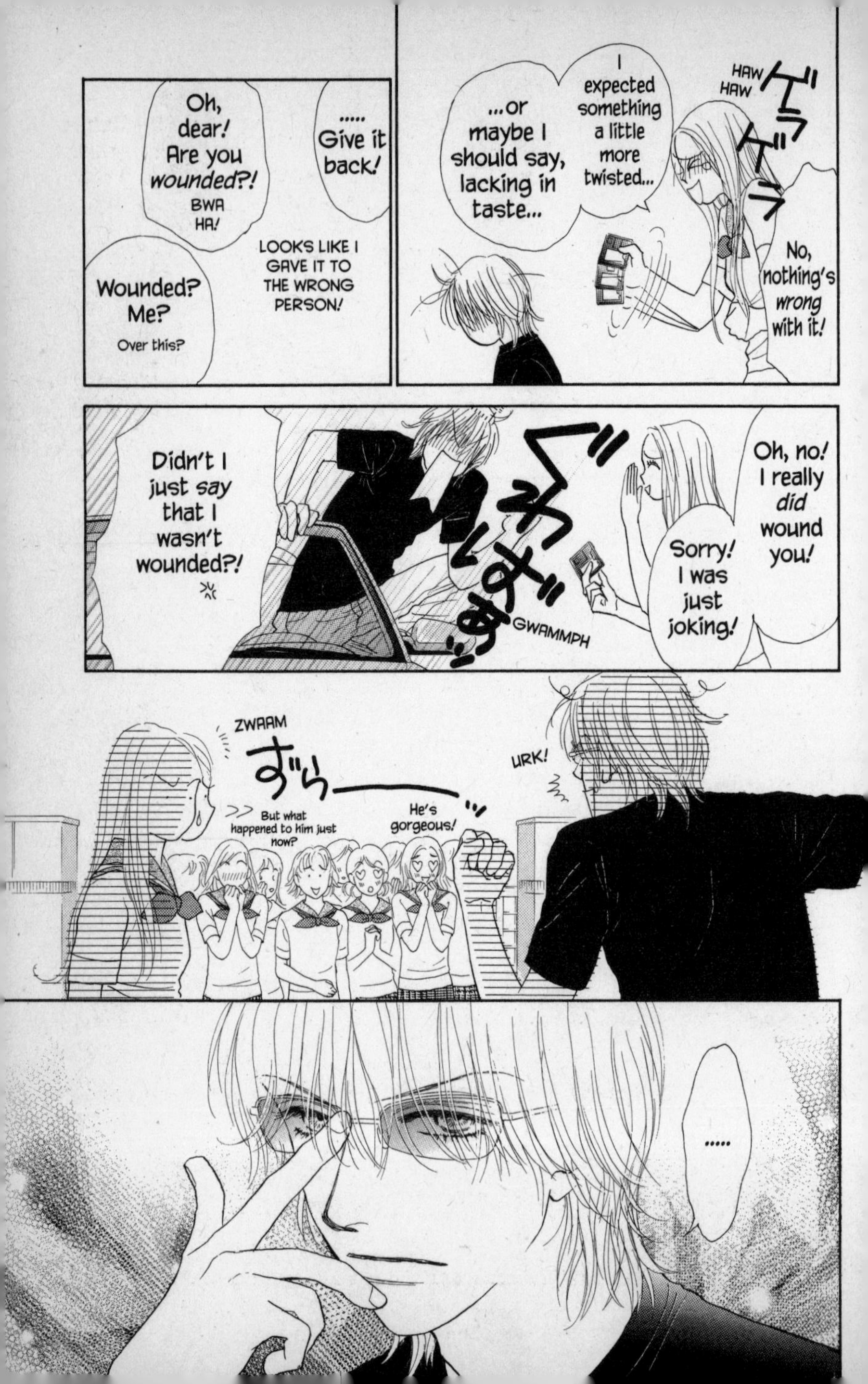
HAW HAW
ゲラゲラ
I expected something a little more twisted...
...or maybe I should say, lacking in taste...
No, nothing's *wrong* with it!
..... Give it back!
Oh, dear! Are you *wounded?!*
BWA HA!
LOOKS LIKE I GAVE IT TO THE WRONG PERSON!
Wounded? Me?
Over this?
Oh, no! I really *did* wound you!
Sorry! I was just joking!
ぐわしずあっ
GWAMMPH
Didn't I just *say* that I wasn't wounded?!
URK!
ZWAAM
ずら——
He's gorgeous!
But what happened to him just now?
.....

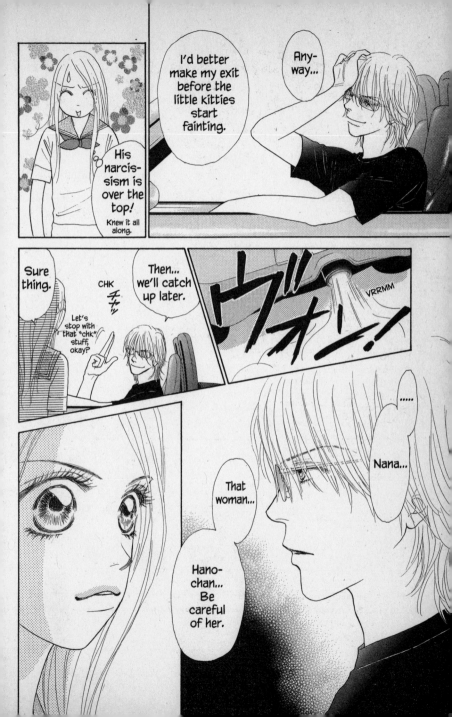

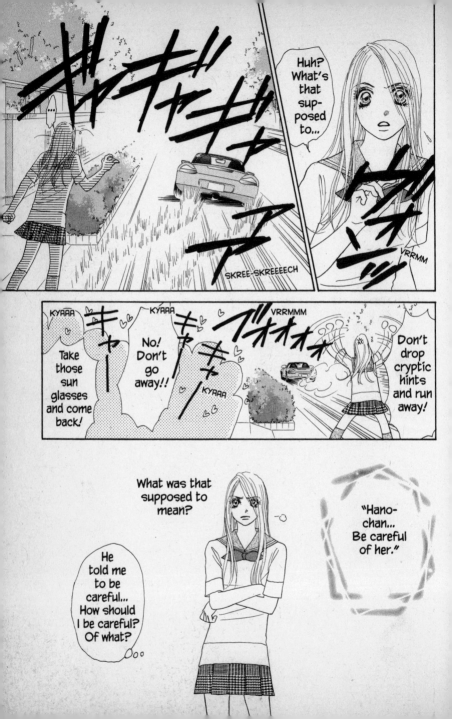

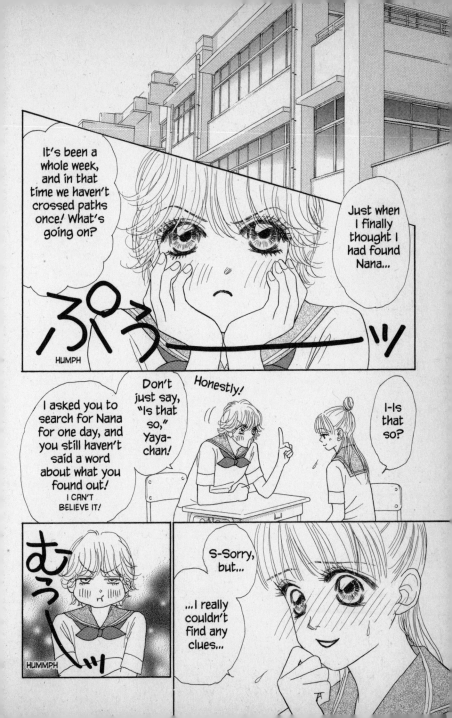

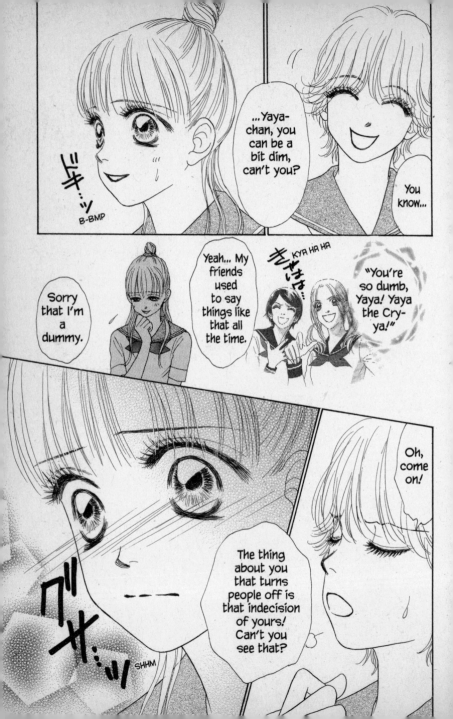

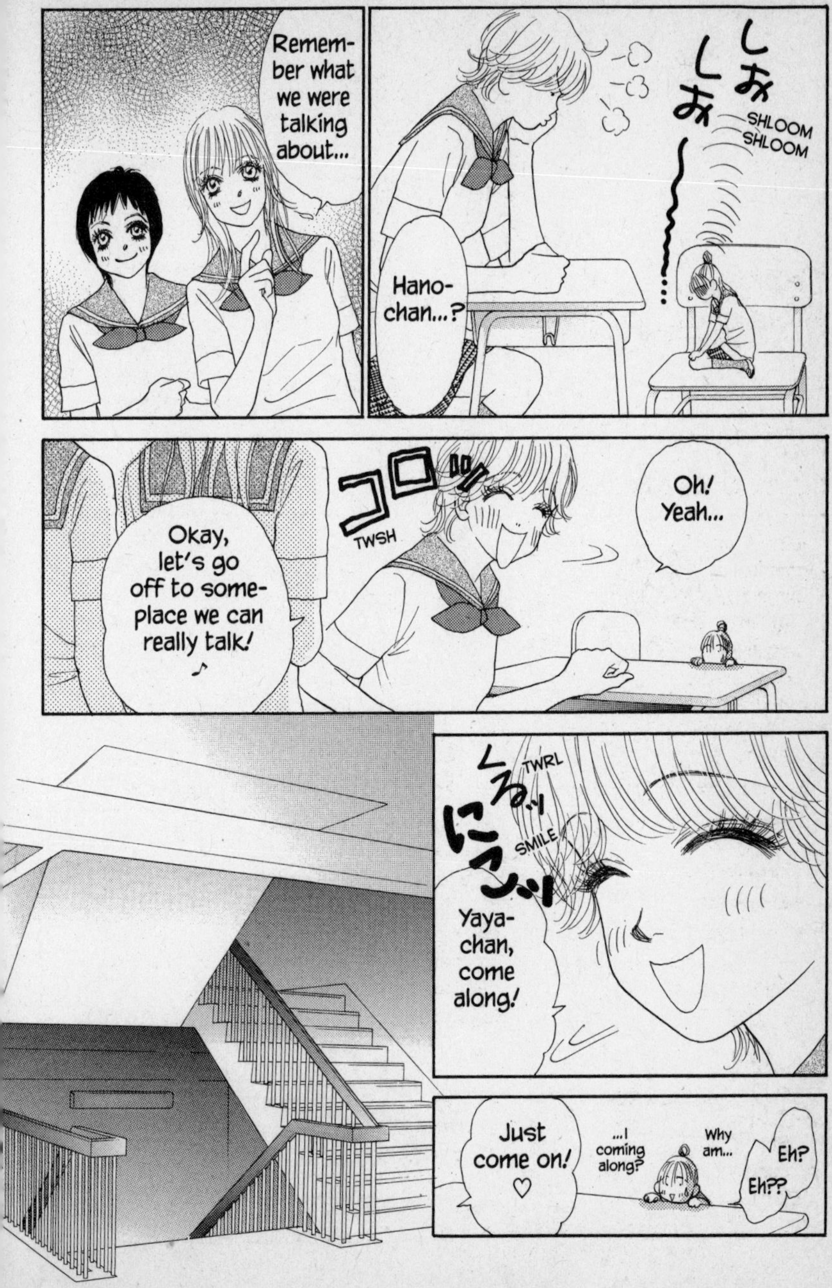
しおしお~…
SHLOOM SHLOOM
Hano-chan...?
Remember what we were talking about...
Oh! Yeah...
コロッ
TWSH
Okay, let's go off to someplace we can really talk! ♪
くるっ
TWRL
にこっ
SMILE
Yaya-chan, come along!
Eh?
Eh??
Why am... ...I coming along?
Just come on! ♡

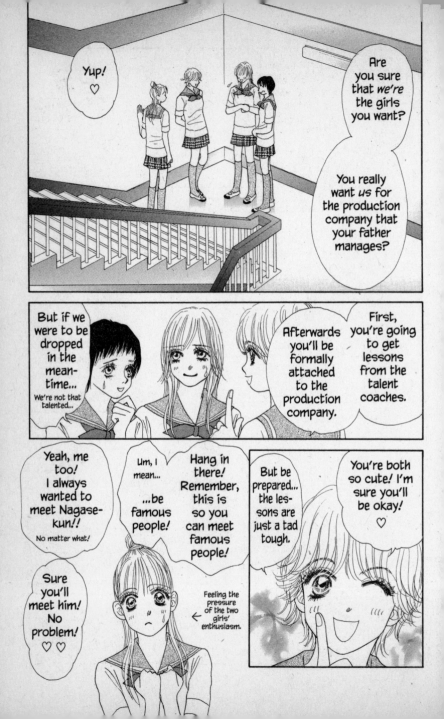

Yup! ♡

Are you sure that *we're* the girls you want?

You really want *us* for the production company that your father manages?

But if we were to be dropped in the meantime...
We're not that talented...

First, you're going to get lessons from the talent coaches.

Afterwards you'll be formally attached to the production company.

Yeah, me too! I always wanted to meet Nagase-kun!!
No matter what!

Um, I mean...
...be famous people!

Hang in there! Remember, this is so you can meet famous people!

Sure you'll meet him! No problem!
♡ ♡

← Feeling the pressure of the two girls' enthusiasm.

But be prepared... the lessons are just a tad tough.

You're both so cute! I'm sure you'll be okay!
♡

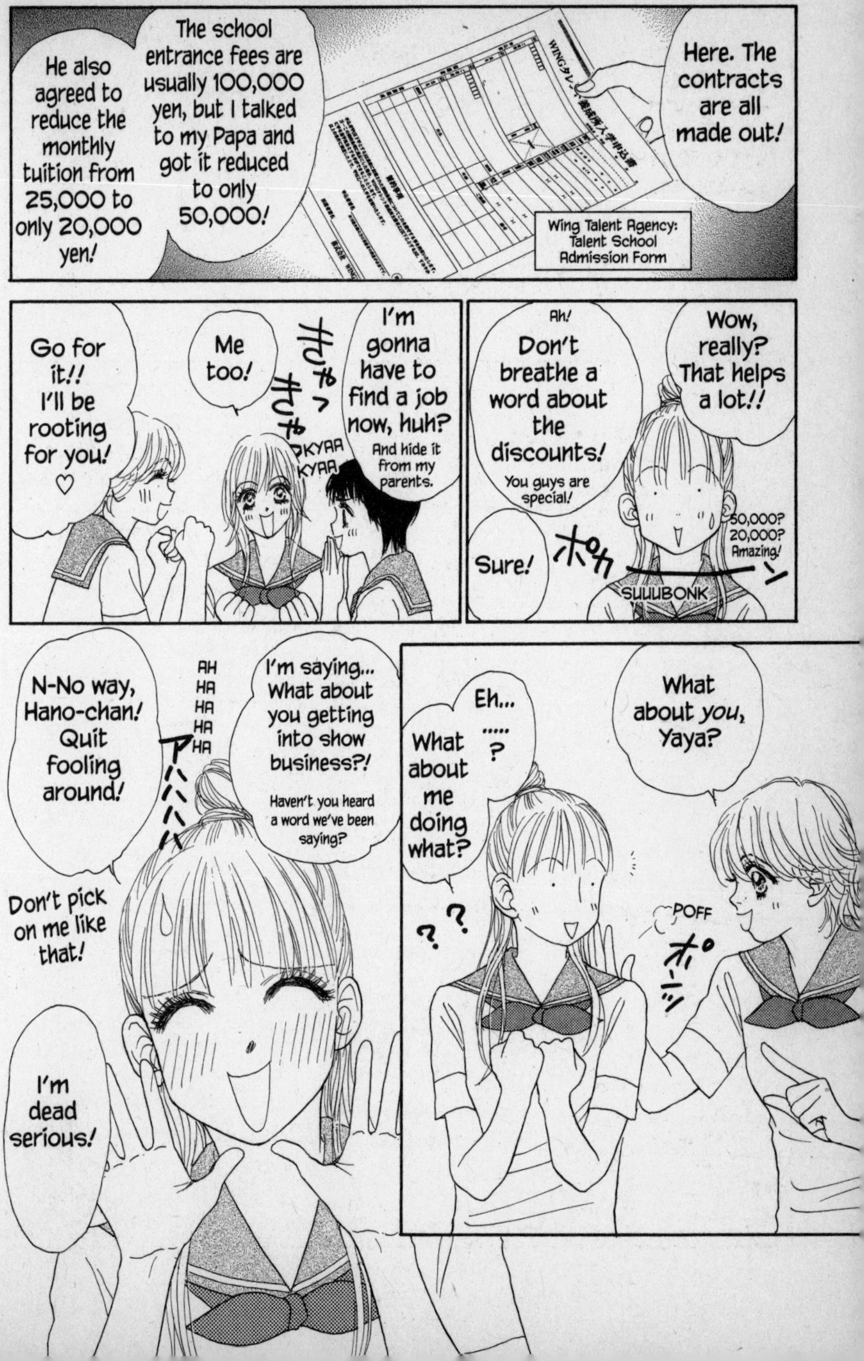
Here. The contracts are all made out!
The school entrance fees are usually 100,000 yen, but I talked to my Papa and got it reduced to only 50,000!
He also agreed to reduce the monthly tuition from 25,000 to only 20,000 yen!
Wing Talent Agency: Talent School Admission Form
Wow, really? That helps a lot!!
Ah! Don't breathe a word about the discounts! You guys are special!
50,000? 20,000? Amazing!
Sure!
SUUUBONK
I'm gonna have to find a job now, huh? And hide it from my parents.
KYAA KYAA
Me too!
Go for it!! I'll be rooting for you! ♡
What about you, Yaya?
POFF
Eh... .....?
What about me doing what?
I'm saying... What about you getting into show business?! Haven't you heard a word we've been saying?
AH HA HA HA HA
N-No way, Hano-chan! Quit fooling around!
Don't pick on me like that!
I'm dead serious!

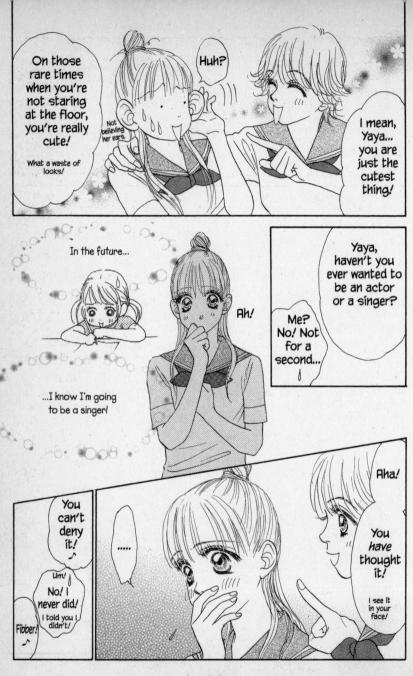

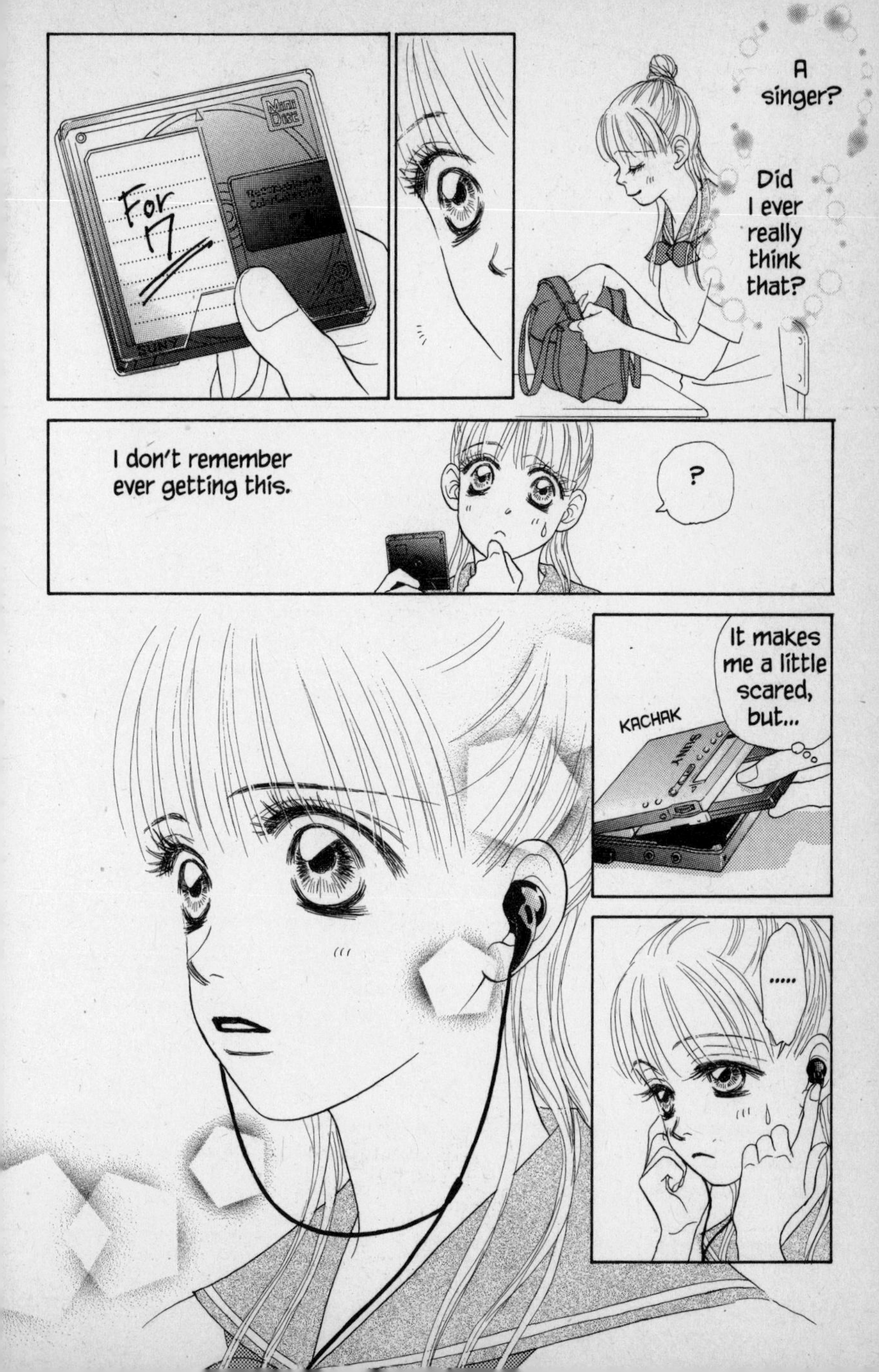
A singer?
Did I ever really think that?
MiniDisc
For 17
?
I don't remember ever getting this.
It makes me a little scared, but...
KACHAK
.....

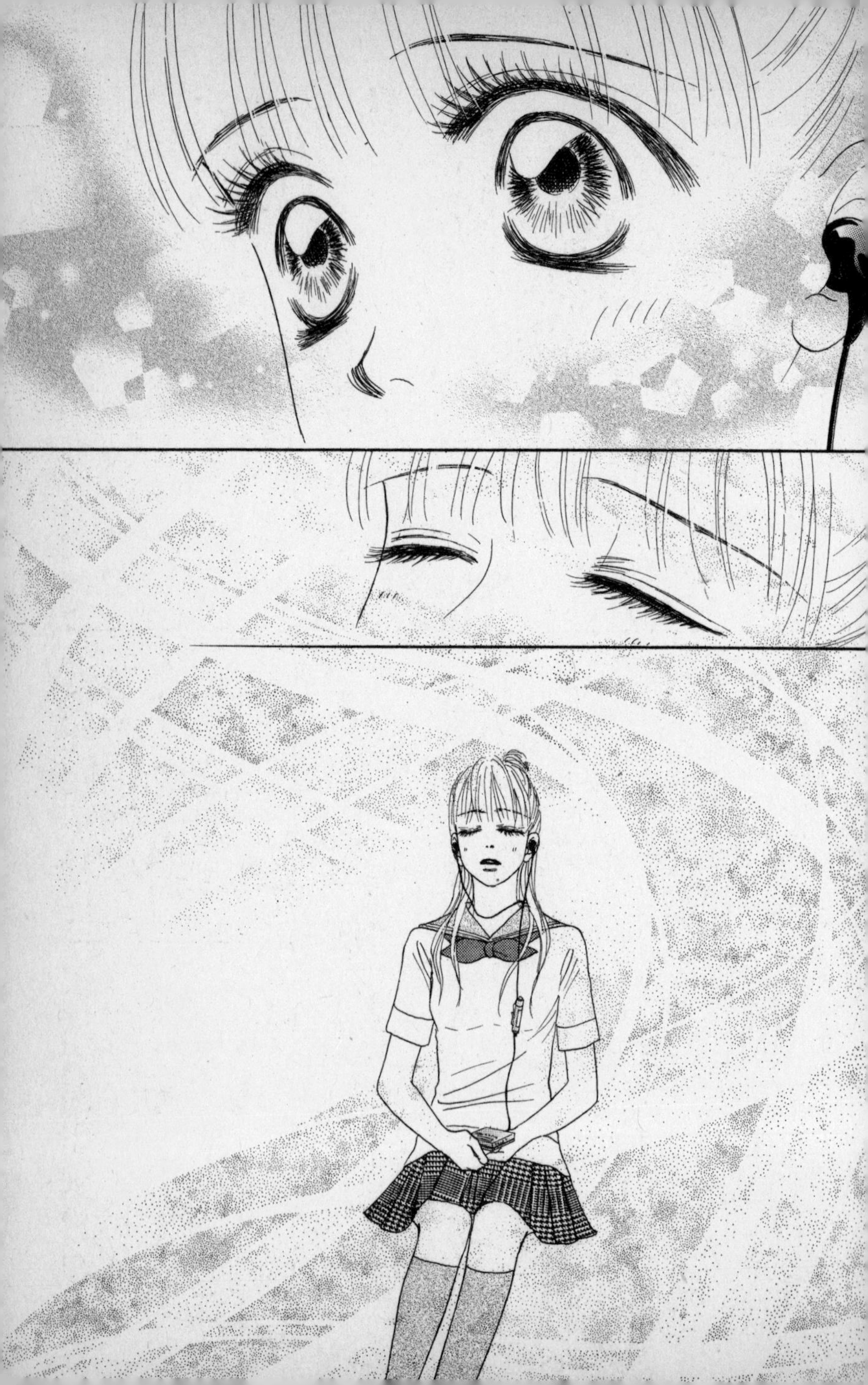

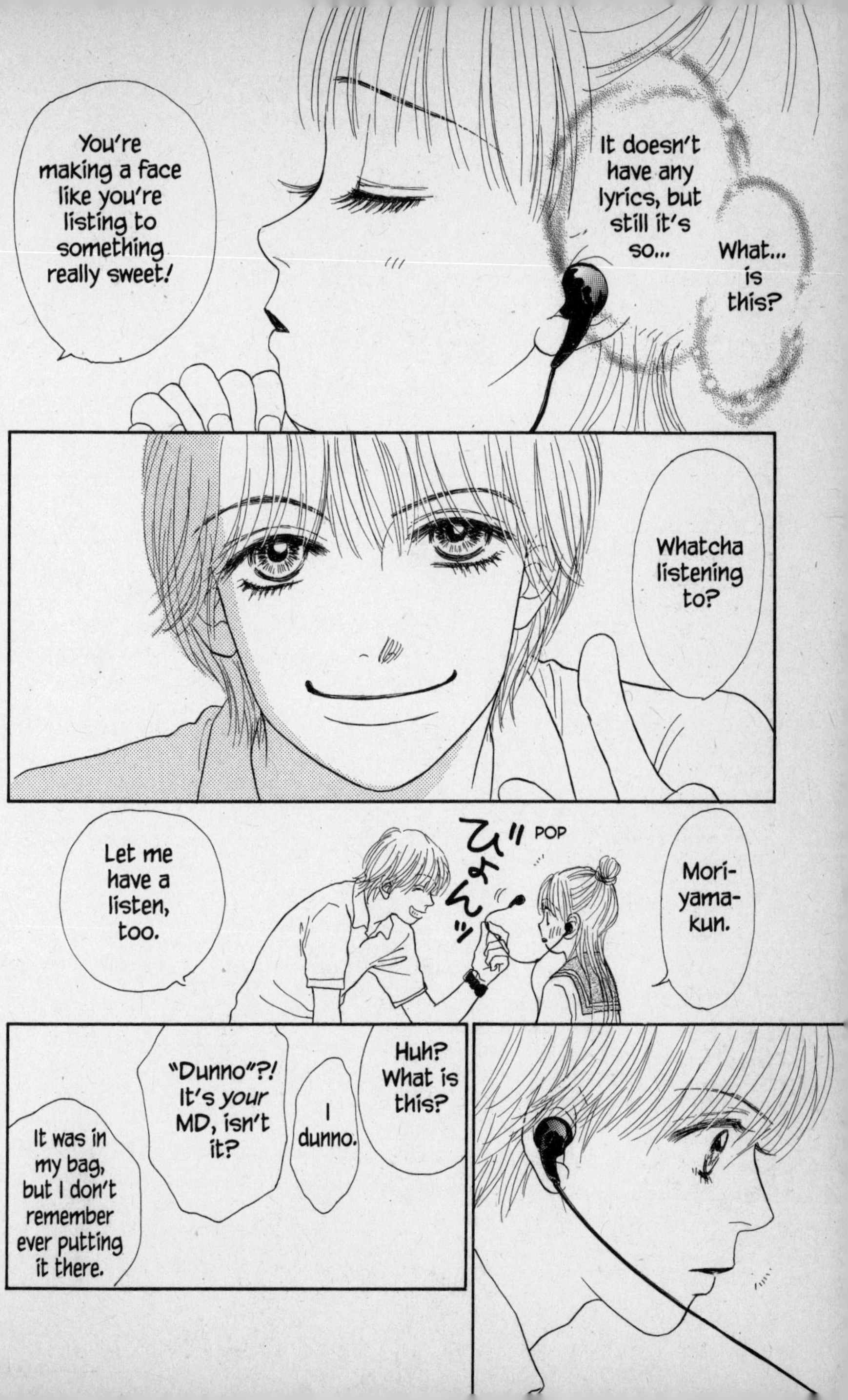
It doesn't have any lyrics, but still it's so...
What... is this?
You're making a face like you're listing to something really sweet!
Whatcha listening to?
Mori-yama-kun.
POP
Let me have a listen, too.
Huh? What is this?
I dunno.
"Dunno"?! It's *your* MD, isn't it?
It was in my bag, but I don't remember ever putting it there.

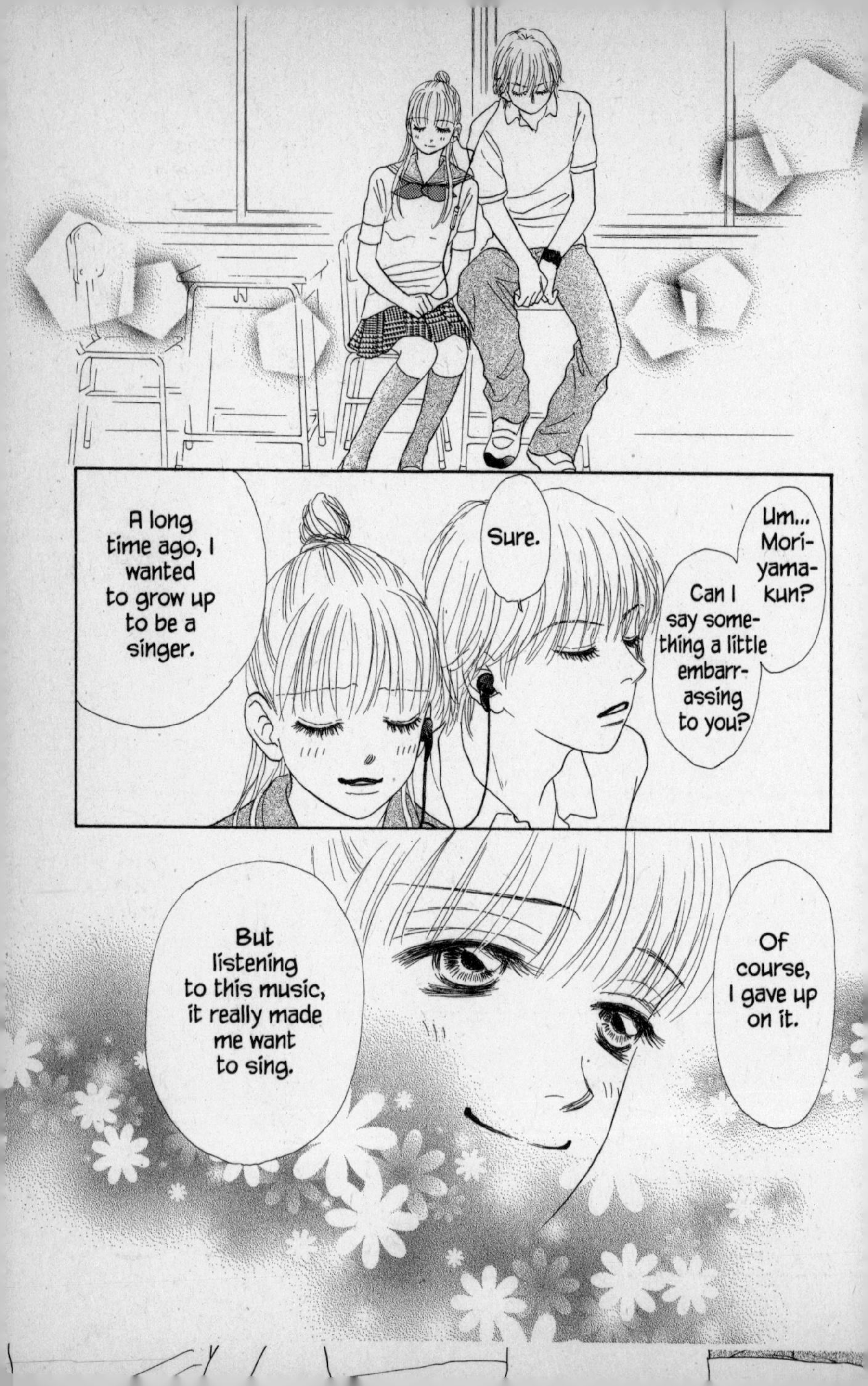

Um... Mori-yama-kun?
Can I say some-thing a little embarr-assing to you?
Sure.
A long time ago, I wanted to grow up to be a singer.
Of course, I gave up on it.
But listening to this music, it really made me want to sing.

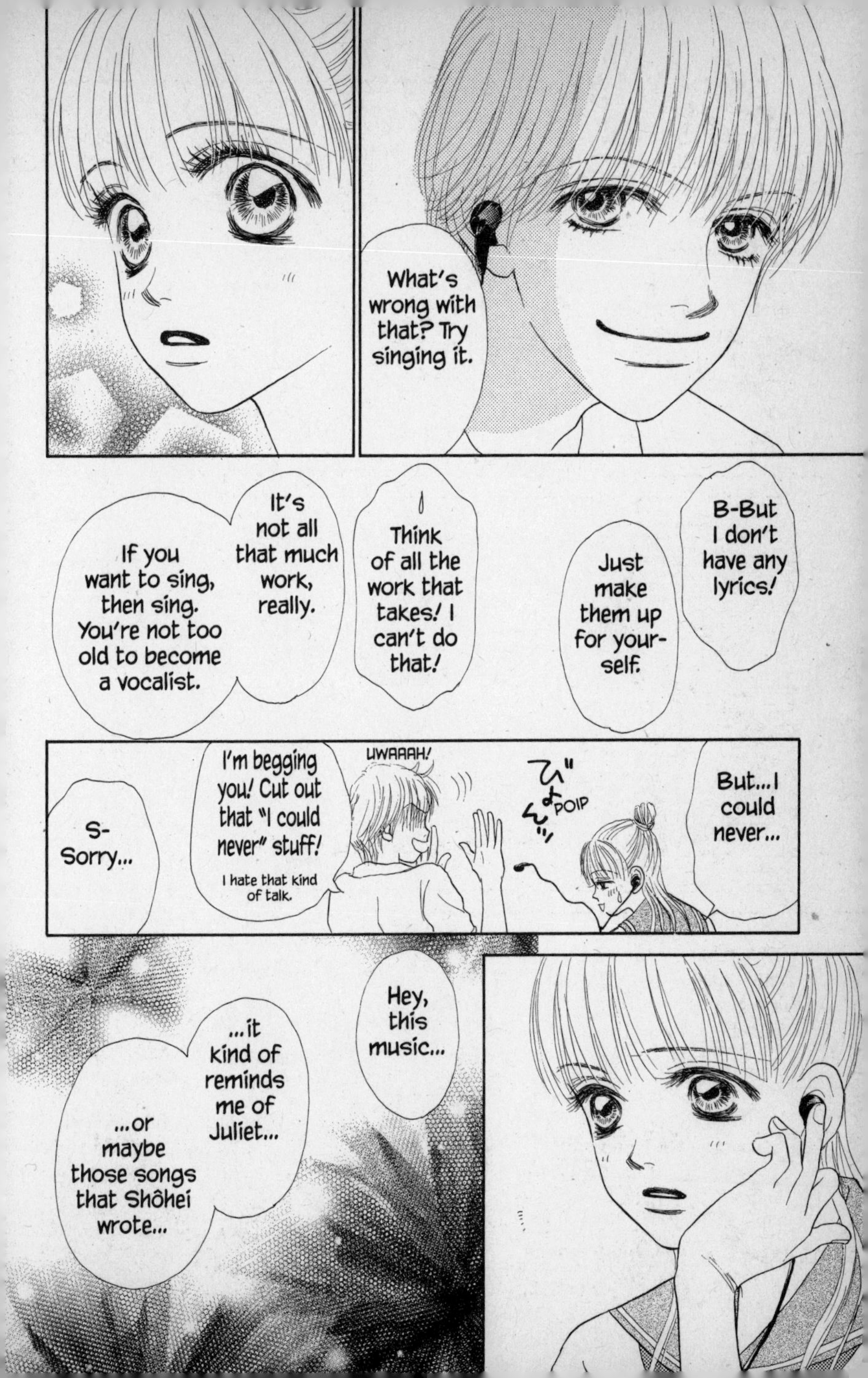
What's wrong with that? Try singing it.
B-But I don't have any lyrics!
Just make them up for your-self.
!
Think of all the work that takes! I can't do that!
It's not all that much work, really.
If you want to sing, then sing. You're not too old to become a vocalist.
But...I could never...
POIP
UWAAAH!
I'm begging you! Cut out that "I could never" stuff!
I hate that kind of talk.
S-Sorry...
Hey, this music...
...it kind of reminds me of Juliet...
...or maybe those songs that Shôhei wrote...

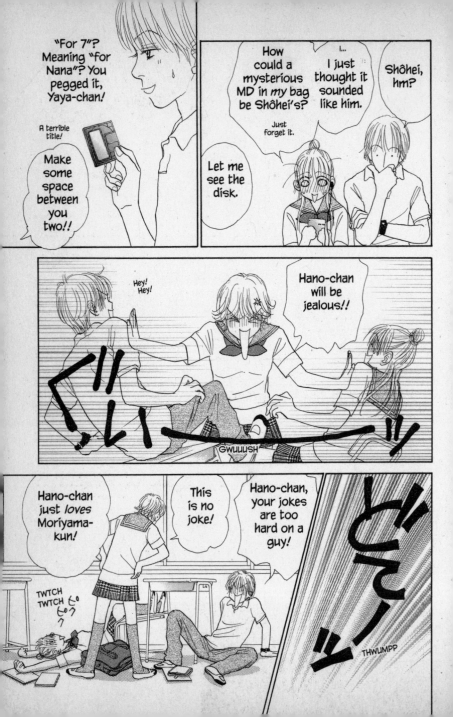

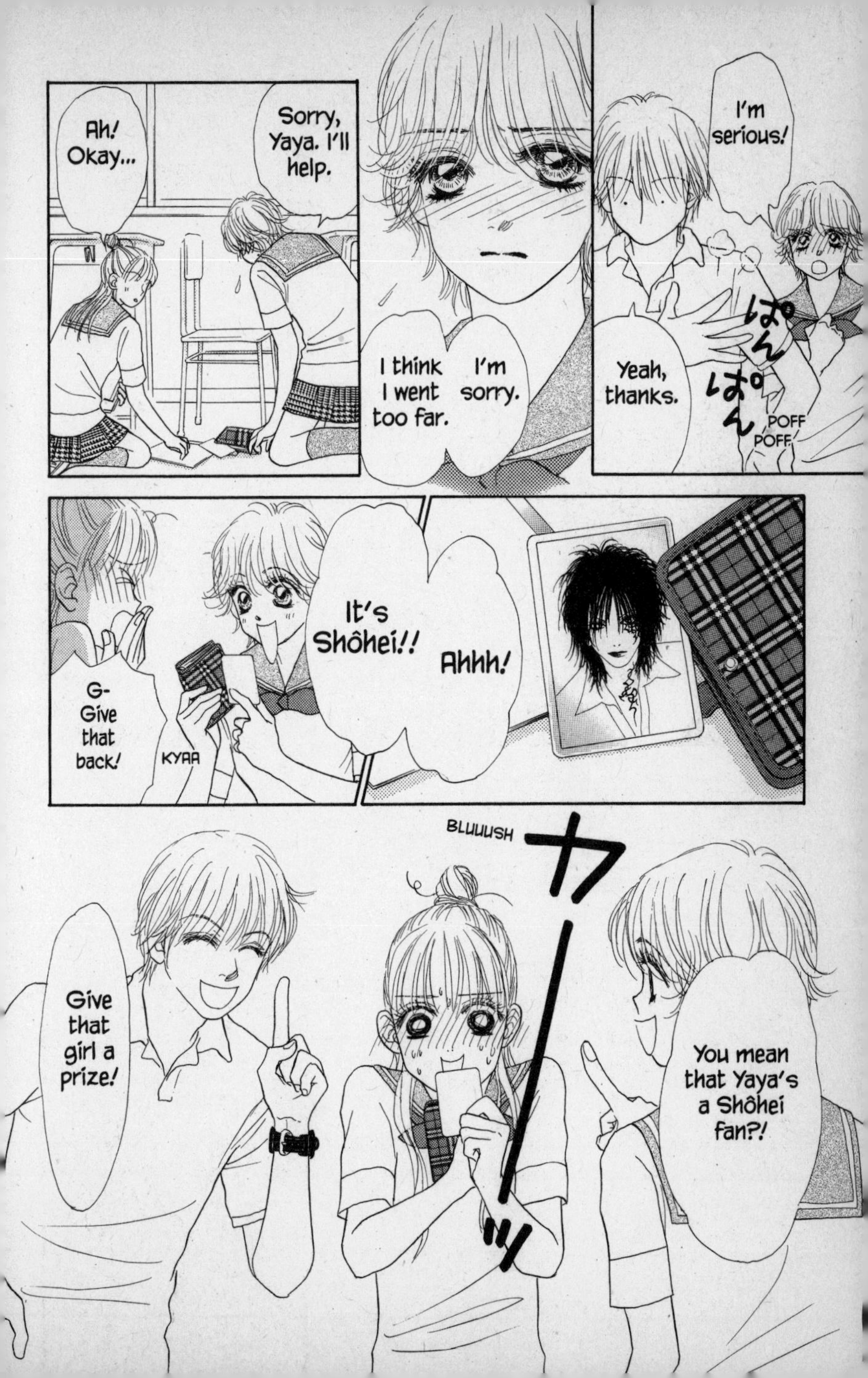
I'm serious!
Yeah, thanks.
ぱん ぱん
POFF POFF
I'm sorry.
I think I went too far.
Sorry, Yaya. I'll help.
Ah! Okay...
Ahhh!
It's Shôhei!!
KYAA
G-Give that back!
BLUUUSH
You mean that Yaya's a Shôhei fan?!
Give that girl a prize!

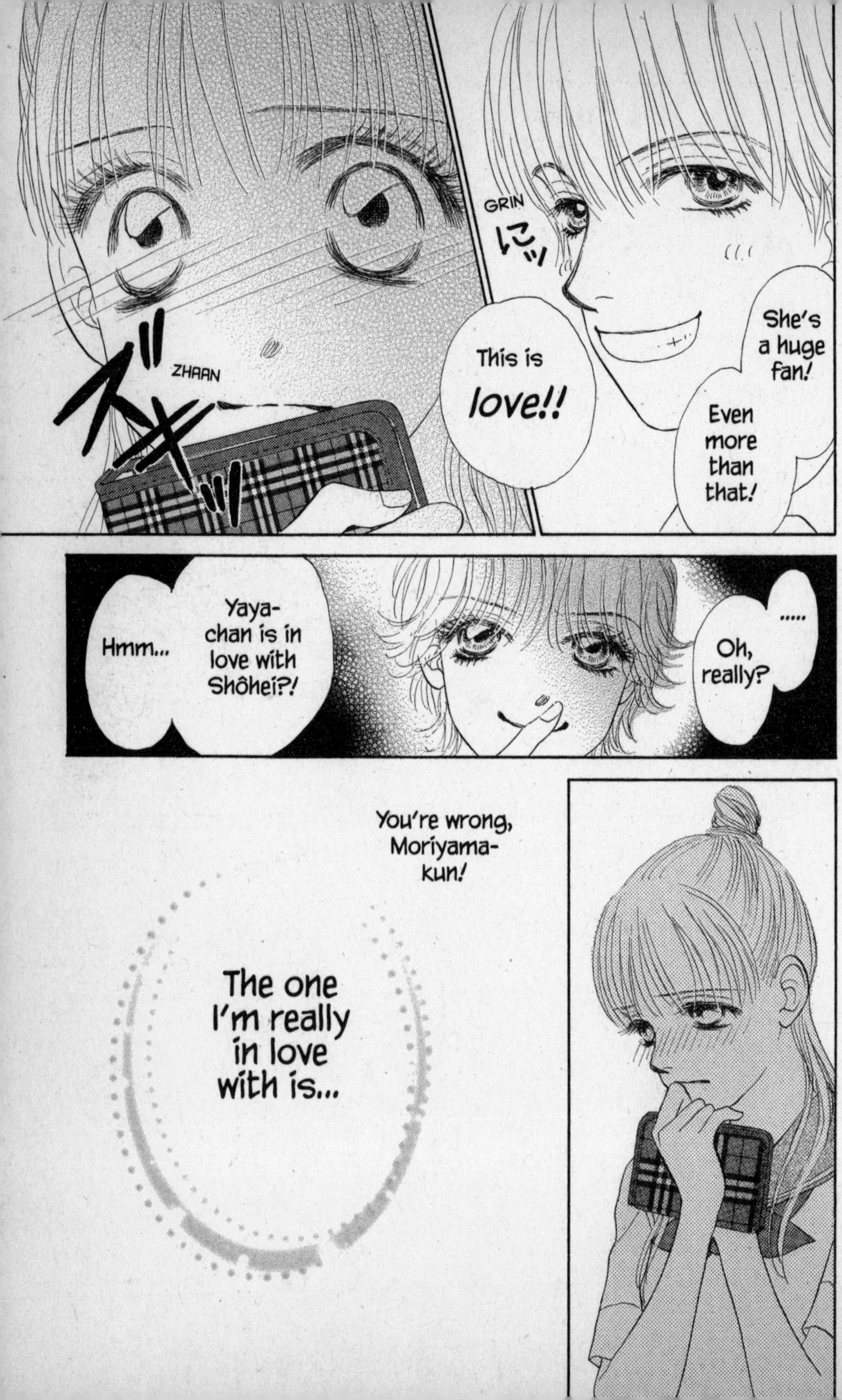
She's a huge fan!
Even more than that!
This is love!!
GRIN
にッ
ZHAAN
ズ
.....
Oh, really?
Yaya-chan is in love with Shôhei?!
Hmm...
You're wrong, Moriyama-kun!
The one I'm really in love with is...

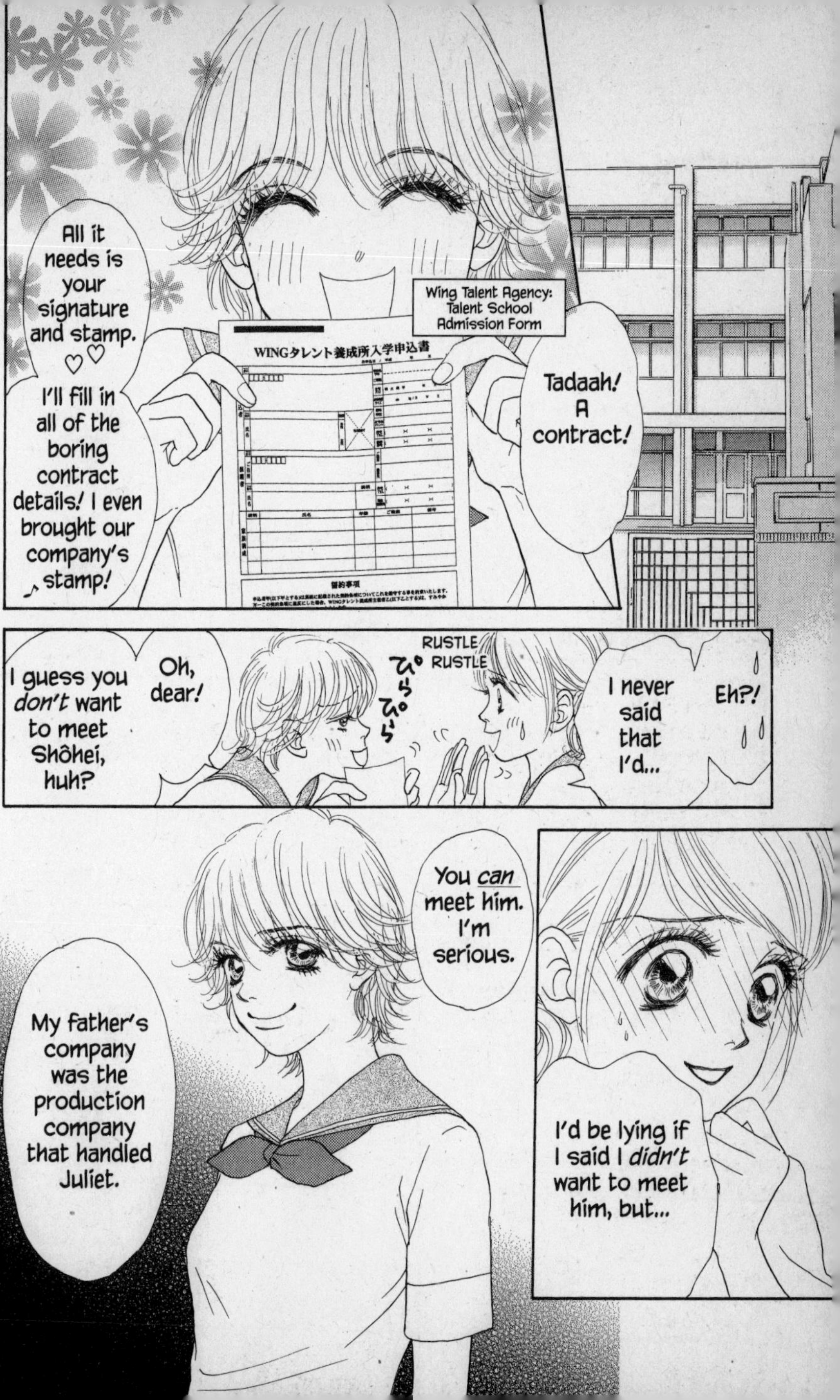
Tadaah! A contract!
Wing Talent Agency: Talent School Admission Form
WINGタレント養成所入学申込書
All it needs is your signature and stamp. ♡♡
I'll fill in all of the boring contract details! I even brought our company's stamp! ♪
Eh?!
I never said that I'd...
RUSTLE RUSTLE
ぴらぴら
Oh, dear!
I guess you *don't* want to meet Shôhei, huh?
I'd be lying if I said I *didn't* want to meet him, but...
You *can* meet him. I'm serious.
My father's company was the production company that handled Juliet.

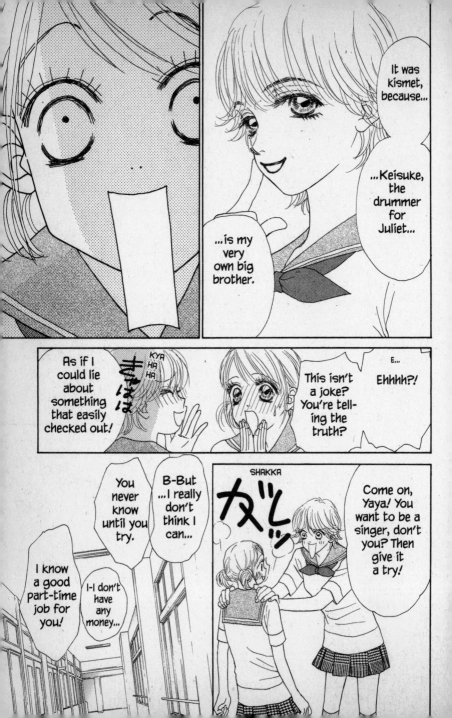

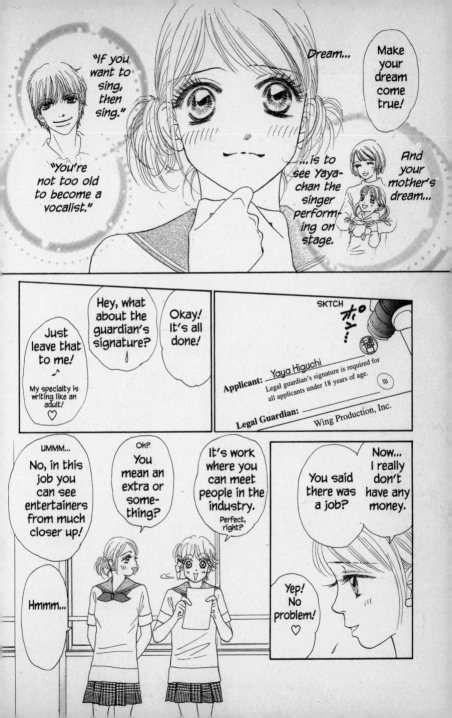

"If you want to sing, then sing."

"You're not too old to become a vocalist."

Dream...

Make your dream come true!

...is to see Yaya-chan the singer performing on stage.

And your mother's dream...

Just leave that to me!

My specialty is writing like an adult! ♡

Hey, what about the guardian's signature?

Okay! It's all done!

SKTCH

Applicant: Yaya Higuchi

Legal guardian's signature is required for all applicants under 18 years of age.

Legal Guardian: _____

Wing Production, Inc.

UMMM... No, in this job you can see entertainers from much closer up!

Hmmm...

Oh? You mean an extra or something?

It's work where you can meet people in the industry. Perfect, right?

You said there was a job?

Now... I really don't have any money.

Yep! No problem! ♡

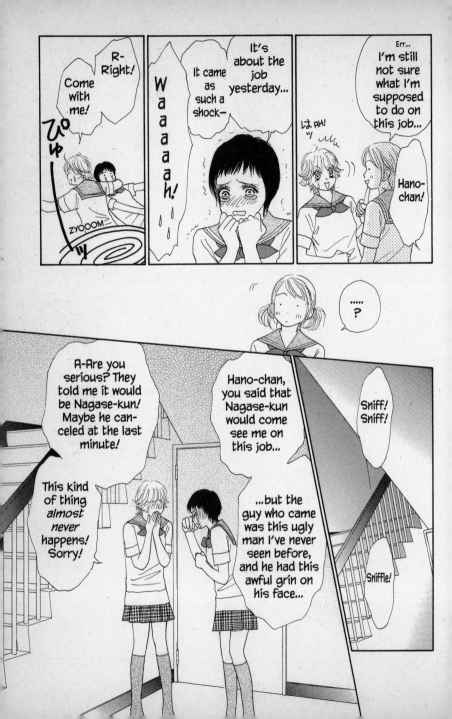

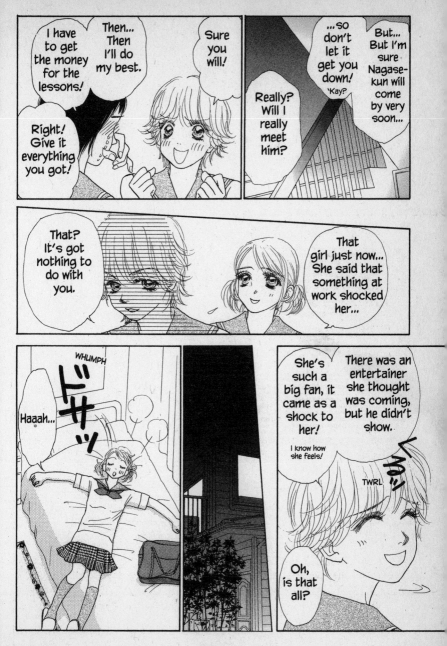

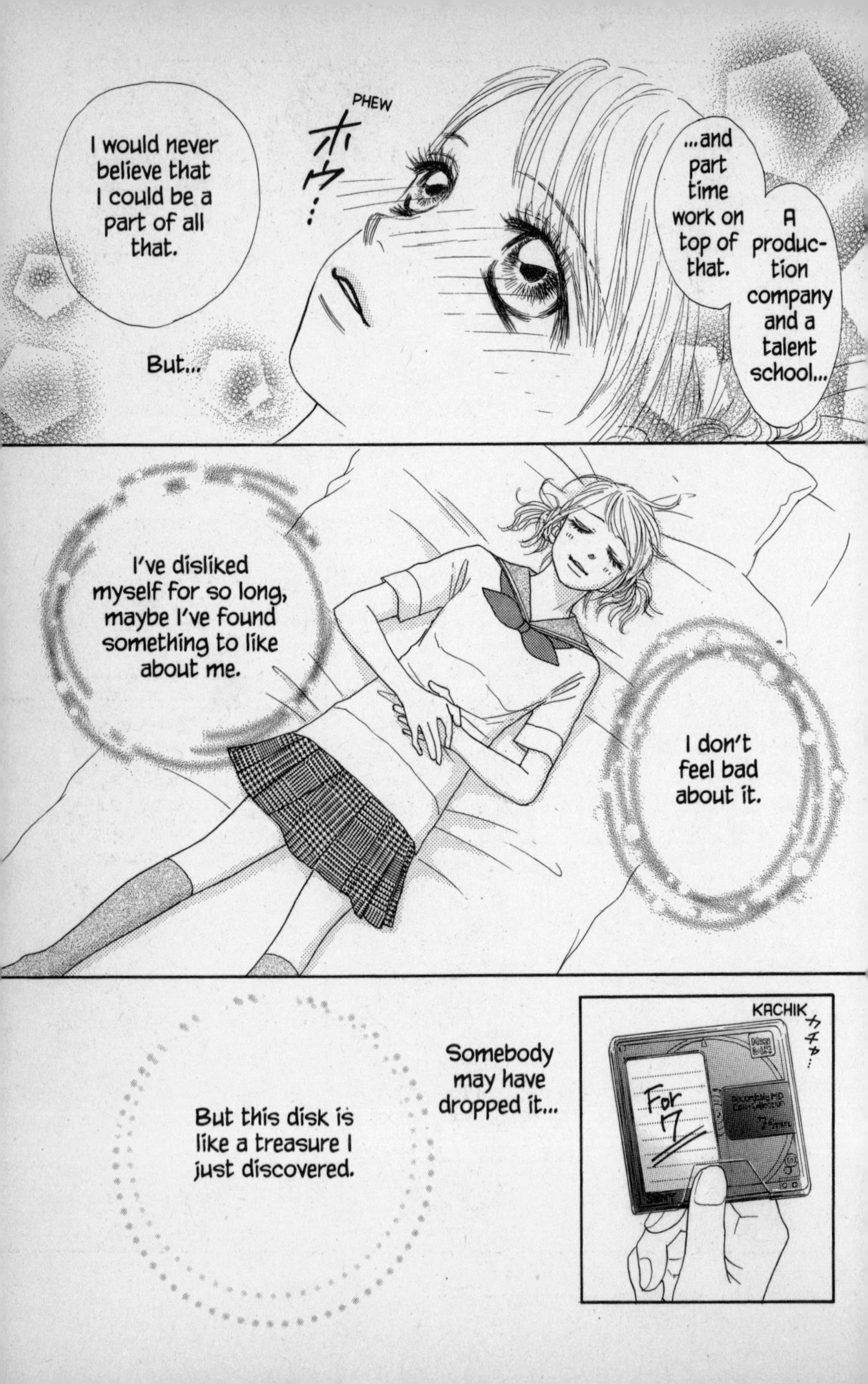
A production-company and a talent school...
...and part time work on top of that.
PHEW
I would never believe that I could be a part of all that.
But...
I've disliked myself for so long, maybe I've found something to like about me.
I don't feel bad about it.
KACHIK
Somebody may have dropped it...
But this disk is like a treasure I just discovered.

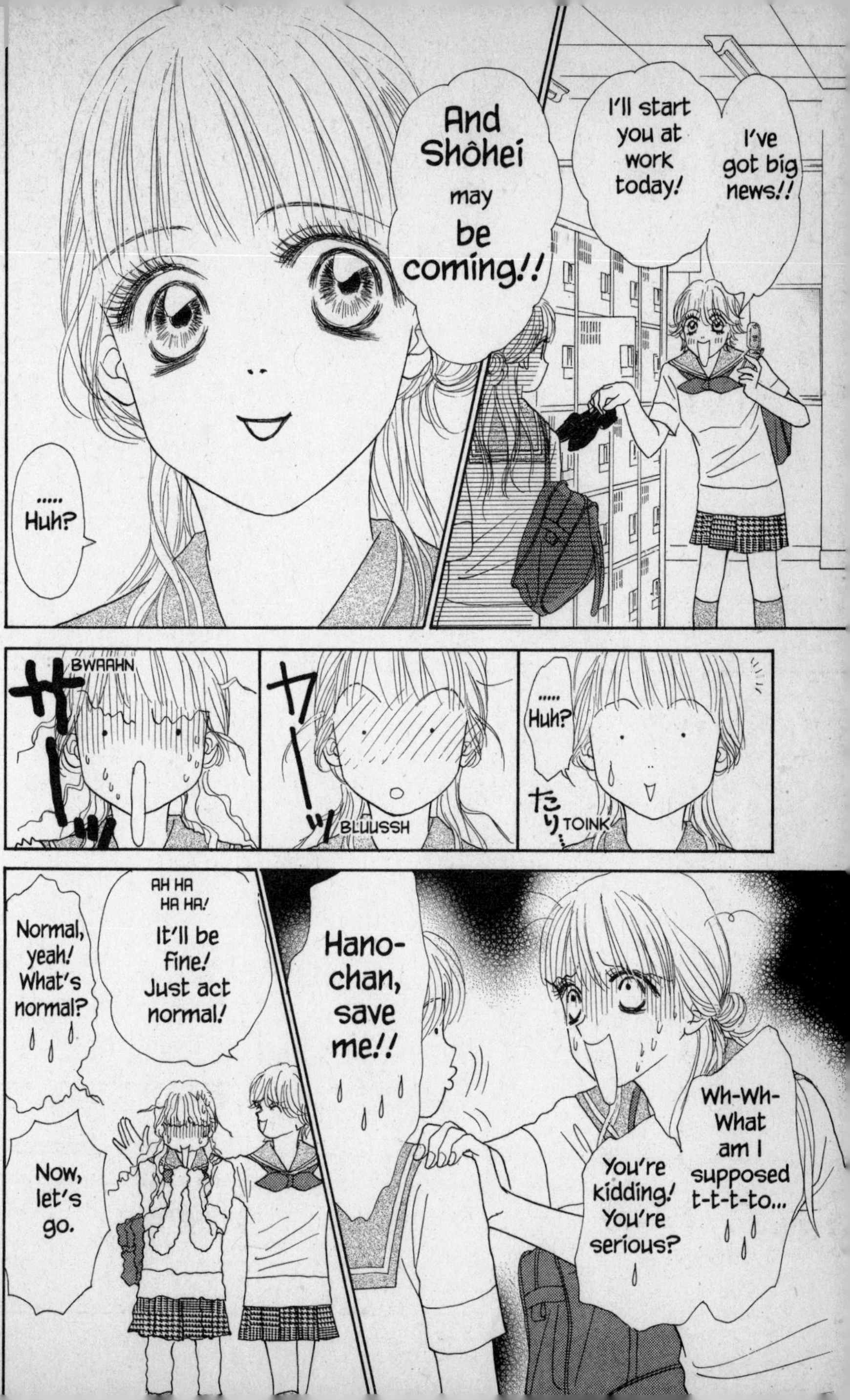
I've got big news!!
I'll start you at work today!
And Shôhei may be coming!!
..... Huh?
..... Huh?
たり TOINK
ヤーッ BLUUSSH
サーッ BWAAHN
Wh-Wh-What am I supposed t-t-t-to...
You're kidding! You're serious?
Hano-chan, save me!!
AH HA HA HA! It'll be fine! Just act normal!
Normal, yeah! What's normal?
Now, let's go.

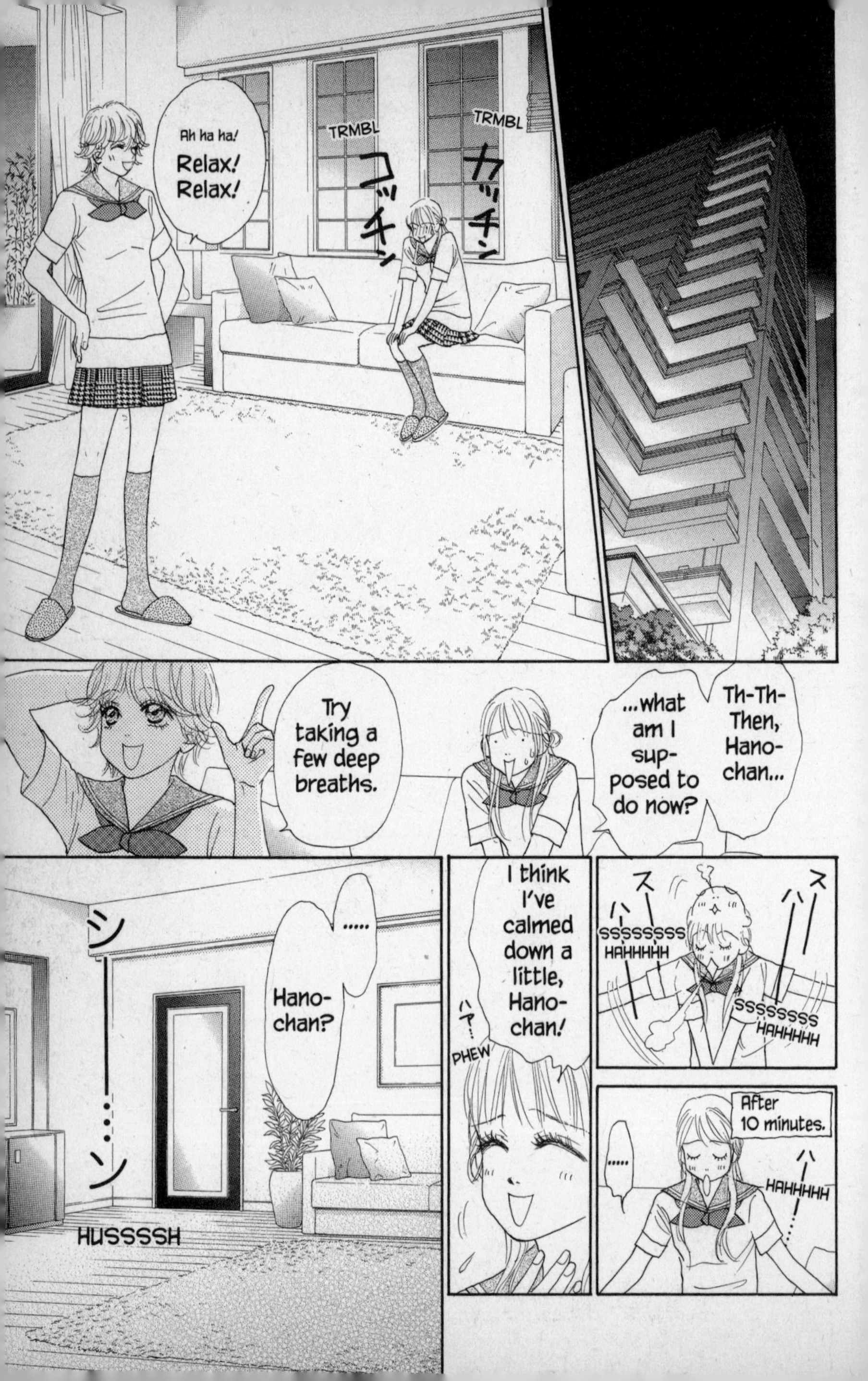

TRMBL
カッチン
TRMBL
コッチン
Ah ha ha!
Relax! Relax!
Th-Th-Then, Hano-chan...
...what am I sup-posed to do now?
Try taking a few deep breaths.
スーハー
SSSSSSSS HAHHHHH
スーハー
SSSSSSSS HAHHHHH
After 10 minutes.
ハー…
HAHHHHH
.....
ハァ…
PHEW
I think I've calmed down a little, Hano-chan!
.....
Hano-chan?
シーン
HUSSSSH

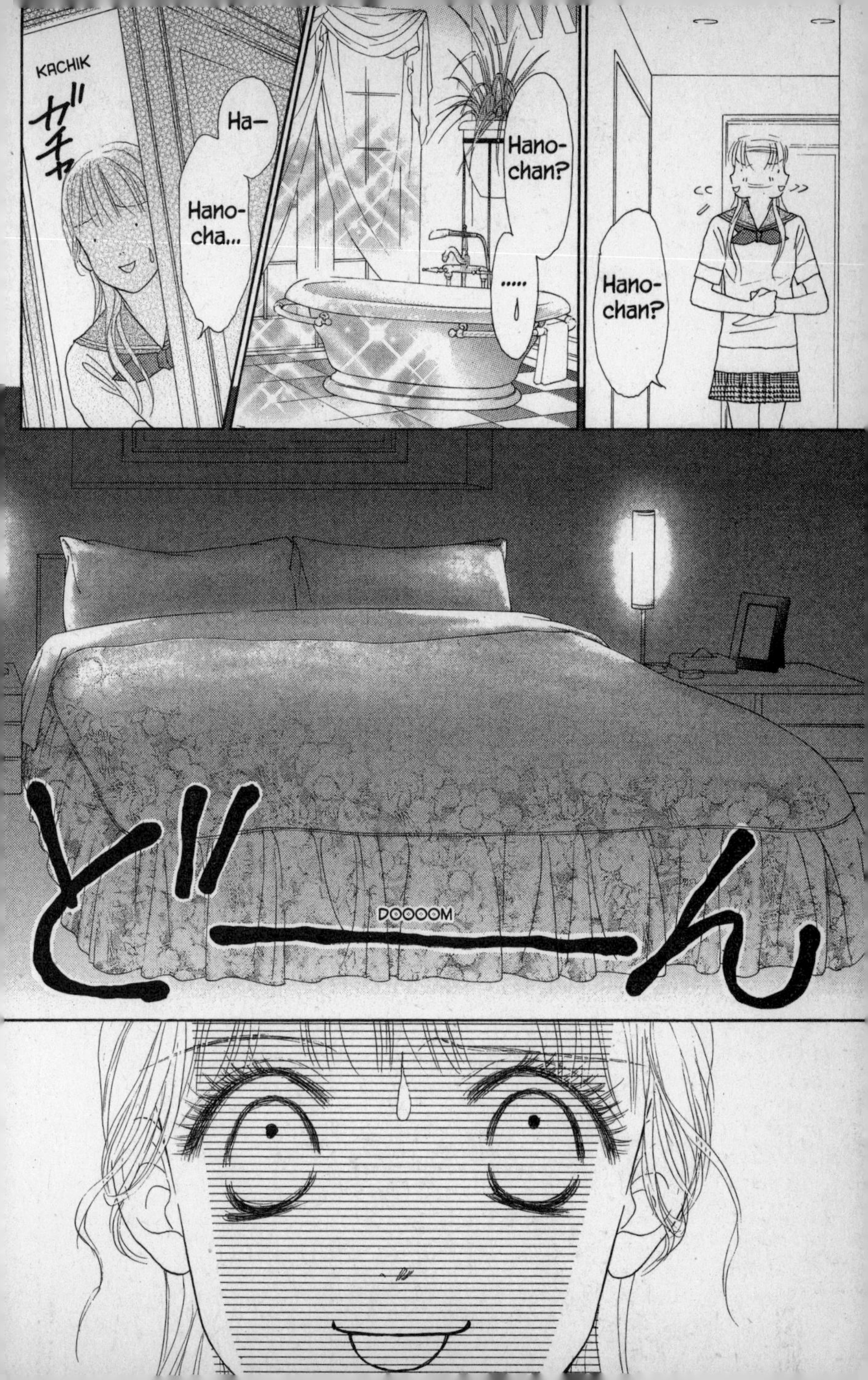
Hano-chan?
Hano-chan?
.....
Ha-
Hano-cha...
KACHIK
ガチャ
どーん
DOOOOM

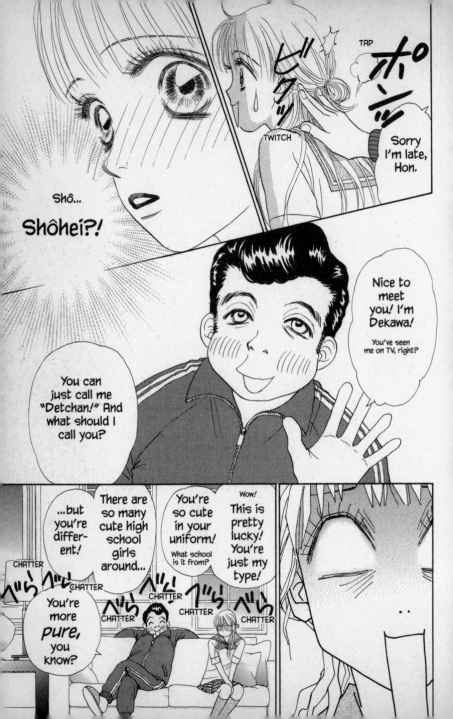

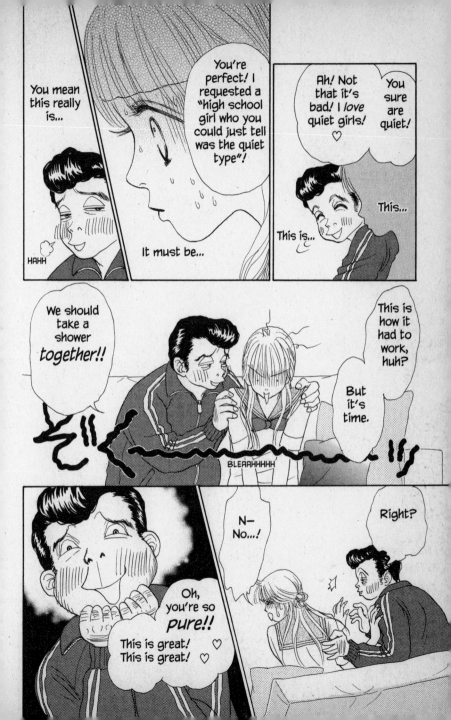

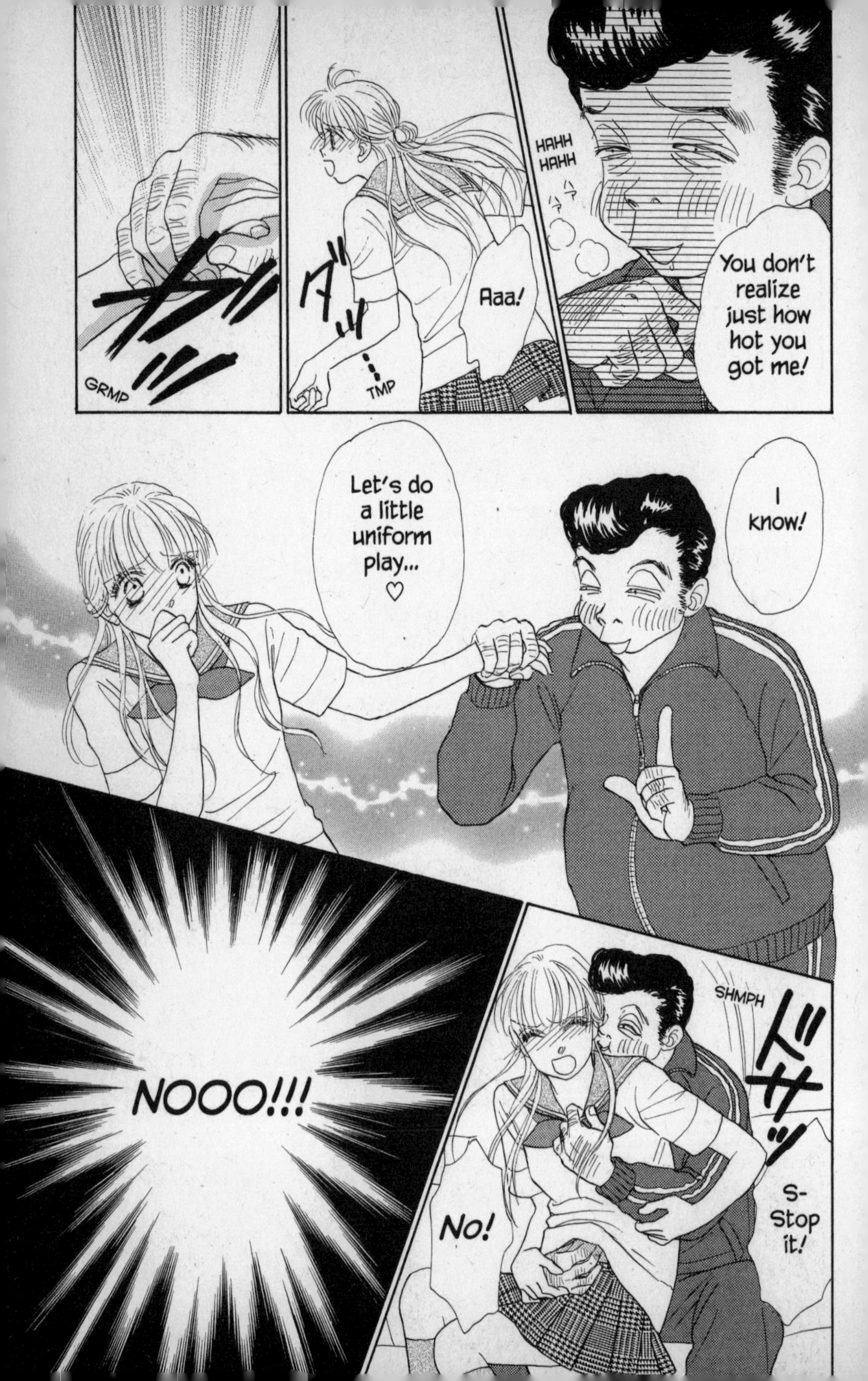
HAHH HAHH
You don't realize just how hot you got me!
Aaa!
TMP
GRMP
I know!
Let's do a little uniform play... ♡
SHMPH
S-Stop it!
No!
NOOO!!!

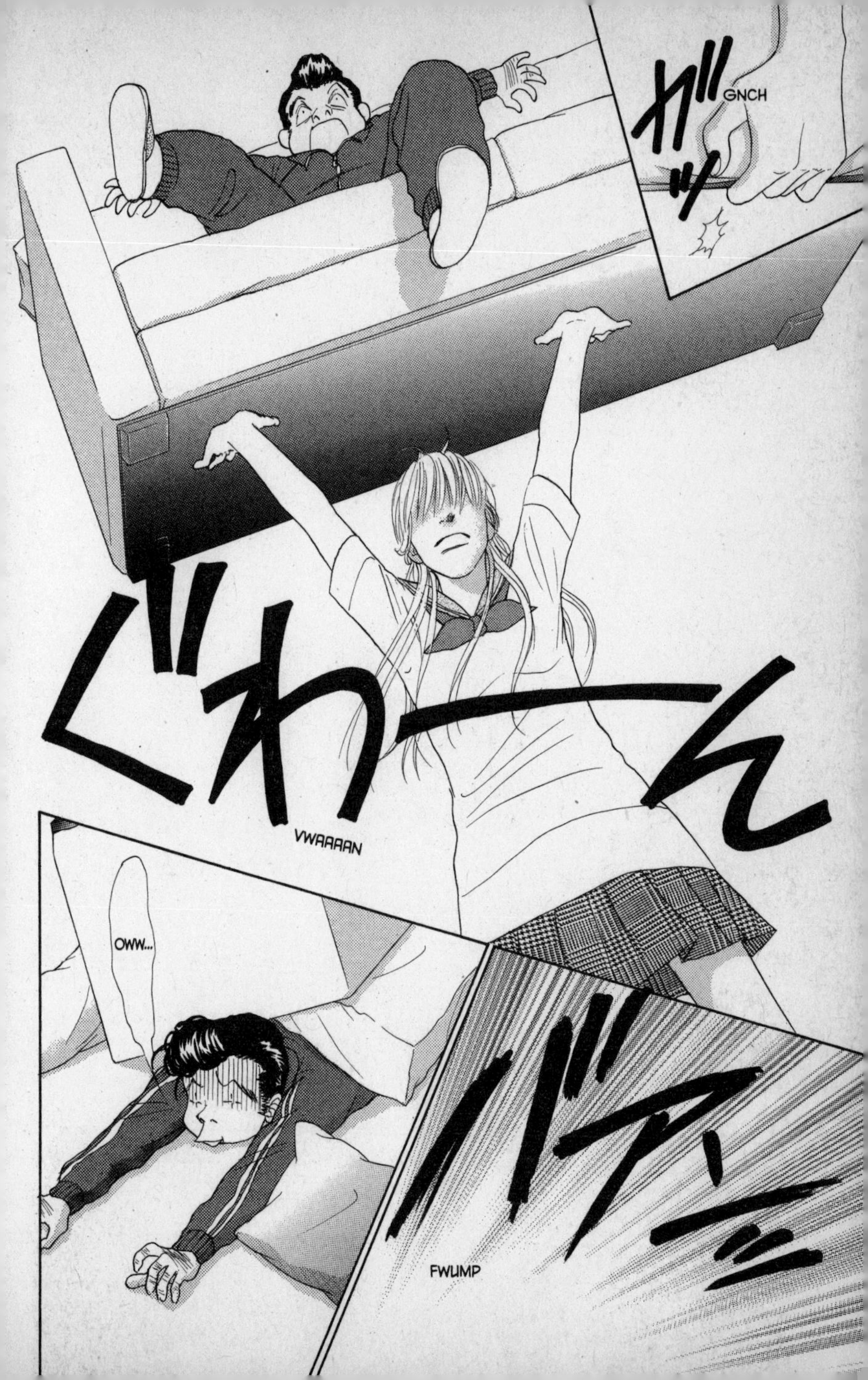
ガッ
GNCH
ぐわーん
VWAAAAN
FWUMP
OWW...

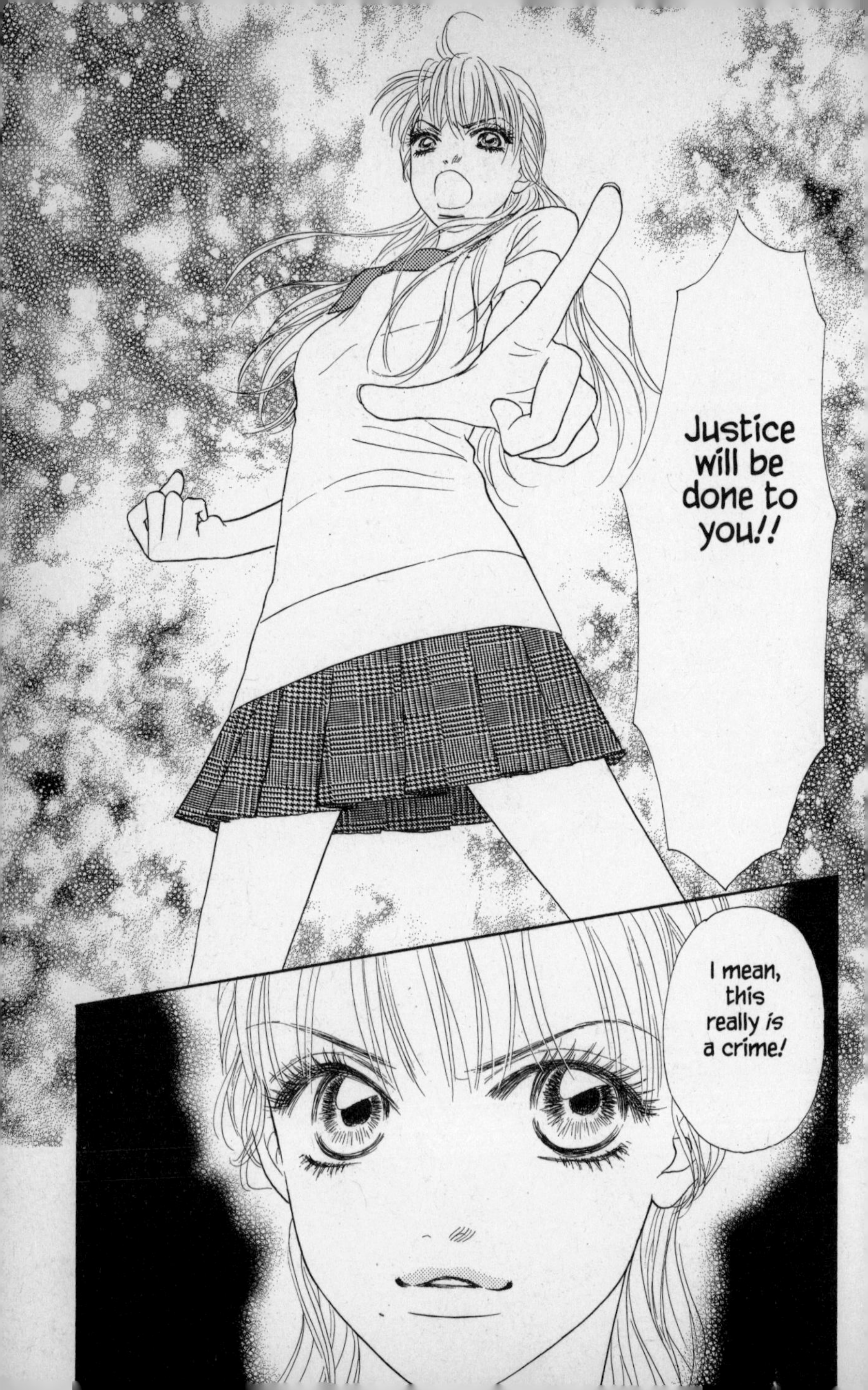
Justice will be done to you!!
I mean, this really *is* a crime!

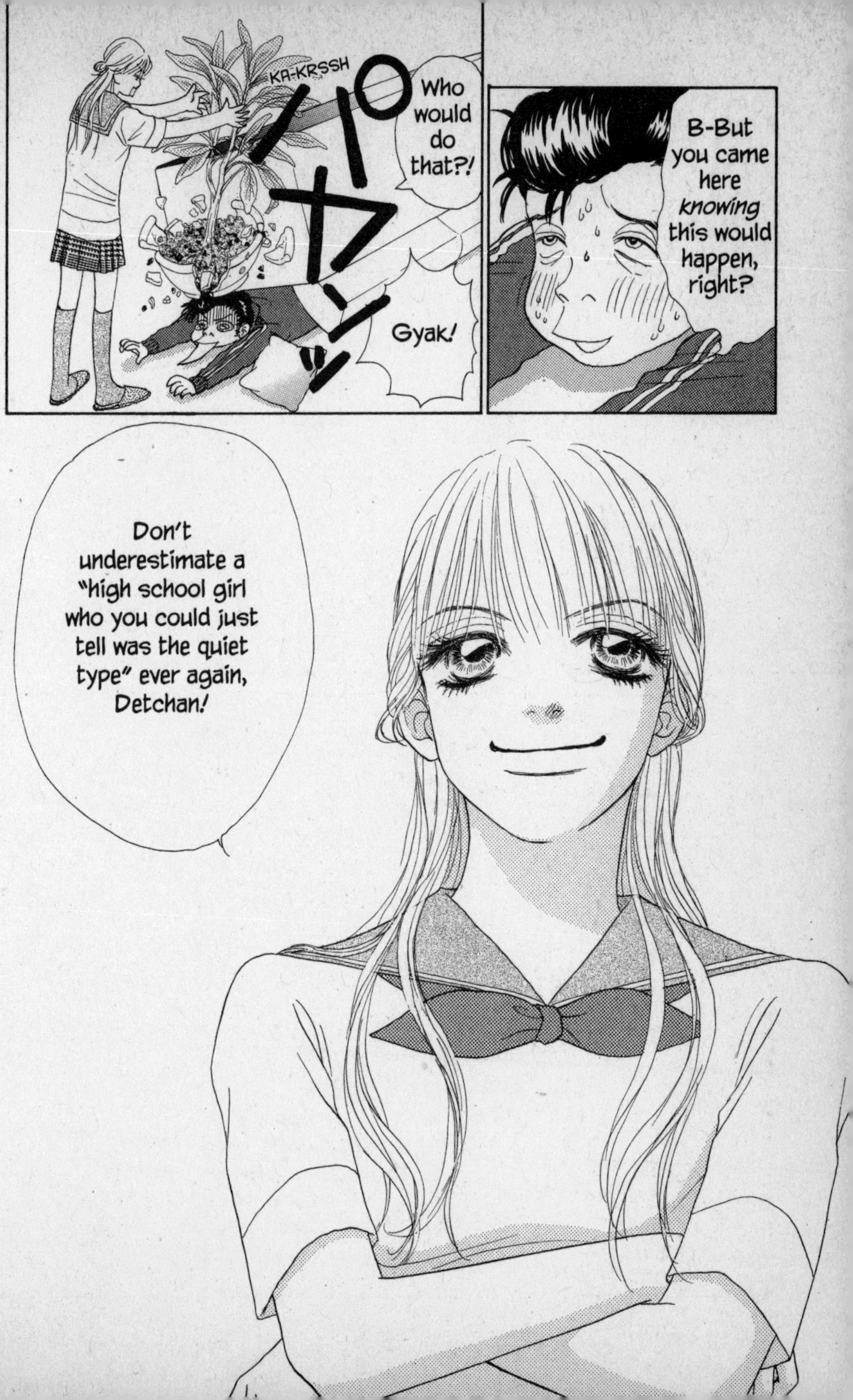
B-But you came here *knowing* this would happen, right?
Who would do that?!
KA-KRSSH
Gyak!
Don't underestimate a "high school girl who you could just tell was the quiet type" ever again, Detchan!

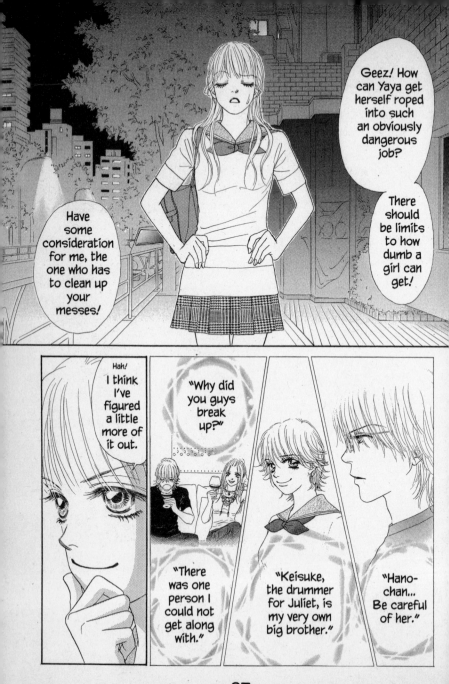

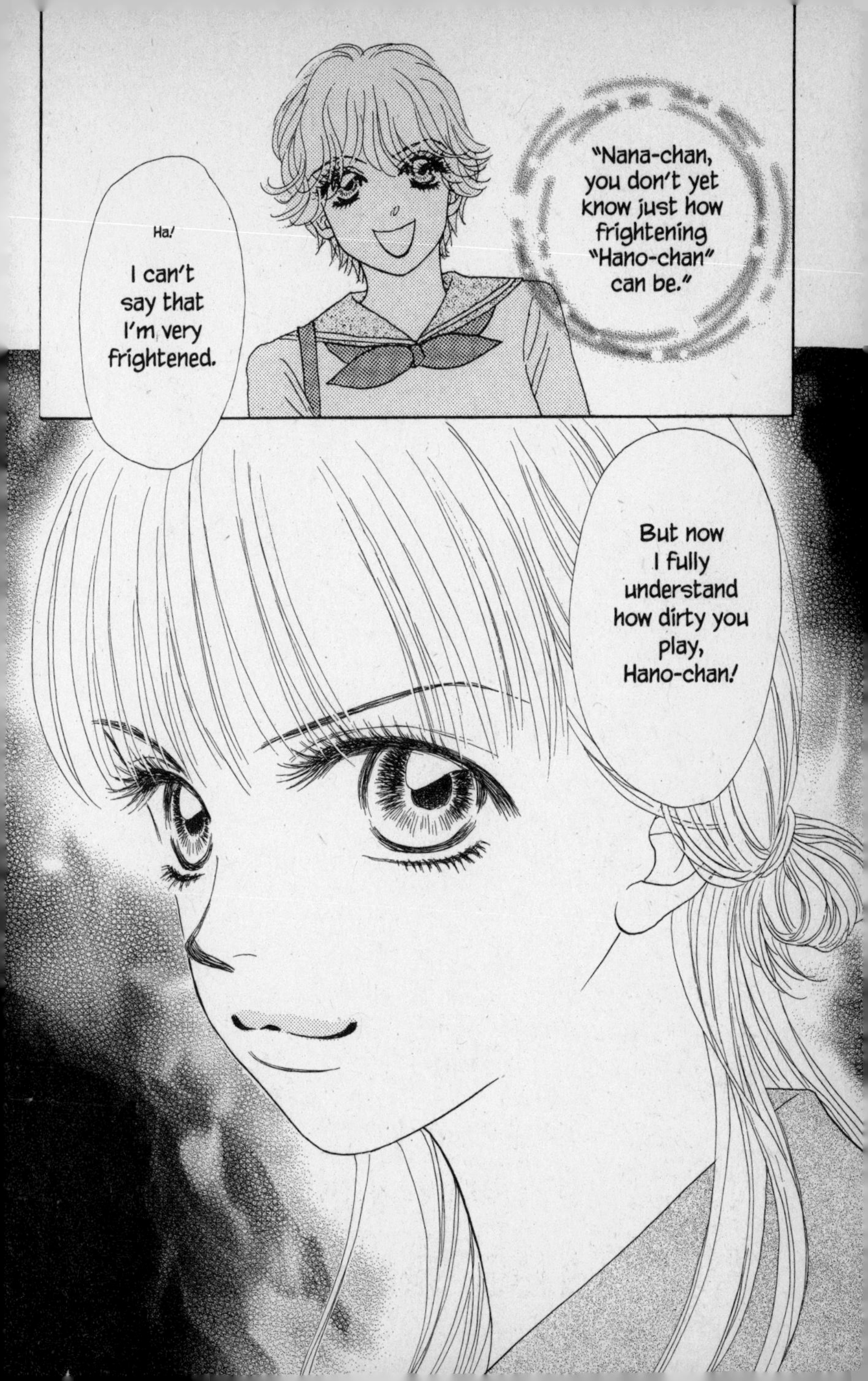
"Nana-chan, you don't yet know just how frightening "Hano-chan" can be."
Ha!
I can't say that I'm very frightened.
But now I fully understand how dirty you play, Hano-chan!

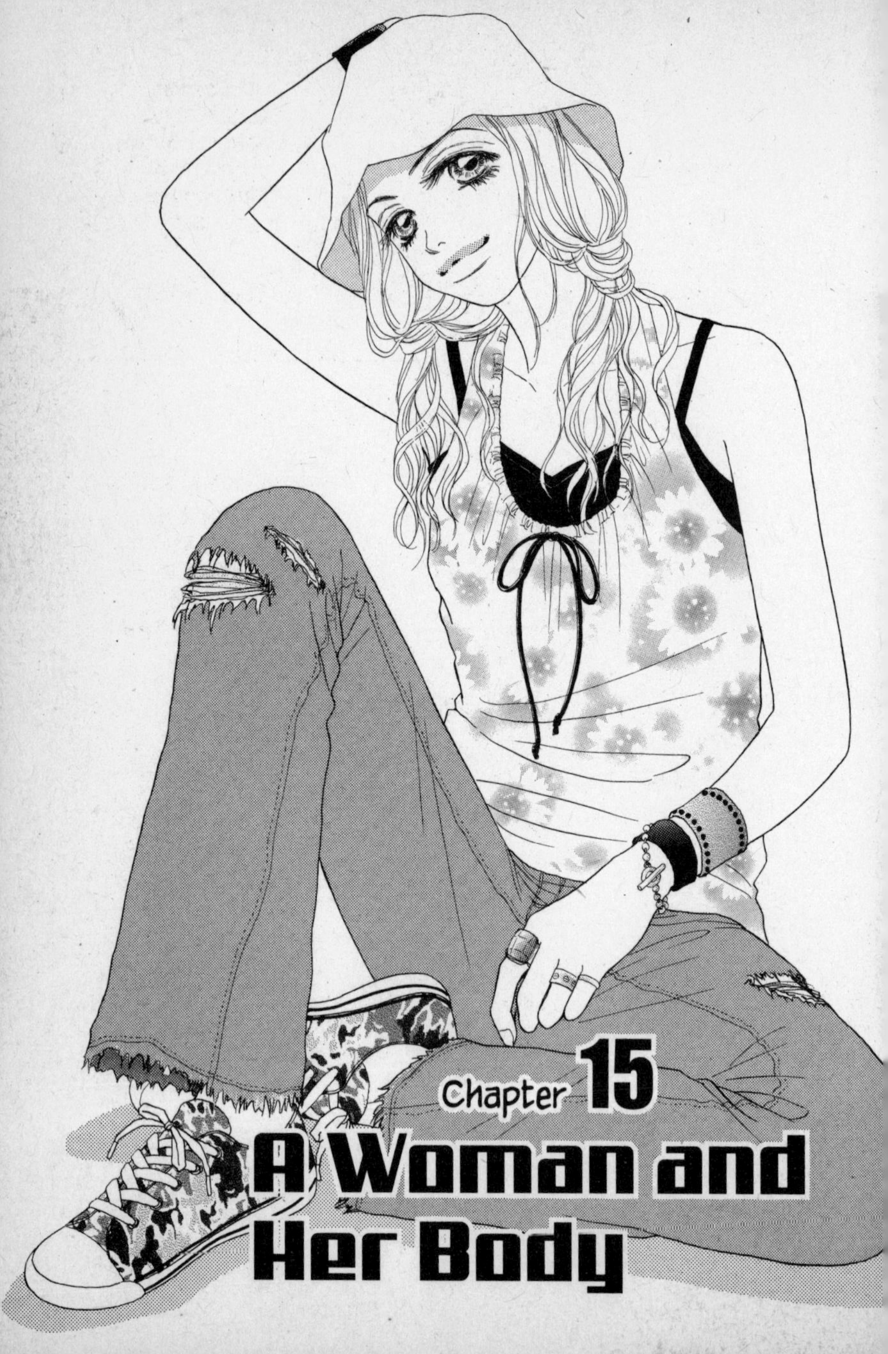
Chapter 15
A Woman and Her Body

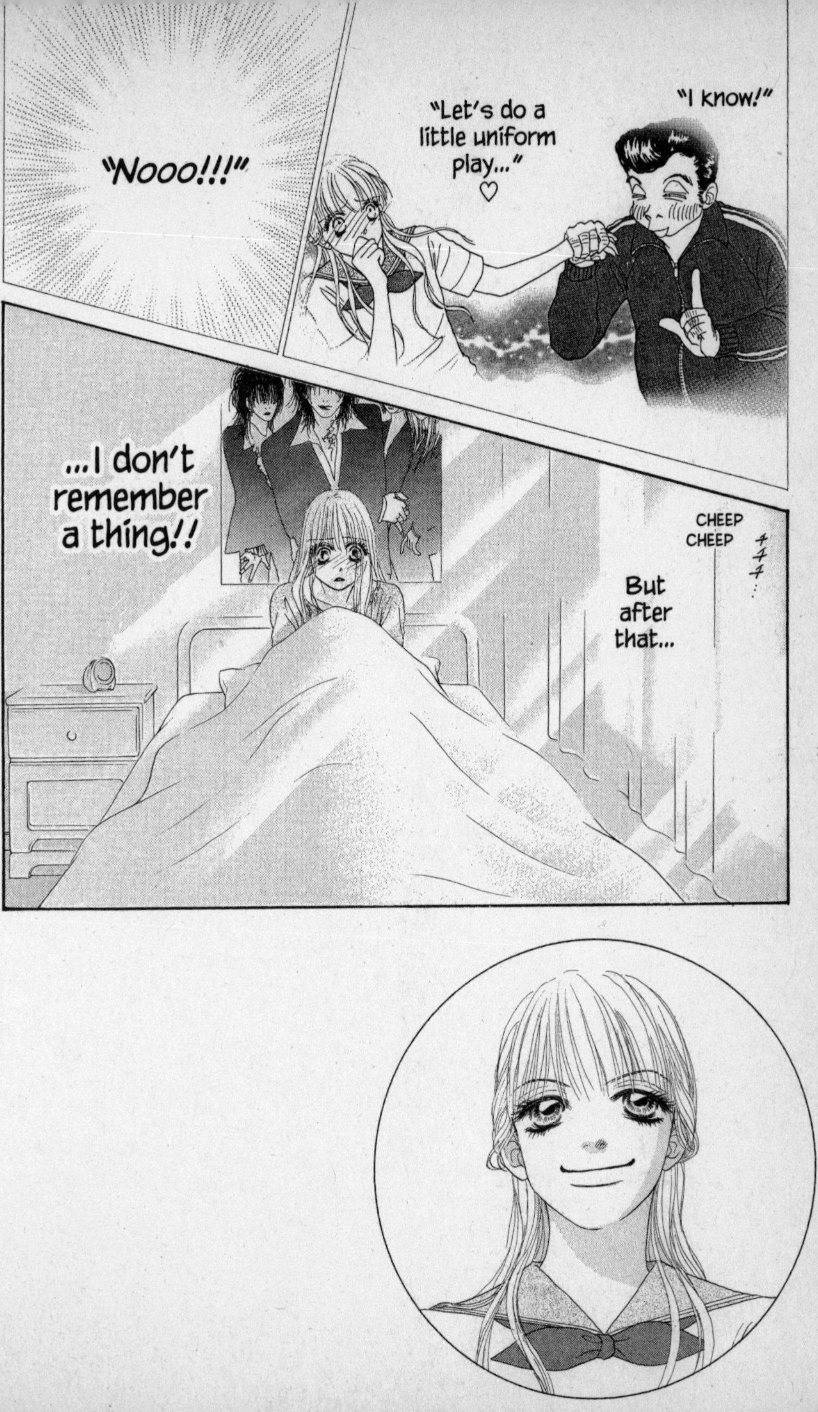
"I know!"
"Let's do a little uniform play..." ♡
"Nooo!!!"
CHEEP CHEEP
But after that...
...I don't remember a thing!!

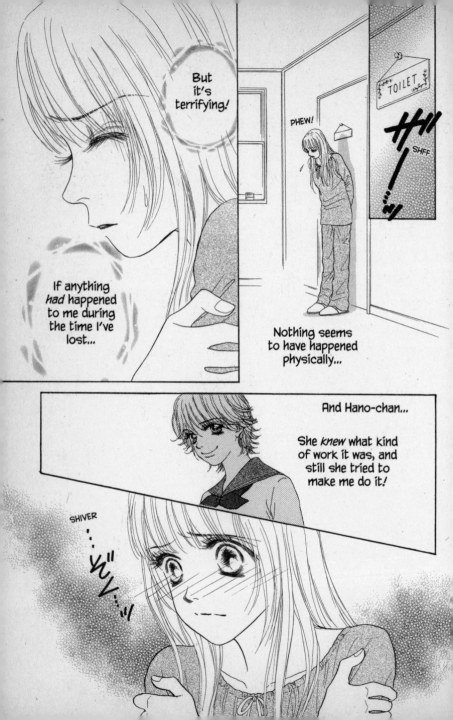

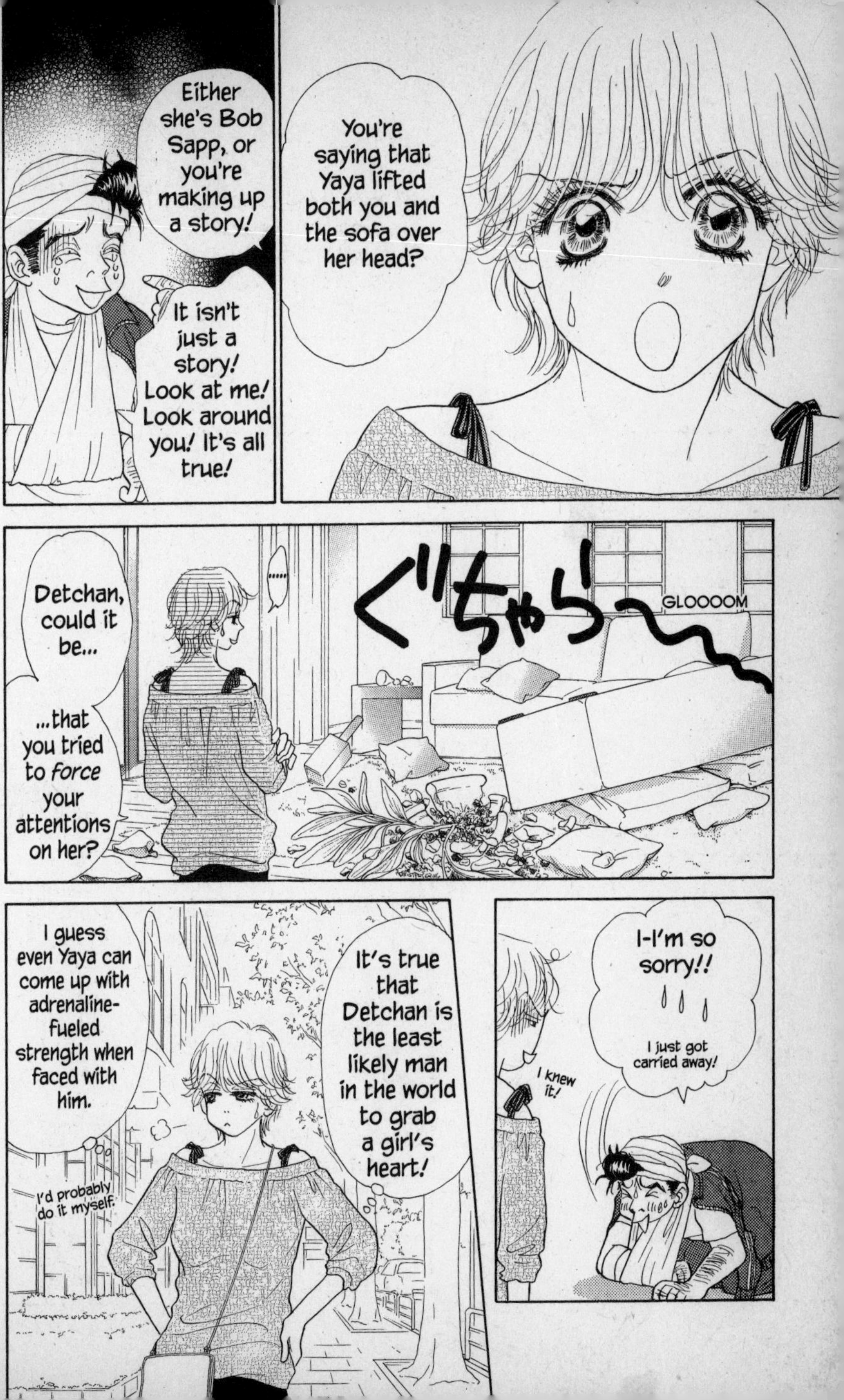
You're saying that Yaya lifted both you and the sofa over her head?
Either she's Bob Sapp, or you're making up a story!
It isn't just a story! Look at me! Look around you! It's all true!
ぐちゃら〜
GLOOOOM
......
Detchan, could it be...
...that you tried to *force* your attentions on her?
I-I'm so sorry!!
I just got carried away!
I knew it!
It's true that Detchan is the least likely man in the world to grab a girl's heart!
I guess even Yaya can come up with adrenaline-fueled strength when faced with him.
I'd probably do it myself.

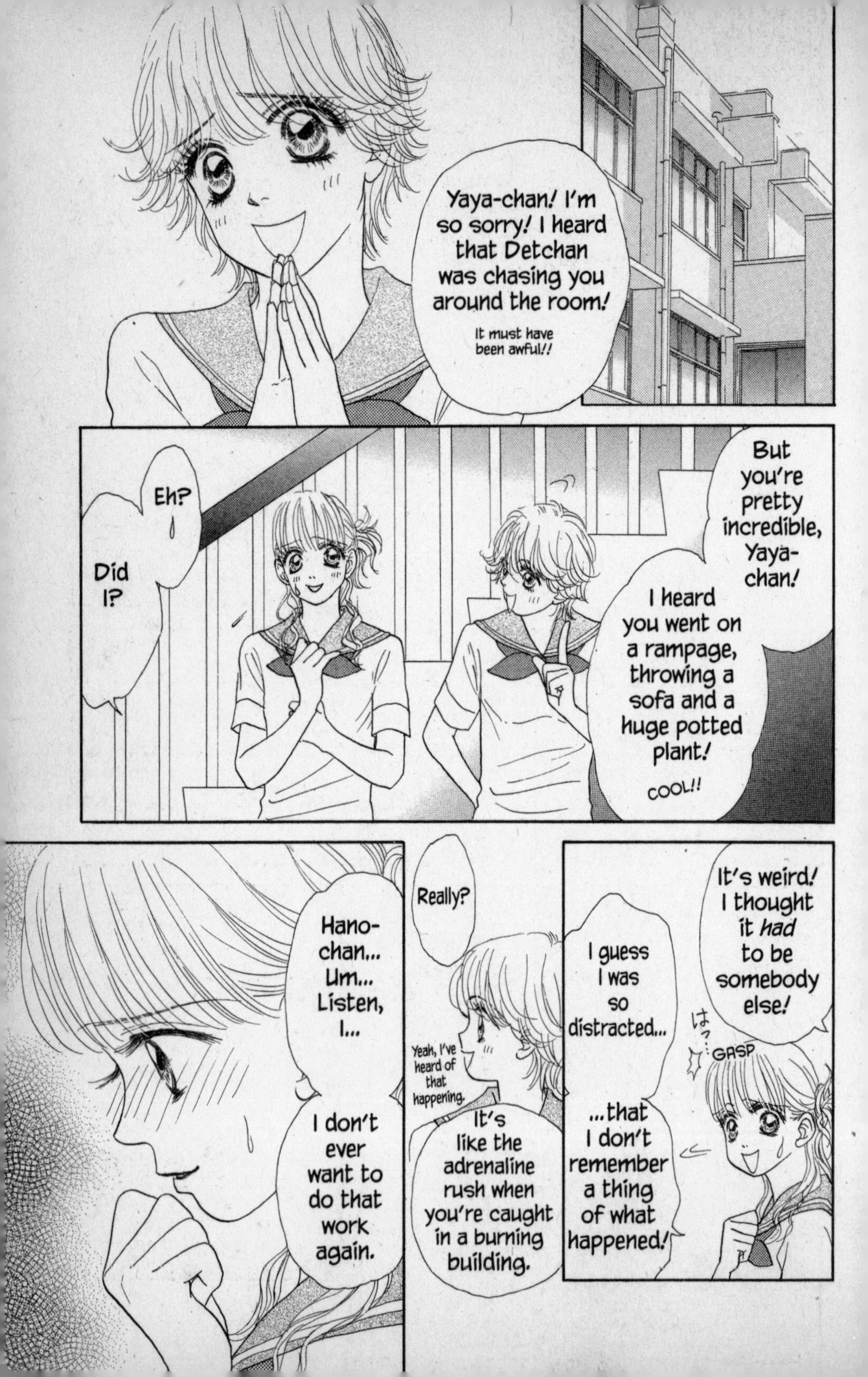
Yaya-chan! I'm so sorry! I heard that Detchan was chasing you around the room!
It must have been awful!!
But you're pretty incredible, Yaya-chan!
I heard you went on a rampage, throwing a sofa and a huge potted plant!
COOL!!
Eh?
Did I?
It's weird! I thought it *had* to be somebody else!
はっ… GASP
I guess I was so distracted...
...that I don't remember a thing of what happened!
Really?
Yeah, I've heard of that happening.
It's like the adrenaline rush when you're caught in a burning building.
Hano-chan... Um... Listen, I...
I don't ever want to do that work again.

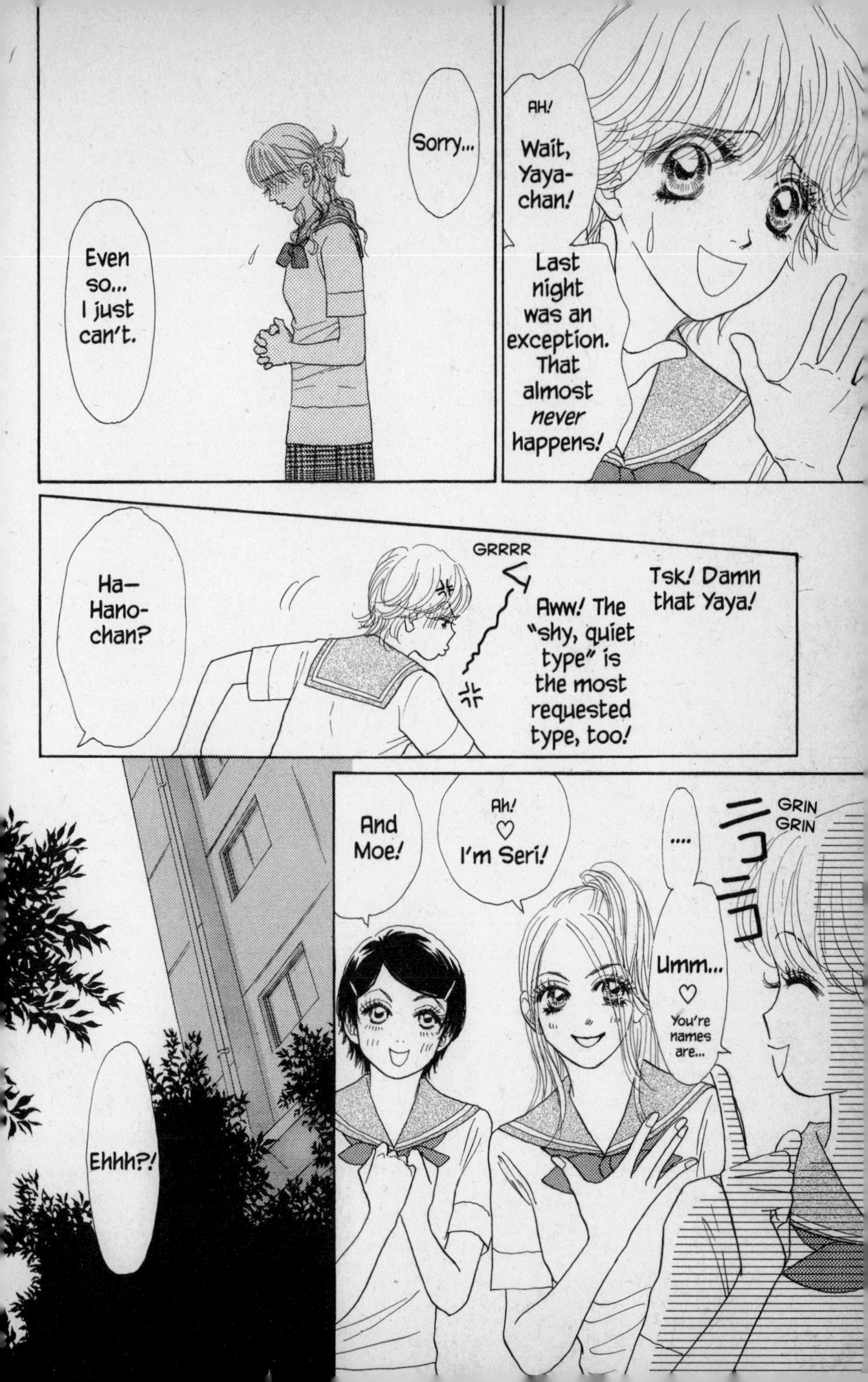
AH!
Wait, Yaya-chan!
Last night was an exception. That almost *never* happens!
Sorry...
Even so... I just can't.
Tsk! Damn that Yaya!
Aww! The "shy, quiet type" is the most requested type, too!
GRRRR
Ha—Hano-chan?
GRIN GRIN
....
Umm... ♡ You're names are...
Ah! ♡ I'm Seri!
And Moe!
Ehhh?!

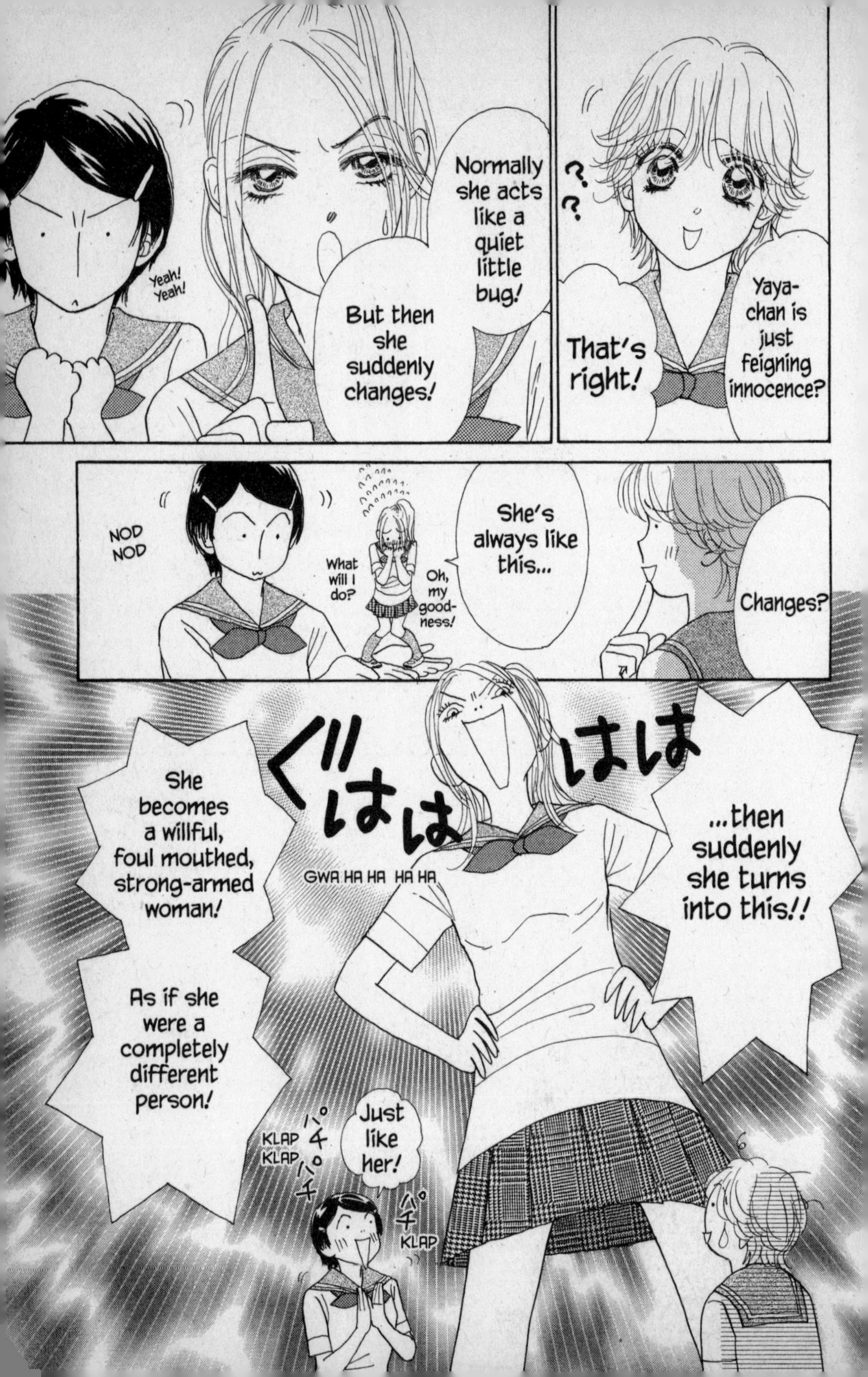

Yaya-chan is just feigning innocence?
That's right!
Normally she acts like a quiet little bug!
But then she suddenly changes!
Yeah! Yeah!
Changes?
She's always like this...
Oh, my goodness!
What will I do?
NOD NOD
...then suddenly she turns into this!!
ぐははははは
GWA HA HA HA HA
She becomes a willful, foul mouthed, strong-armed woman!
As if she were a completely different person!
パチ
KLAP
Just like her!
パチパチ
KLAP KLAP

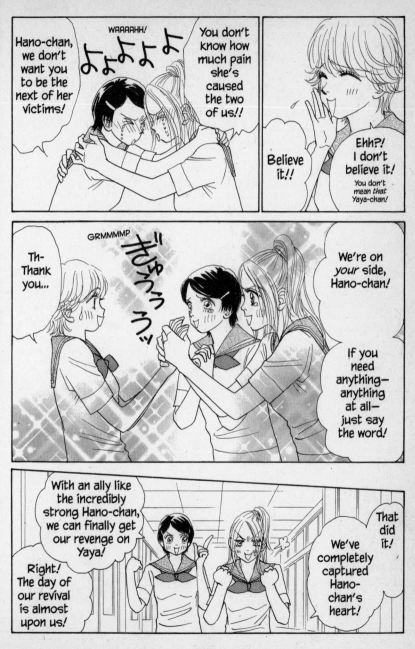

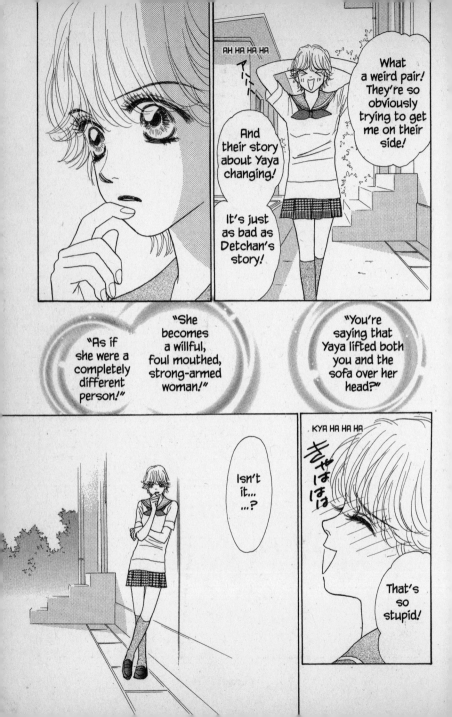

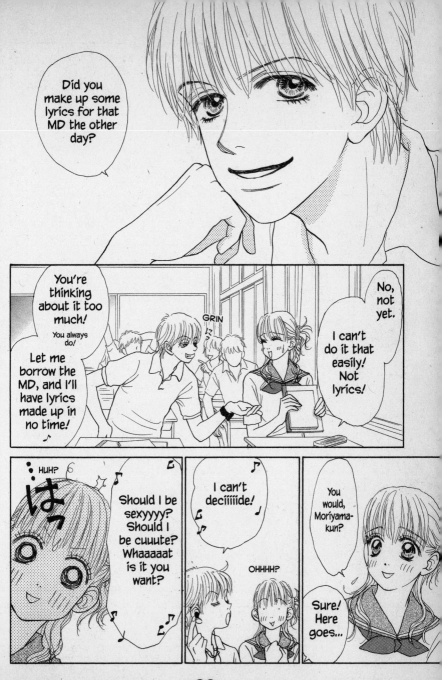

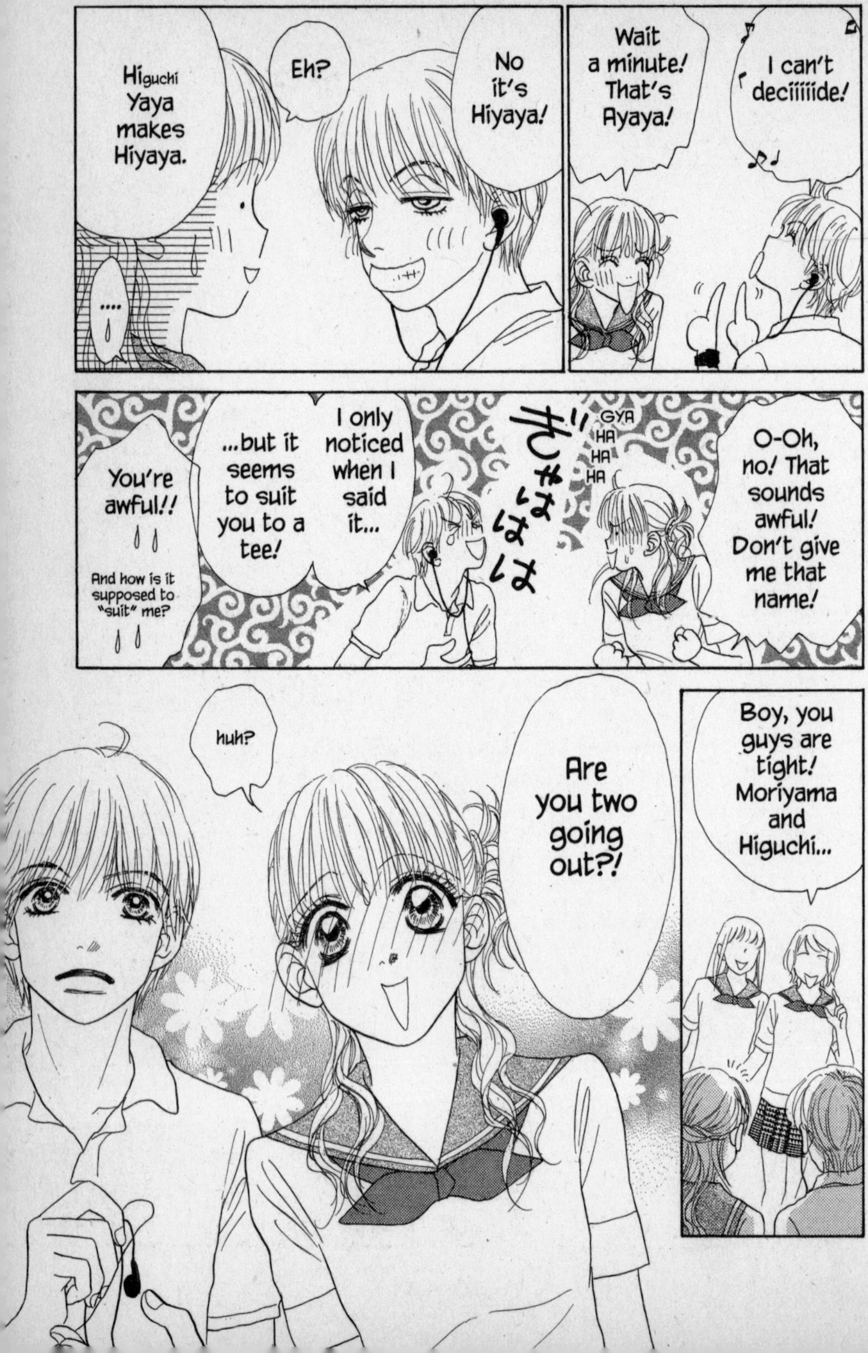

I can't deciiiiide!
Wait a minute! That's Ayaya!
No it's Hiyaya!
Eh?
Higuchi Yaya makes Hiyaya.
....
O-Oh, no! That sounds awful! Don't give me that name!
ぎゃはははは
GYA HA HA HA
I only noticed when I said it...
...but it seems to suit you to a tee!
You're awful!!
And how is it supposed to "suit" me?
Boy, you guys are tight! Moriyama and Higuchi...
Are you two going out?!
huh?

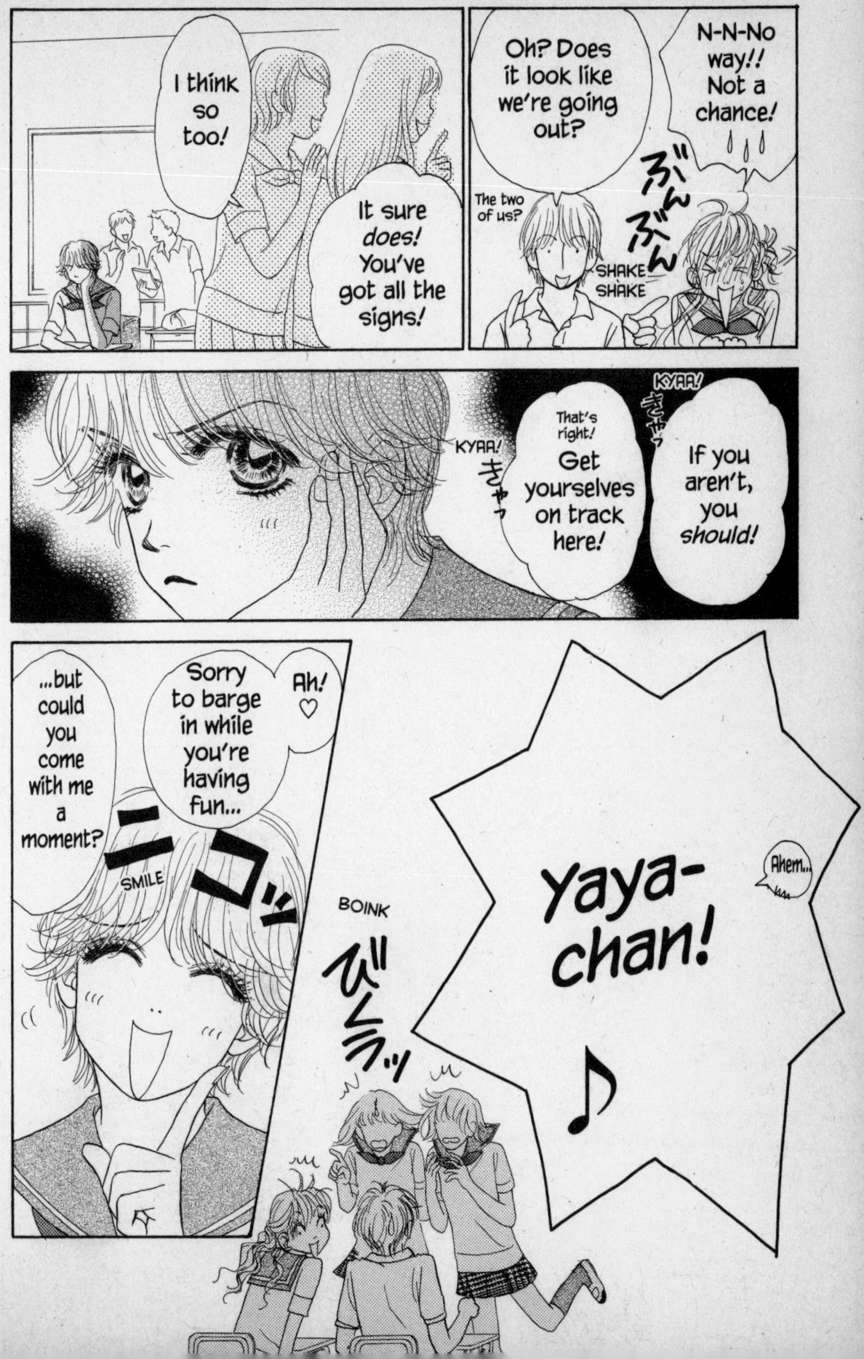
N-N-No way!! Not a chance!
Oh? Does it look like we're going out?
ぶんぶん
The two of us?
SHAKE SHAKE
It sure does! You've got all the signs!
I think so too!
KYAA!
きゃっ
If you aren't, you should!
That's right! Get yourselves on track here!
KYAA!
きゃっ
Yaya-chan! ♪
Ahem...
BOINK
Ah! ♡
Sorry to barge in while you're having fun...
...but could you come with me a moment?
ニコッ
SMILE

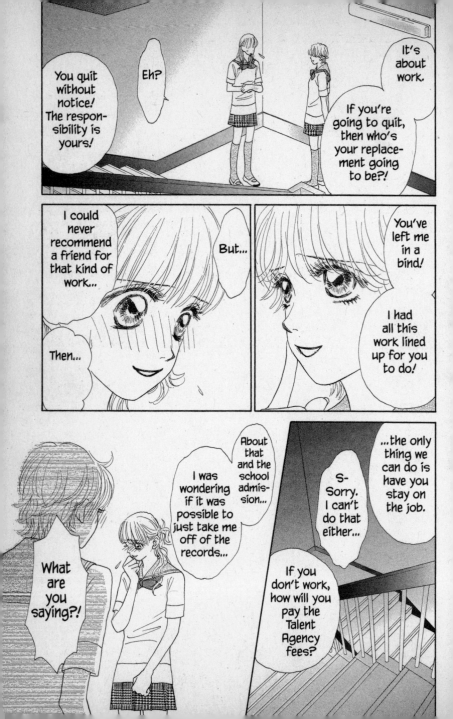

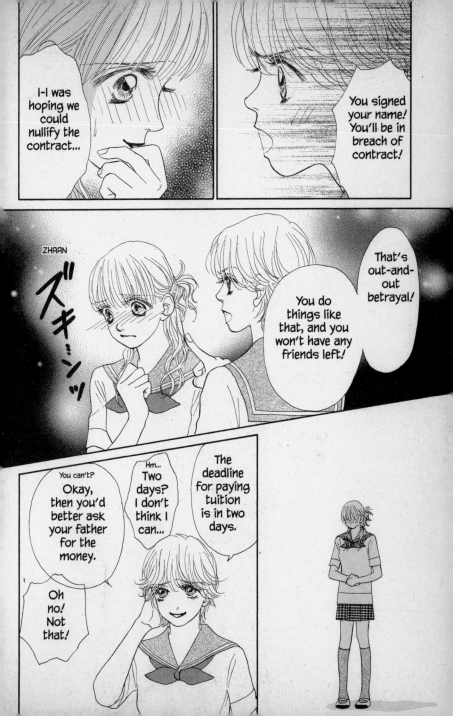

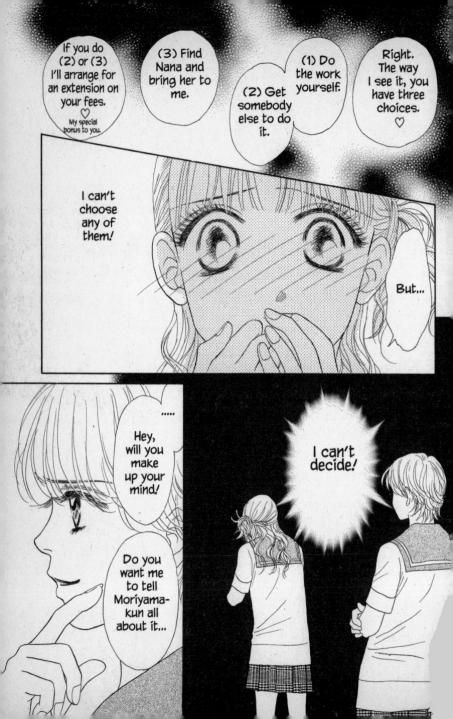

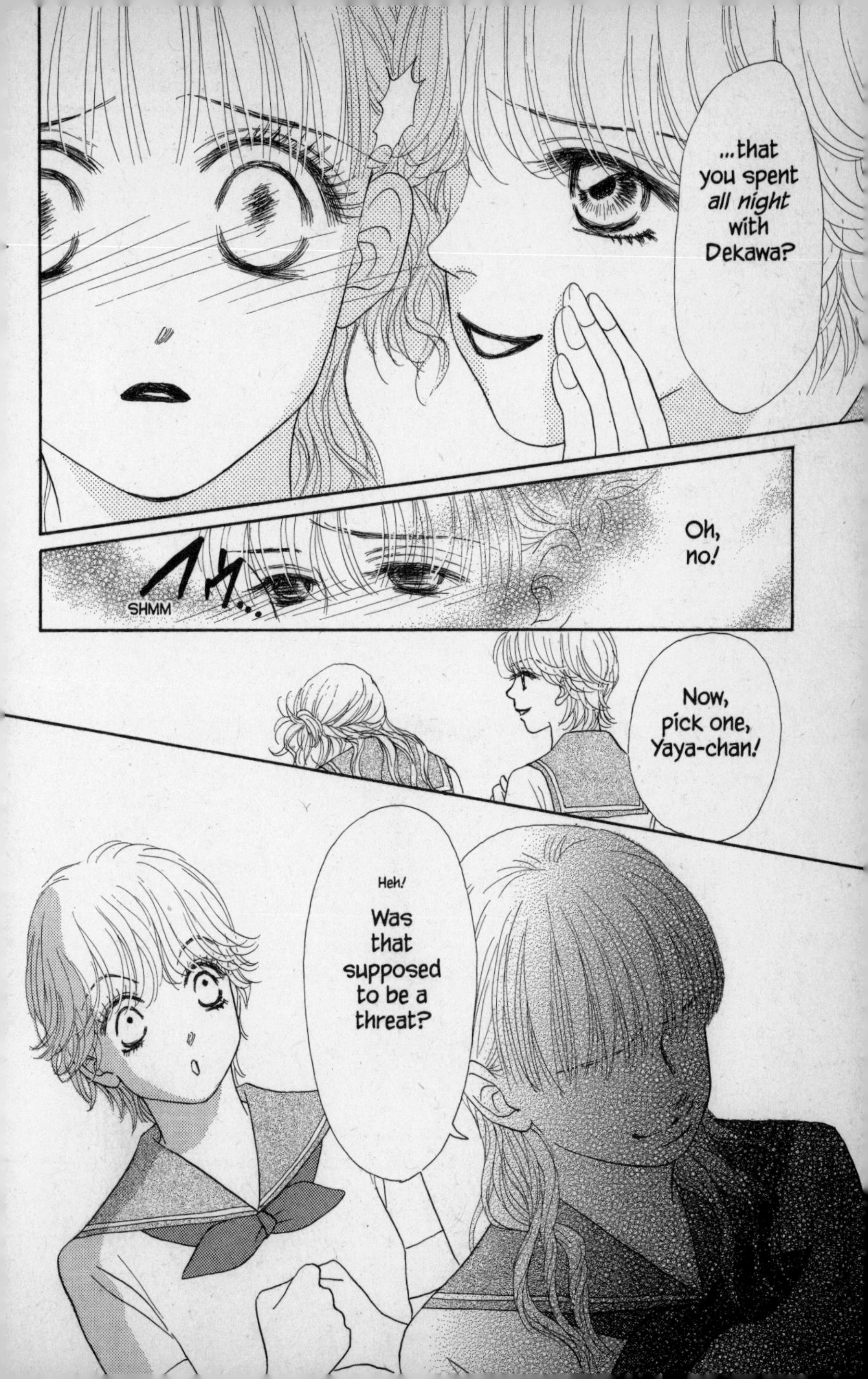
...that you spent *all night* with Dekawa?
Oh, no!
SHMM
Now, pick one, Yaya-chan!
Heh!
Was that supposed to be a threat?

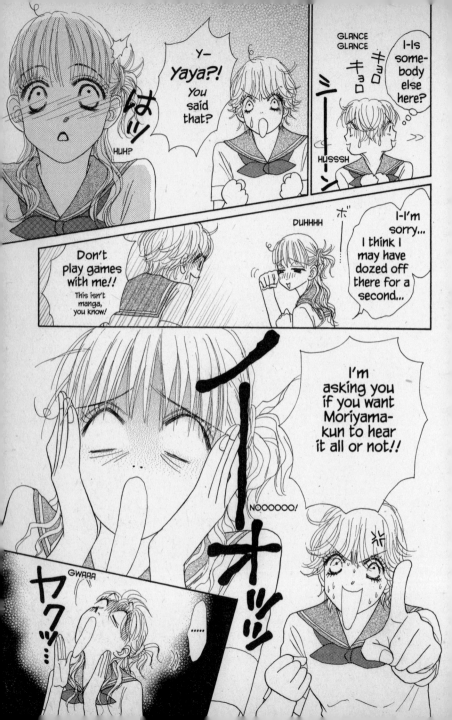

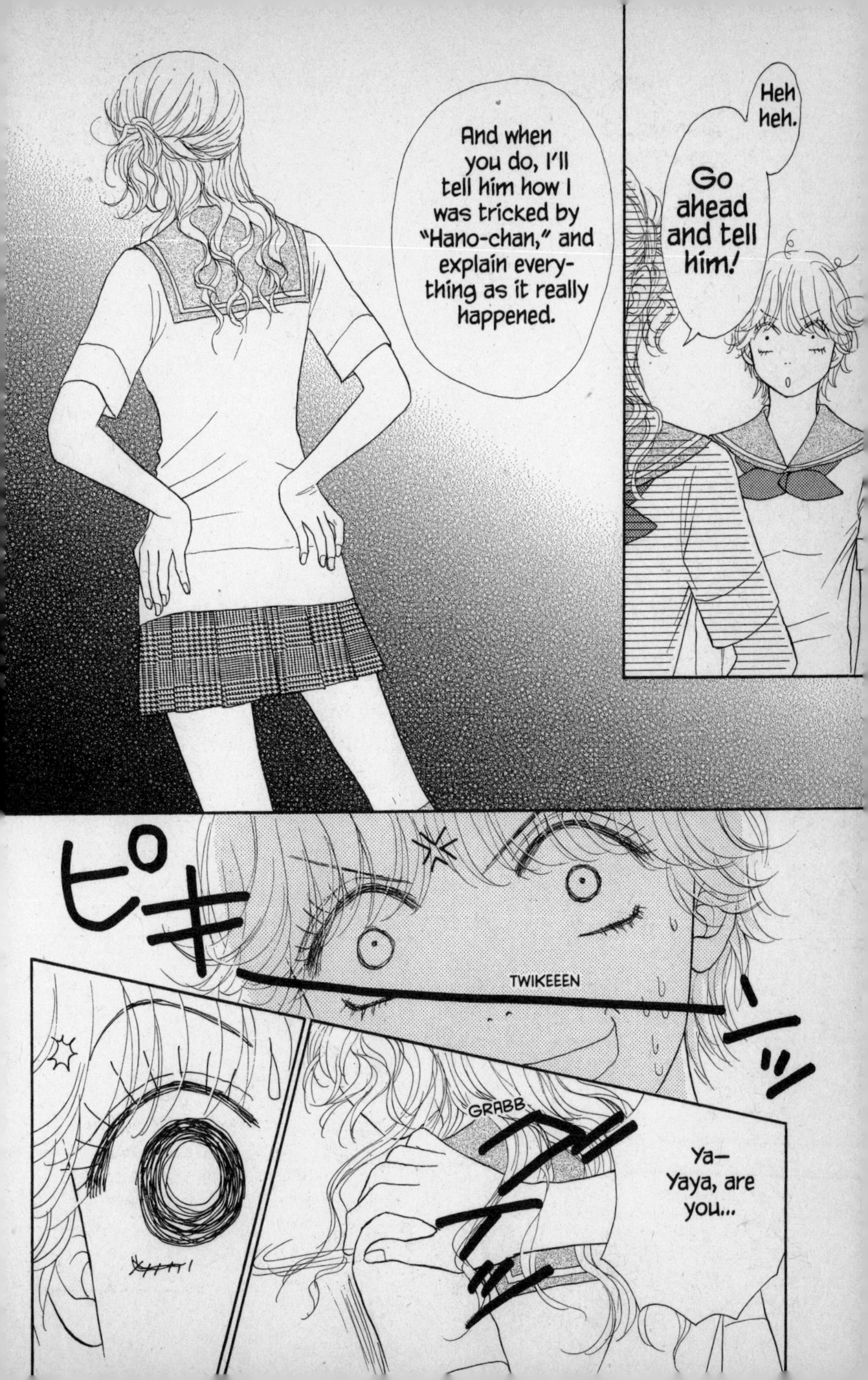
Heh heh.
Go ahead and tell him!
And when you do, I'll tell him how I was tricked by "Hano-chan," and explain everything as it really happened.
TWIKEEEN
GRABB
Ya— Yaya, are you...

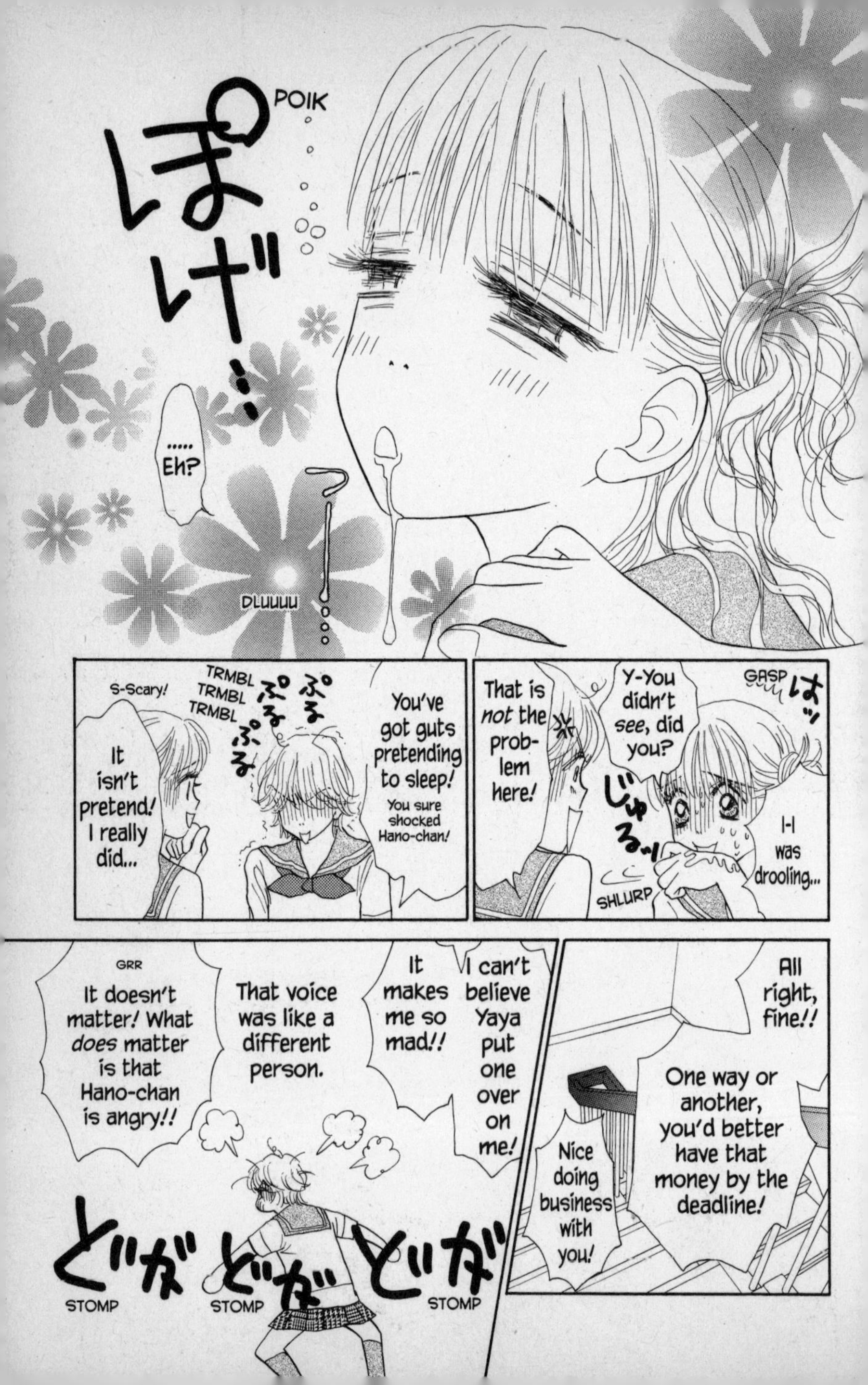
POIK
ぽげ…
.....
Eh?
つー…
DLUUUU
はッ
GASP
Y-You didn't see, did you?
That is *not* the problem here!
I-I was drooling...
じゅるッ
SHLURP
You've got guts pretending to sleep!
You sure shocked Hano-chan!
ぷるぷるぷる
TRMBL TRMBL TRMBL
S-Scary!
It isn't pretend! I really did...
All right, fine!!
One way or another, you'd better have that money by the deadline!
Nice doing business with you!
I can't believe Yaya put one over on me!
It makes me so mad!!
That voice was like a different person.
GRR
It doesn't matter! What *does* matter is that Hano-chan is angry!!
どがどがどが
STOMP
STOMP
STOMP

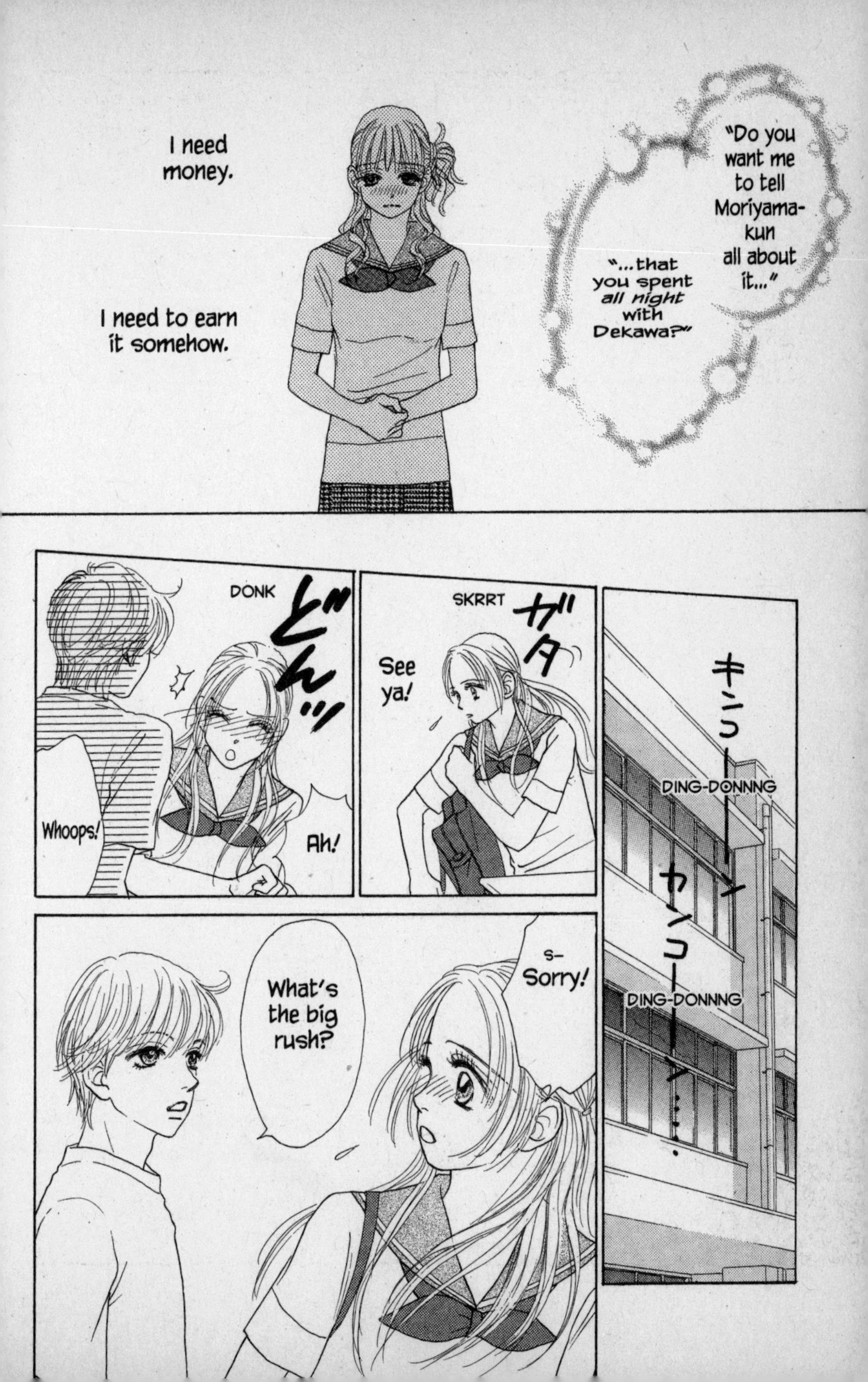
"Do you want me to tell Moriyama-kun all about it..."
"...that you spent *all night* with Dekawa?"
I need money.
I need to earn it somehow.
キンコーン
DING-DONNNG
カンコーン……
DING-DONNNG
ガタ
SKRRT
See ya!
どんッ
DONK
Whoops!
Ah!
S-Sorry!
What's the big rush?

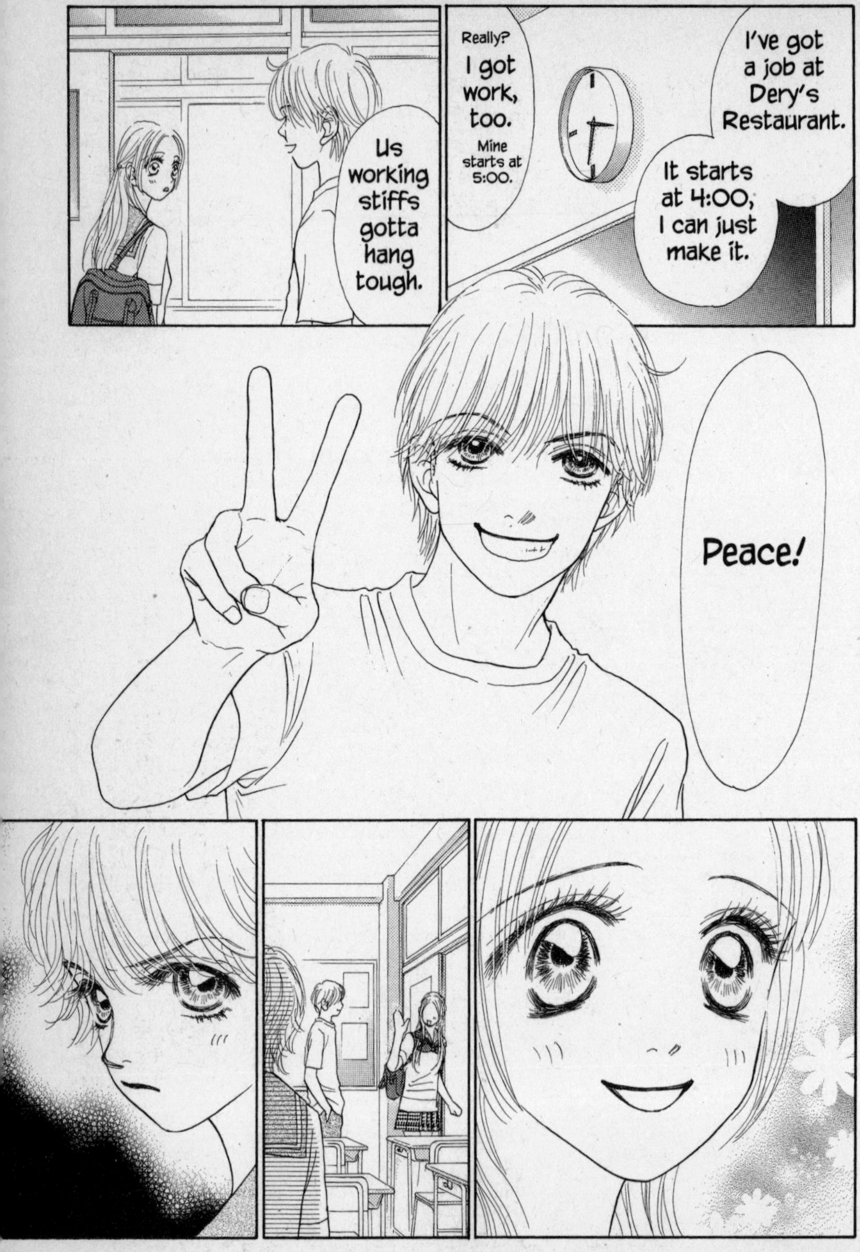
I've got a job at Dery's Restaurant.
It starts at 4:00, I can just make it.
Really?
I got work, too.
Mine starts at 5:00.
Us working stiffs gotta hang tough.
Peace!

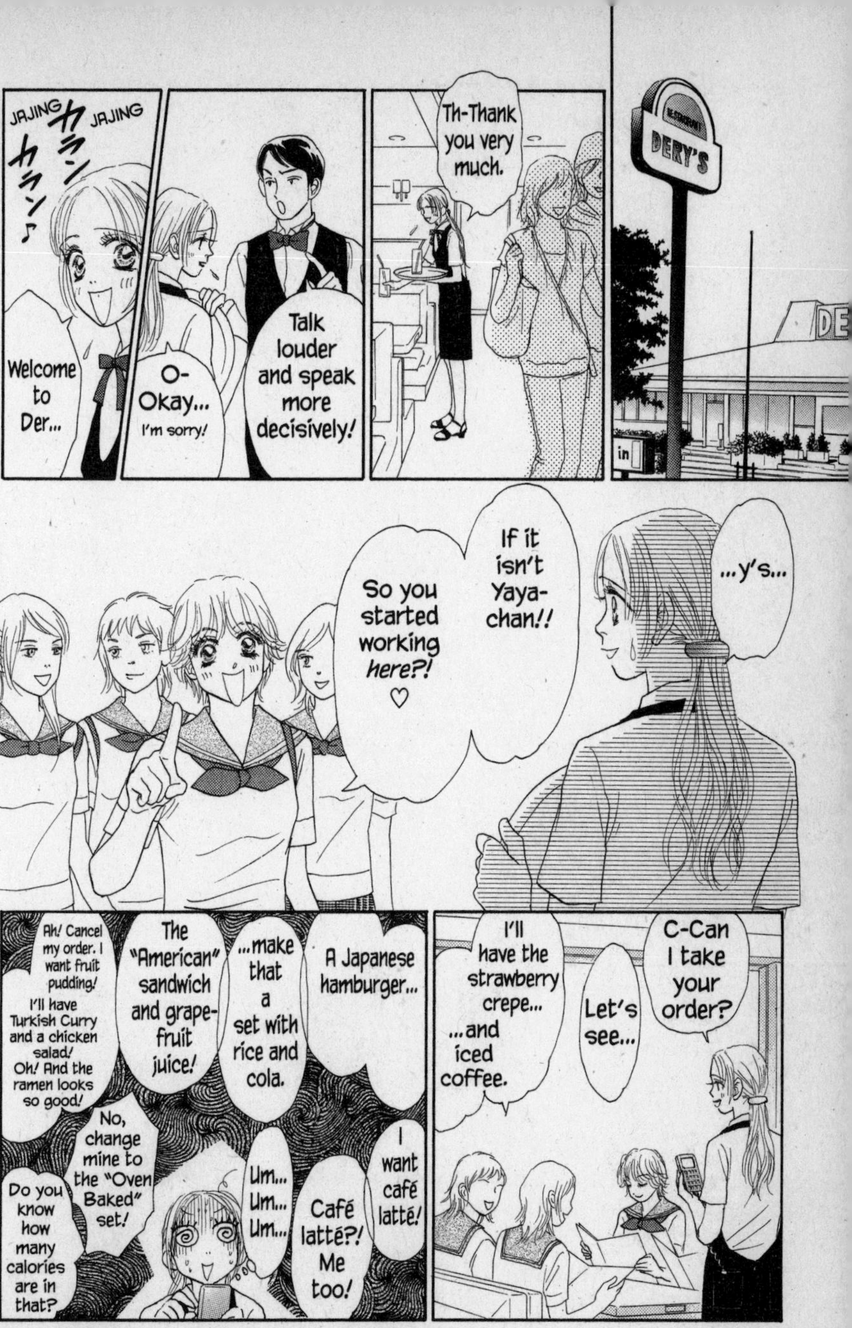
DERY'S
in
DE
Th-Thank you very much.
Talk louder and speak more decisively!
O-Okay... I'm sorry!
JAJING JAJING
カラン
カラン♪
Welcome to Der...
...y's...
If it isn't Yaya-chan!!
So you started working here?! ♡
C-Can I take your order?
Let's see...
I'll have the strawberry crepe... ...and iced coffee.
A Japanese hamburger...
...make that a set with rice and cola.
The "American" sandwich and grape-fruit juice!
Ah! Cancel my order. I want fruit pudding!
I'll have Turkish Curry and a chicken salad! Oh! And the ramen looks so good!
I want café latté!
Café latté?! Me too!
Um... Um... Um...
No, change mine to the "Oven Baked" set!
Do you know how many calories are in that?

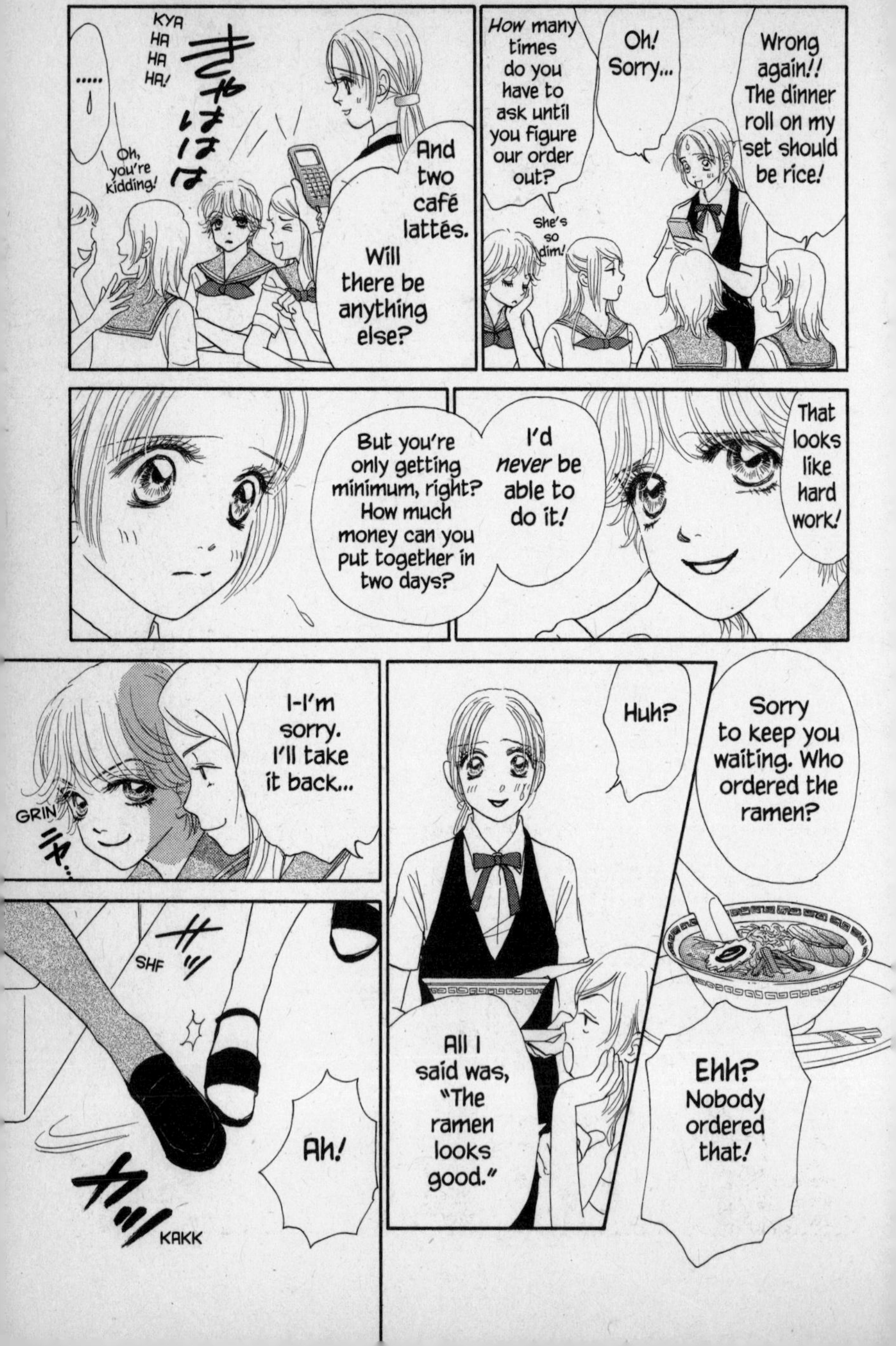
Wrong again!! The dinner roll on my set should be rice!
Oh! Sorry...
How many times do you have to ask until you figure our order out?
She's so dim!
And two café lattés. Will there be anything else?
きゃははは
KYA HA HA HA!
Oh, you're kidding!
......
That looks like hard work!
I'd *never* be able to do it!
But you're only getting minimum, right? How much money can you put together in two days?
Sorry to keep you waiting. Who ordered the ramen?
Huh?
Ehh? Nobody ordered that!
All I said was, "The ramen looks good."
I-I'm sorry. I'll take it back...
GRIN
ニヤ...
サッ
SHF
Ah!
カッ
KAKK

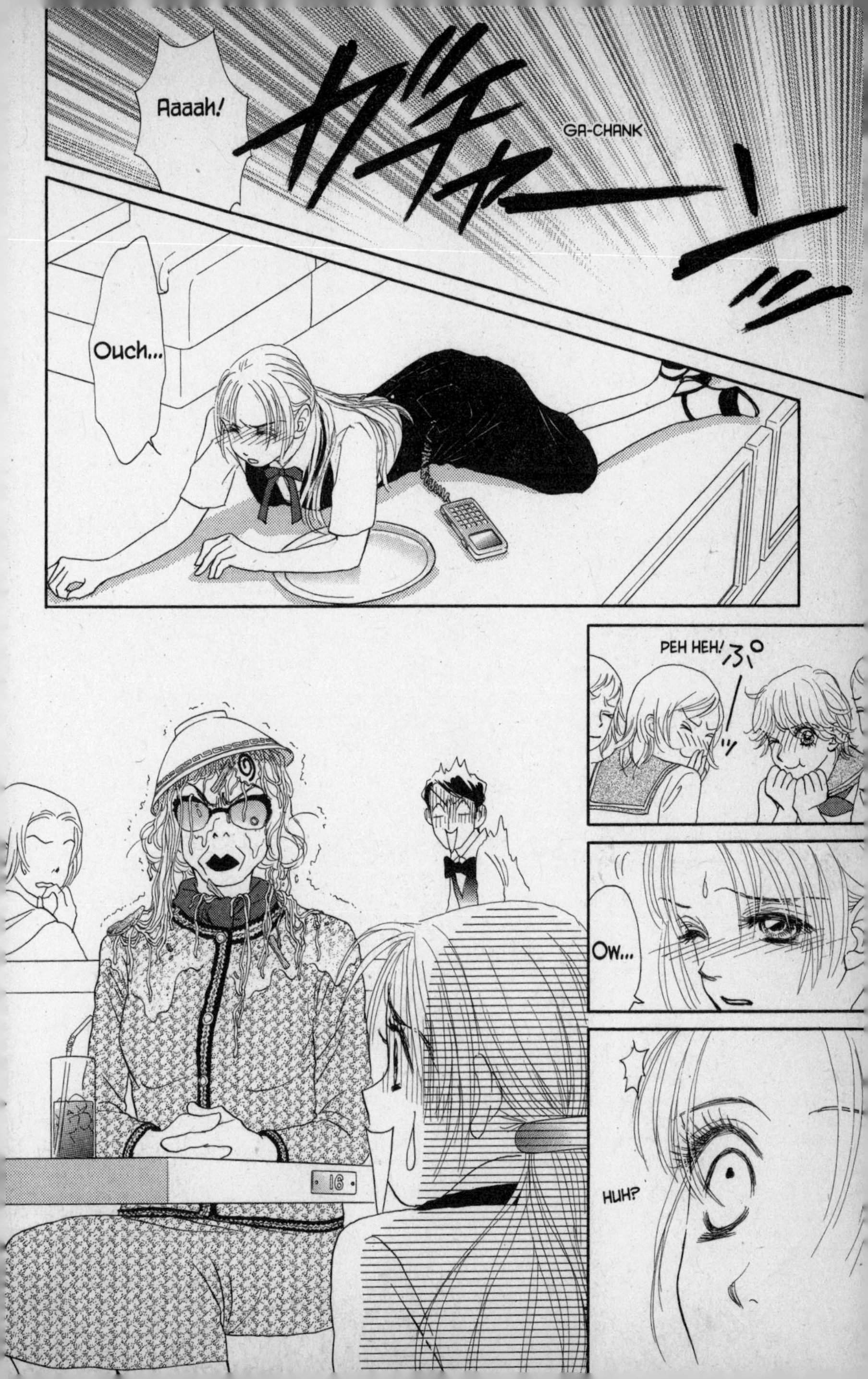
GA-CHANK
Aaaah!
Ouch...
PEH HEH!
Ow...
HUH?
16

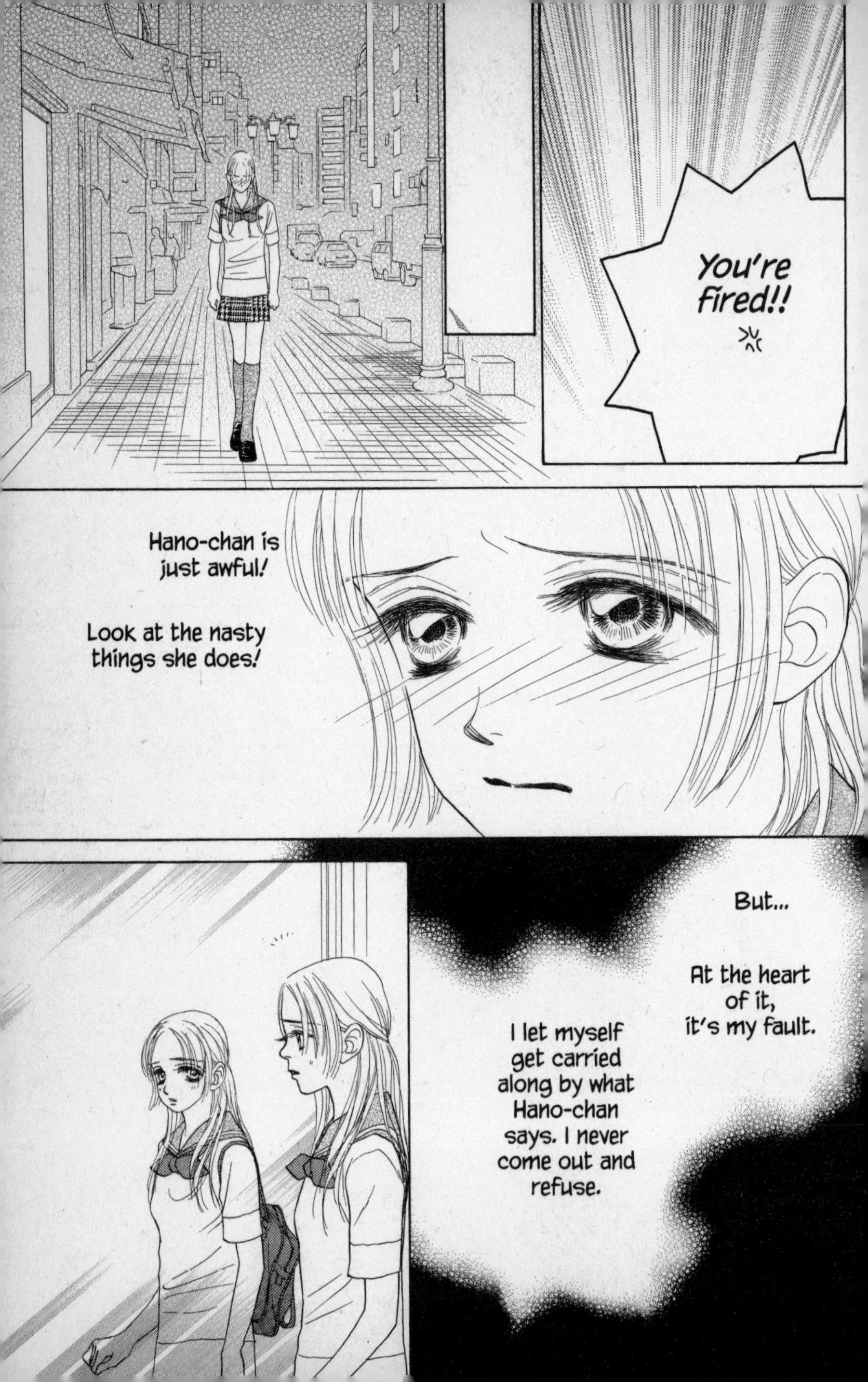
You're fired!!
Hano-chan is just awful!
Look at the nasty things she does!
But...
At the heart of it, it's my fault.
I let myself get carried along by what Hano-chan says. I never come out and refuse.

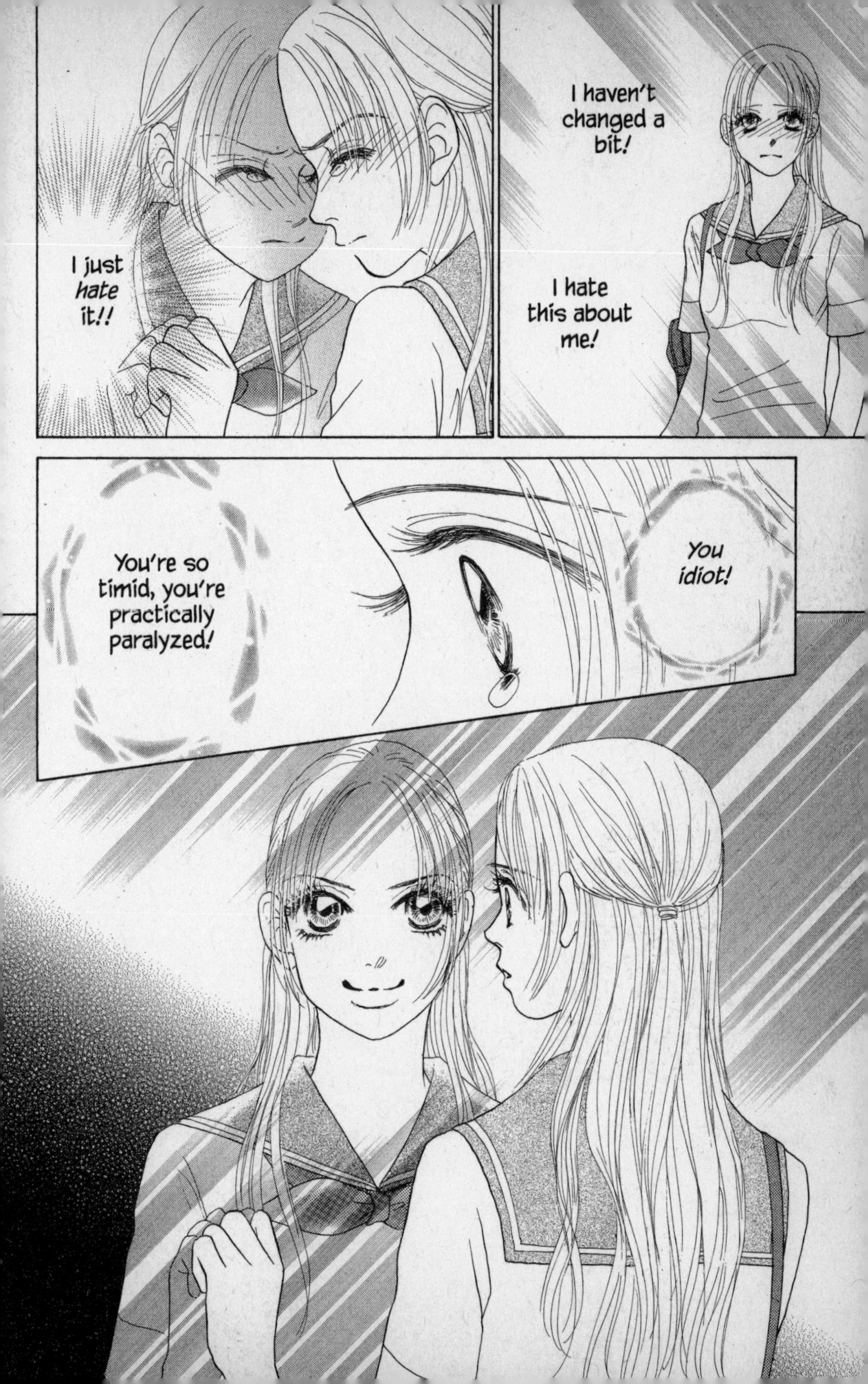
I haven't changed a bit!
I hate this about me!
I just *hate* it!!
You idiot!
You're so timid, you're practically paralyzed!

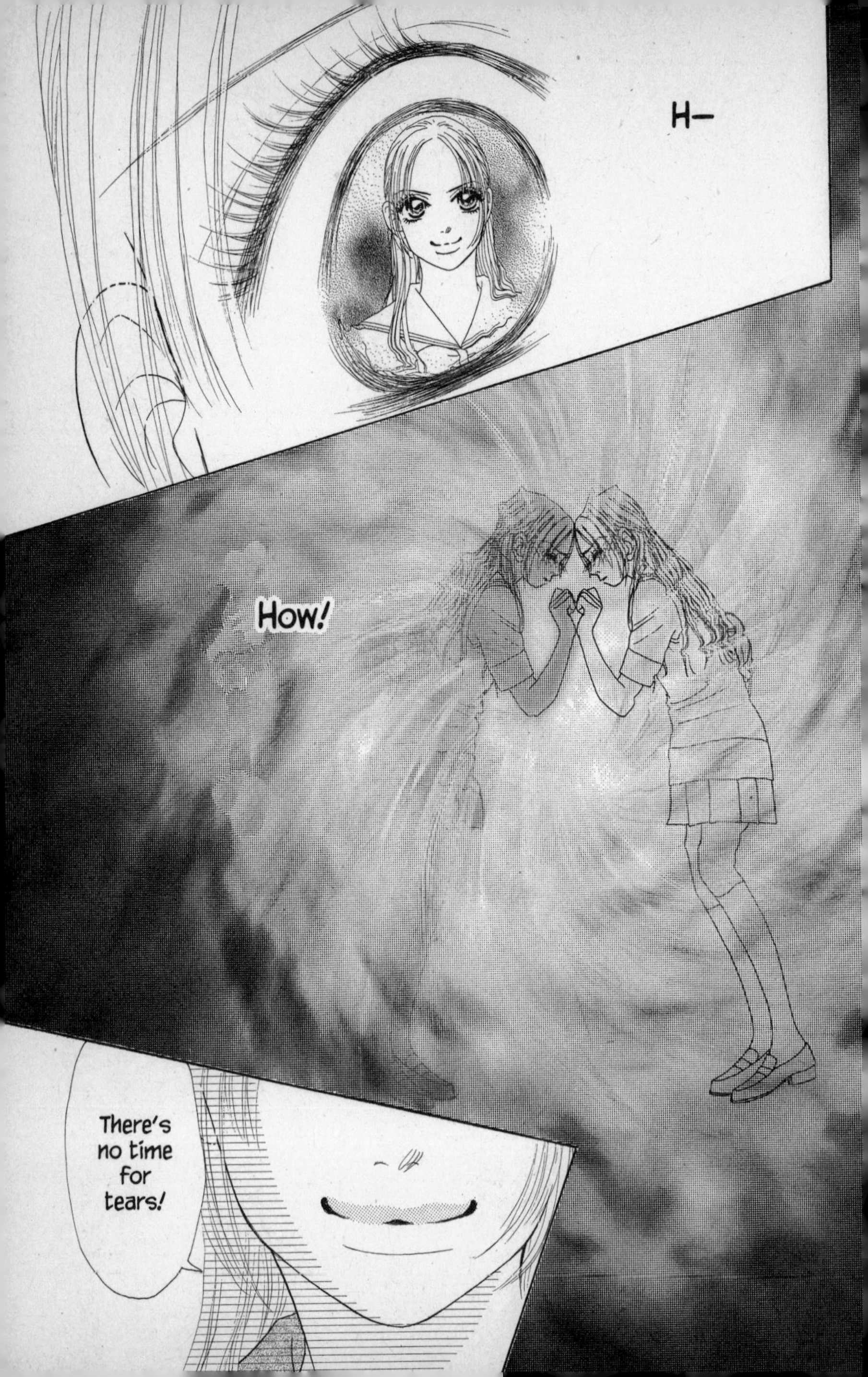
H—
How!
There's no time for tears!

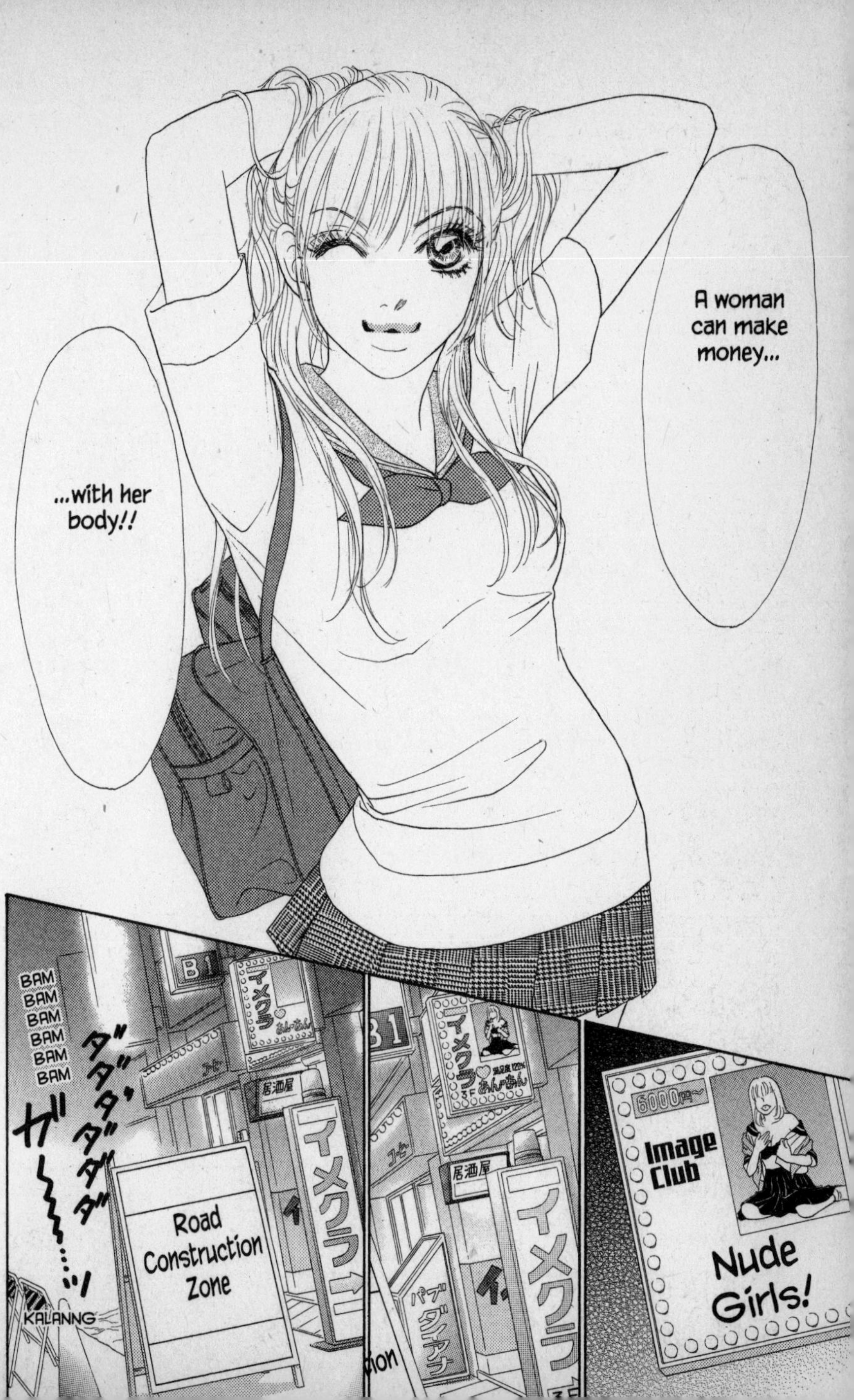
A woman can make money...
...with her body!!
6000円~
Image Club
Nude Girls!
イメクラ あんあん
居酒屋
イメクラ
パブ ダイアナ
BAM BAM BAM BAM BAM BAM
ダダダダダ
KALANNG
Road Construction Zone
イメクラ

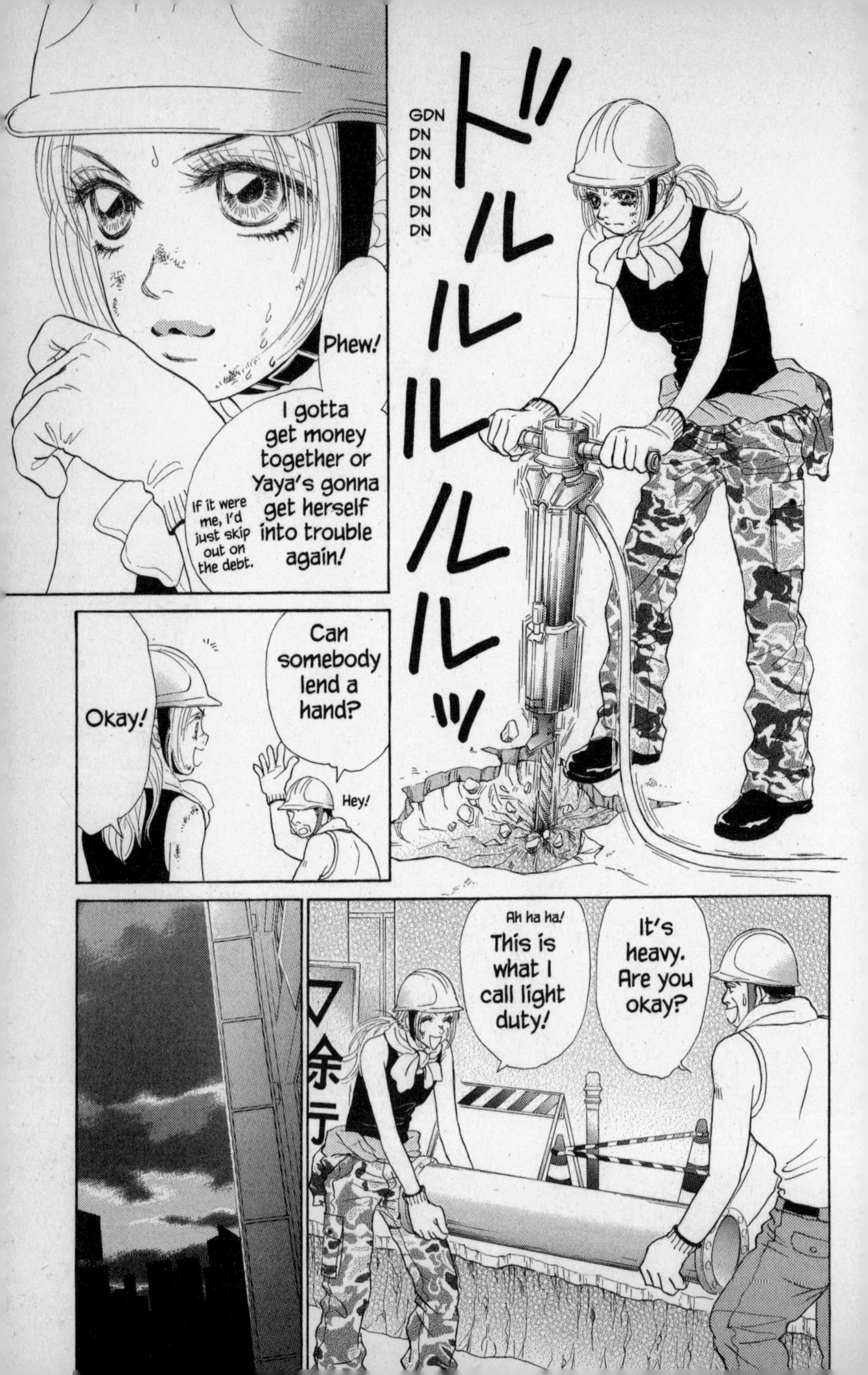
GDN DN DN DN DN DN DN
ドルルルルルッ
Phew!
I gotta get money together or Yaya's gonna get herself into trouble again!
If it were me, I'd just skip out on the debt.
Can somebody lend a hand?
Hey!
Okay!
It's heavy. Are you okay?
Ah ha ha!
This is what I call light duty!

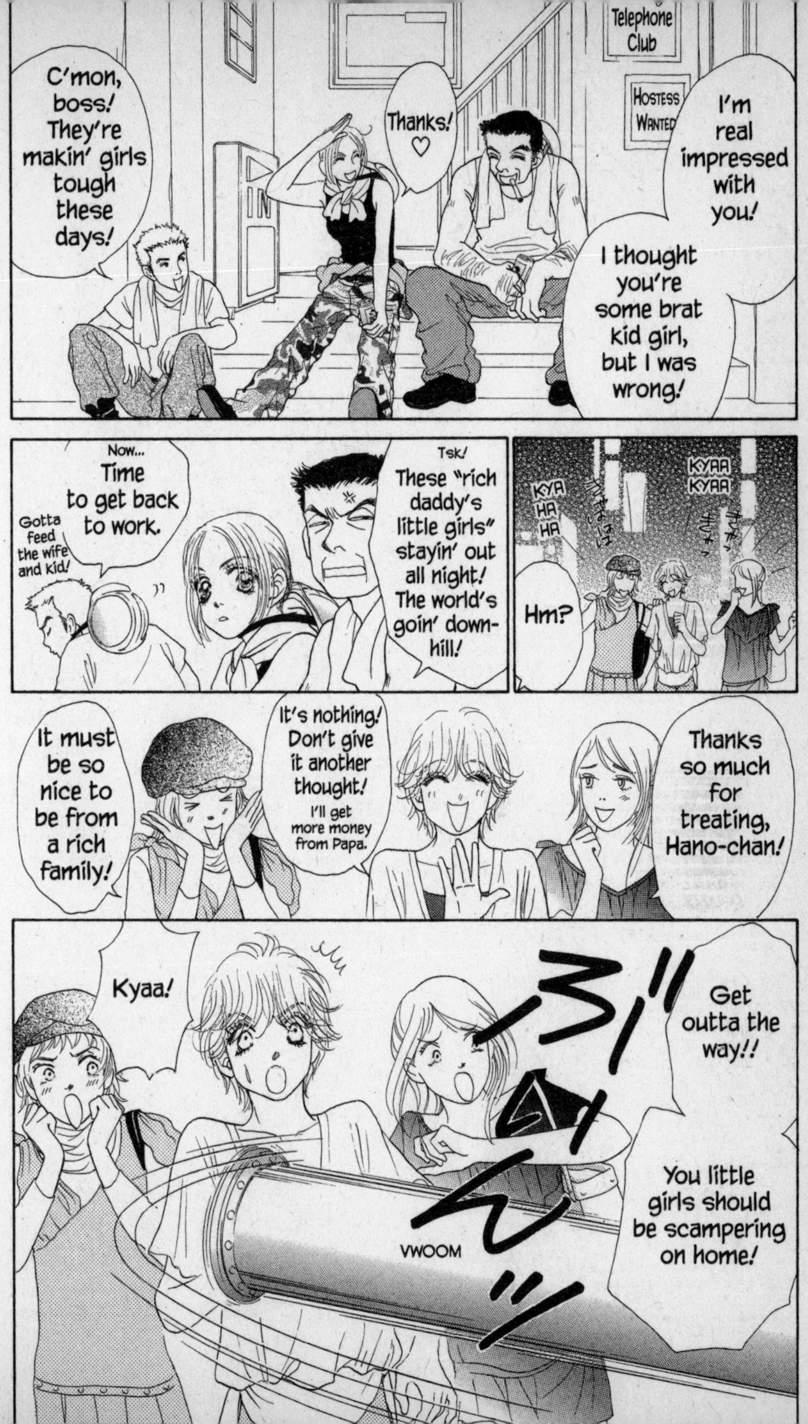
Telephone Club
Hostess Wanted
I'm real impressed with you!
I thought you're some brat kid girl, but I was wrong!
Thanks! ♡
C'mon, boss! They're makin' girls tough these days!
KYAA KYAA
KYA HA HA
Hm?
Tsk!
These "rich daddy's little girls" stayin' out all night! The world's goin' down-hill!
Now... Time to get back to work.
Gotta feed the wife and kid!
Thanks so much for treating, Hano-chan!
It's nothing! Don't give it another thought!
I'll get more money from Papa.
It must be so nice to be from a rich family!
Get outta the way!!
You little girls should be scampering on home!
VWOOM
Kyaa!

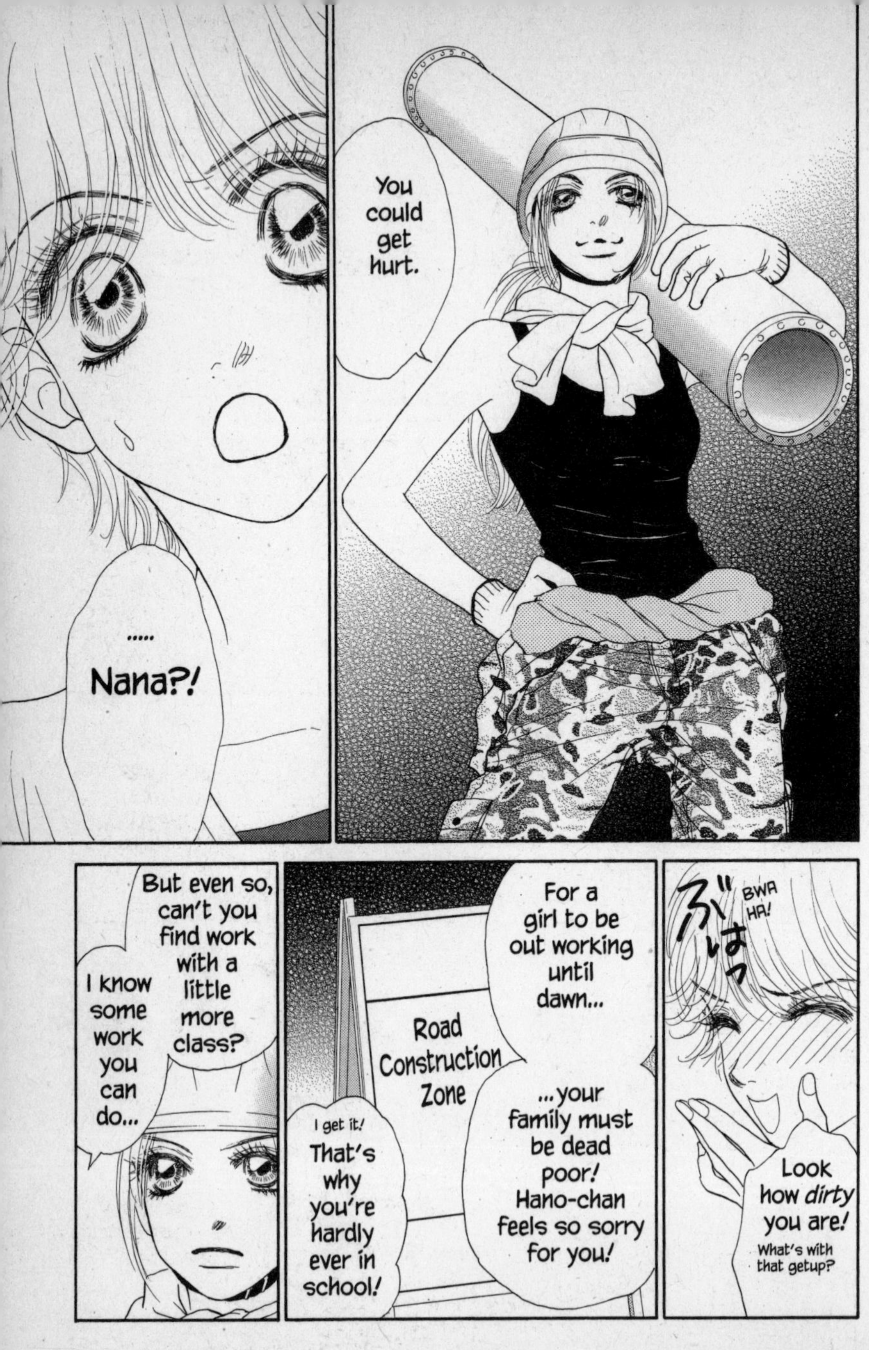
You could get hurt.
..... Nana?!
ぶはっ
BWA HA!
Look how *dirty* you are!
What's with that getup?
For a girl to be out working until dawn...
...your family must be dead poor! Hano-chan feels so sorry for you!
Road Construction Zone
I get it! That's why you're hardly ever in school!
But even so, can't you find work with a little more class?
I know some work you can do...

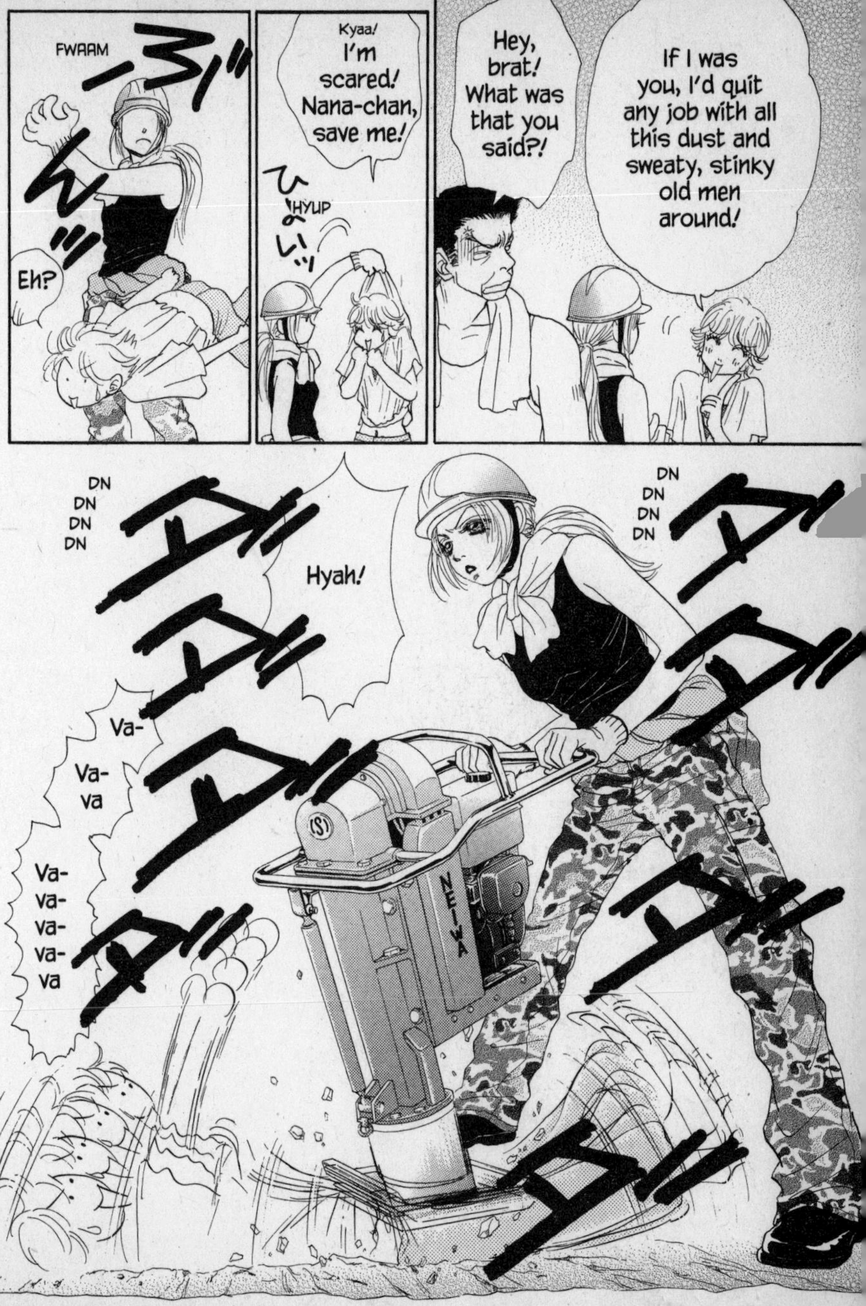
If I was you, I'd quit any job with all this dust and sweaty, stinky old men around!
Hey, brat! What was that you said?!
Kyaa! I'm scared! Nana-chan, save me!
HYUP
FWAAM
Eh?
DN DN DN DN
Hyah!
DN DN DN DN
Va- Va-va
Va-va-va-va-va
NEIWA

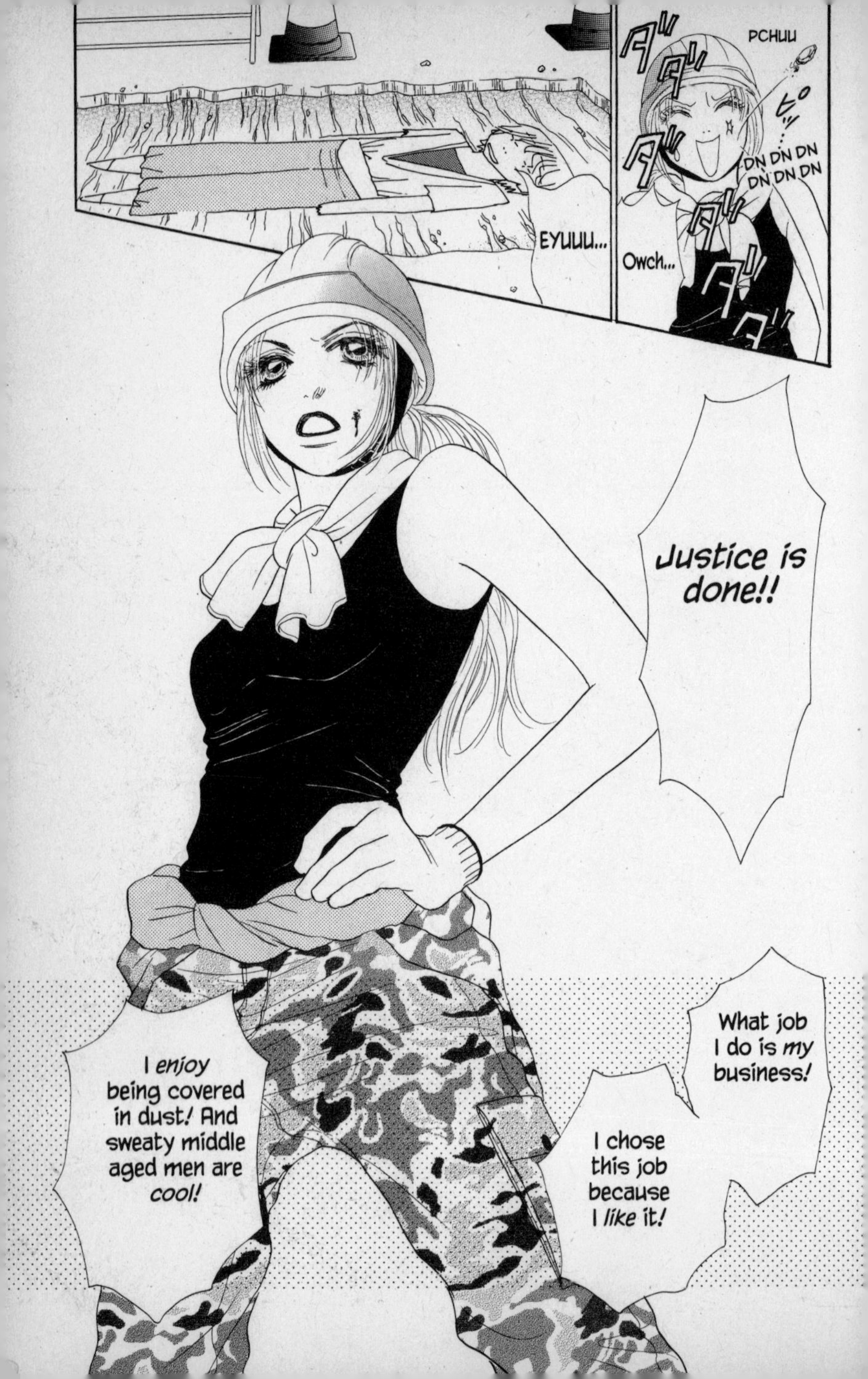
PCHUU
DN DN DN
DN DN DN
Owch...
EYUUU...
Justice is done!!
What job I do is *my* business!
I chose this job because I *like* it!
I *enjoy* being covered in dust! And sweaty middle aged men are *cool!*

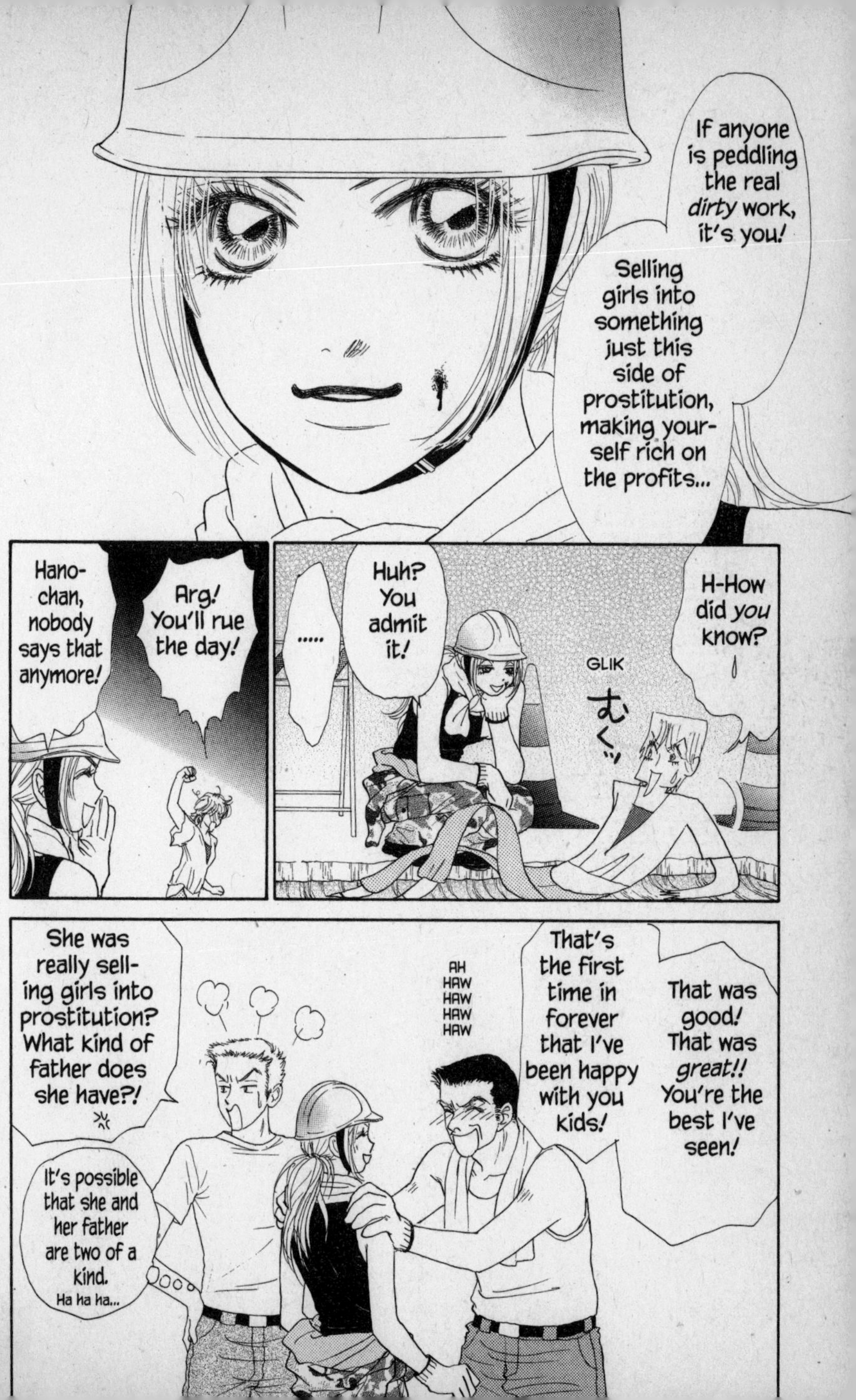
If anyone is peddling the real *dirty* work, it's you!
Selling girls into something just this side of prostitution, making your-self rich on the profits...
H-How did *you* know?
GLIK
むくッ
Huh? You admit it!
.....
Arg! You'll rue the day!
Hano-chan, nobody says that anymore!
That was good! That was *great!!* You're the best I've seen!
That's the first time in forever that I've been happy with you kids!
AH HAW HAW HAW HAW
She was really sell-ing girls into prostitution? What kind of father does she have?!
It's possible that she and her father are two of a kind. Ha ha ha...

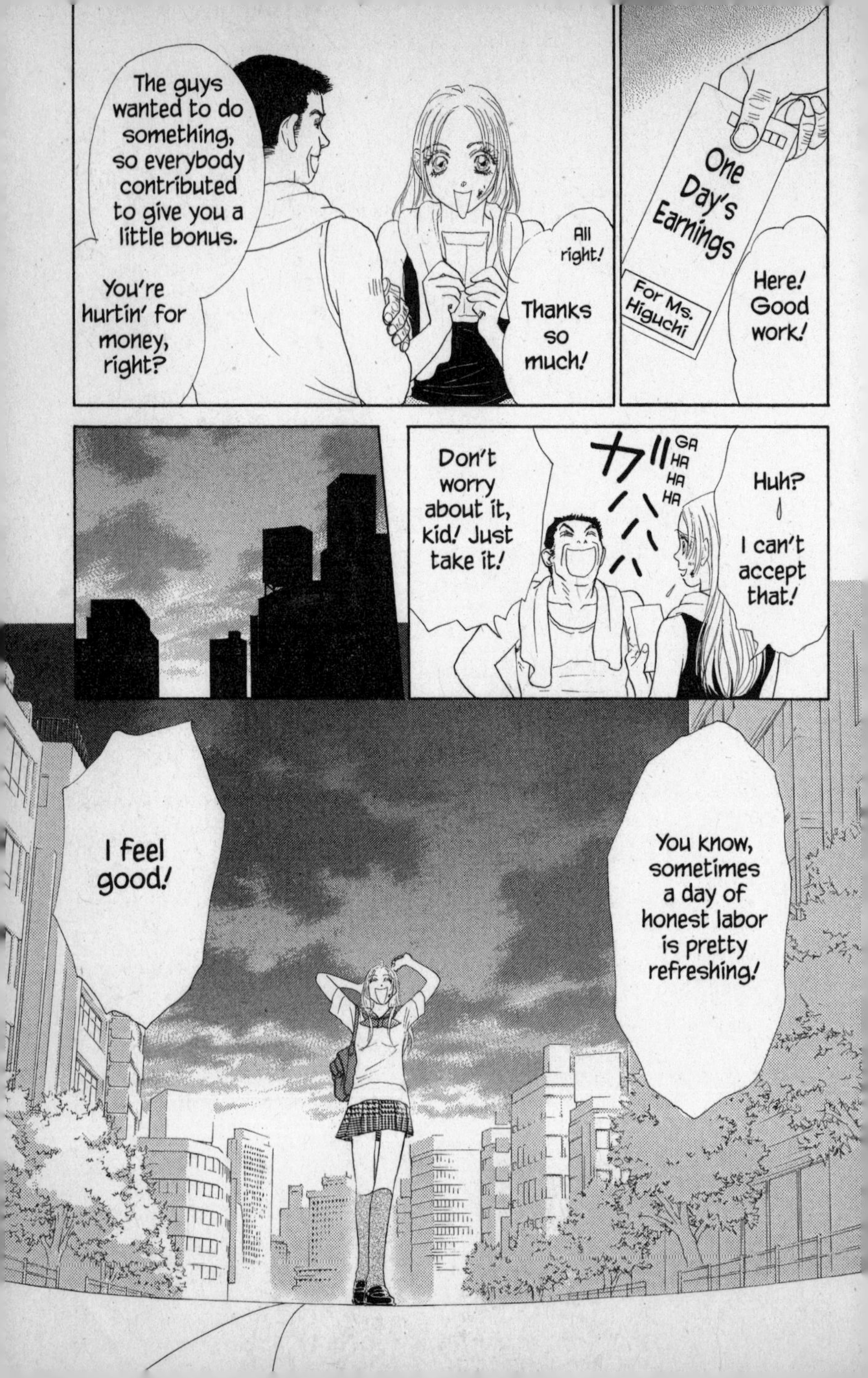
One Day's Earnings
For Ms. Higuchi
Here! Good work!
All right!
Thanks so much!
The guys wanted to do something, so everybody contributed to give you a little bonus.
You're hurtin' for money, right?
Huh?
I can't accept that!
GA HA HA HA
Don't worry about it, kid! Just take it!
You know, sometimes a day of honest labor is pretty refreshing!
I feel good!

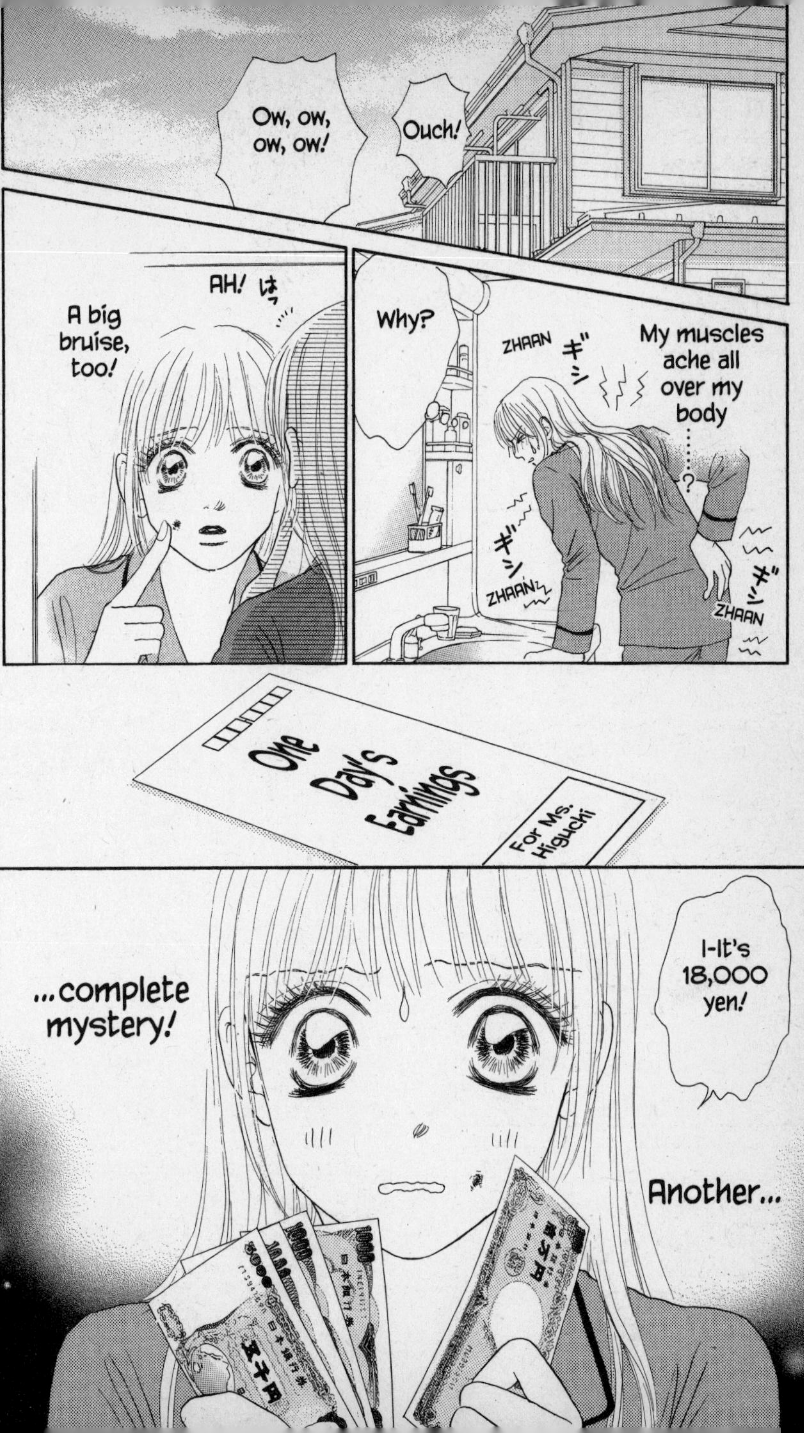
Ouch!
Ow, ow, ow, ow!
My muscles ache all over my body ......?
ギシ
ZHAAN
ギシ
ZHAAN
ギシ
ZHAAN
Why?
AH! は
A big bruise, too!
One Day's Earnings
For Ms. Higuchi
I-It's 18,000 yen!
Another...
...complete mystery!

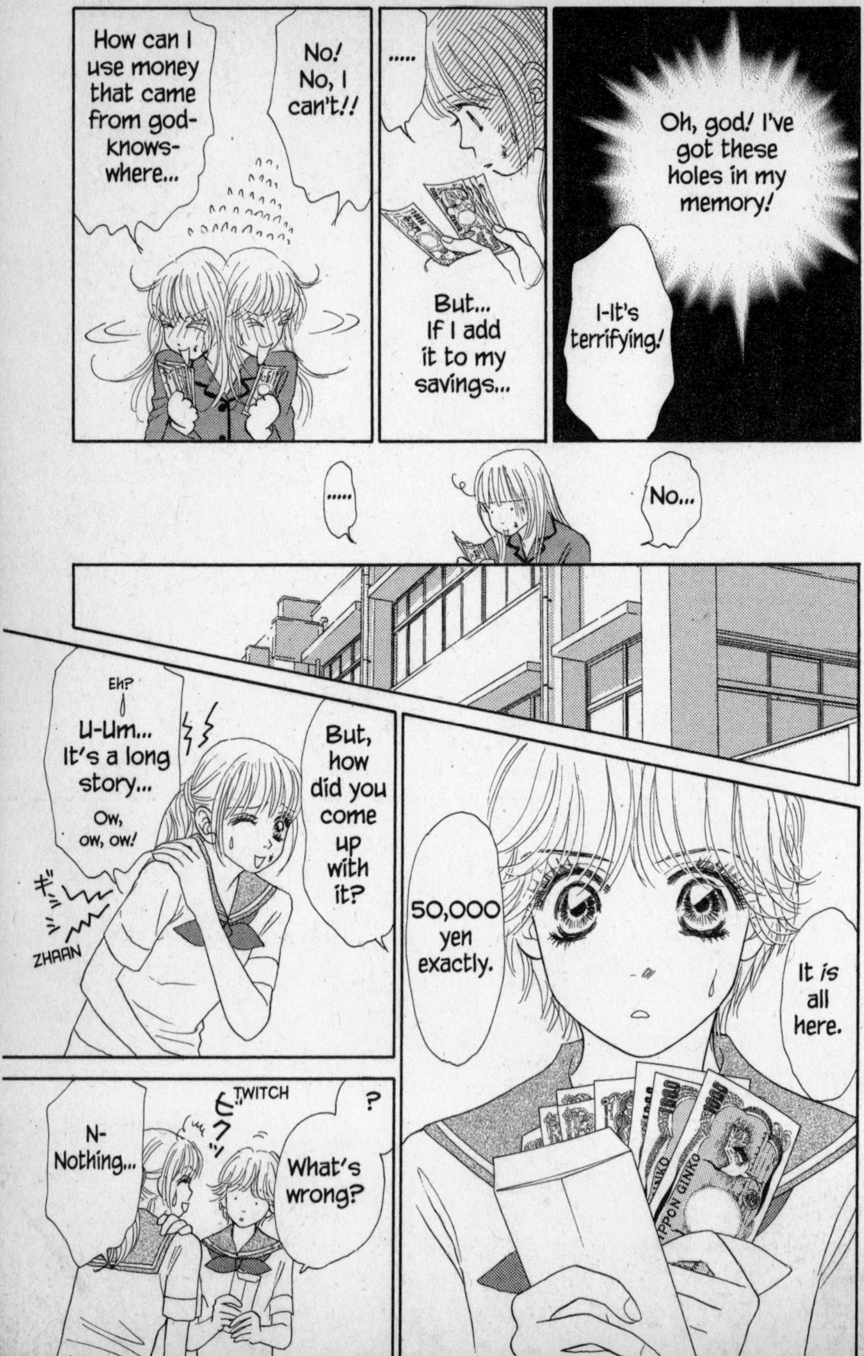
Oh, god! I've got these holes in my memory!
I-It's terrifying!
.....
But... If I add it to my savings...
No! No, I can't!!
How can I use money that came from god-knows-where...
No...
.....
It *is* all here.
50,000 yen exactly.
But, how did you come up with it?
Eh?
U-Um... It's a long story...
Ow, ow, ow!
ZHAAN
?
What's wrong?
TWITCH
N-Nothing...

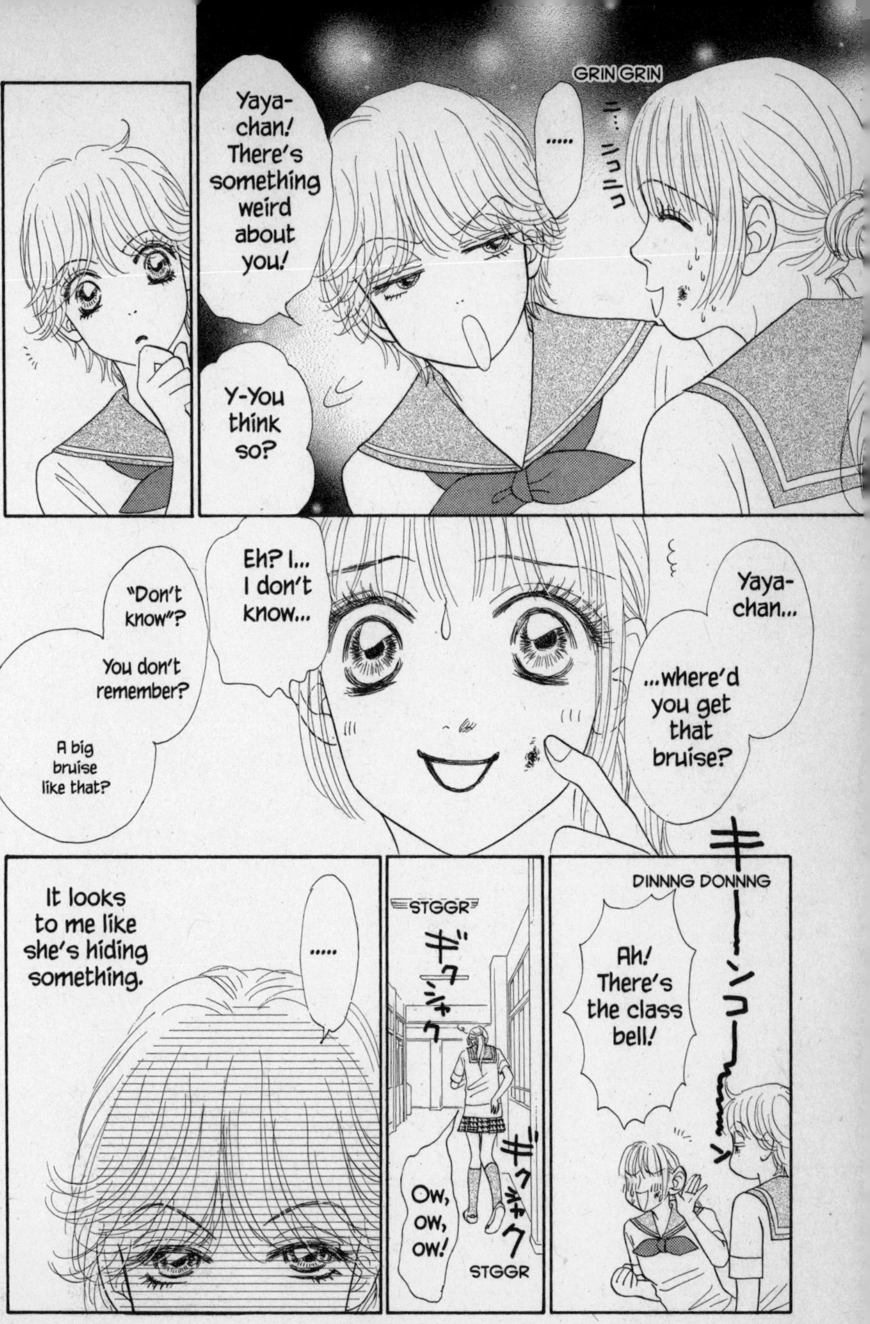
GRIN GRIN
.....
Yaya-chan! There's something weird about you!
Y-You think so?
Yaya-chan...
...where'd you get that bruise?
Eh? I... I don't know...
"Don't know"?
You don't remember?
A big bruise like that?
DINNNG DONNNG
Ah! There's the class bell!
STGGR
Ow, ow, ow!
STGGR
It looks to me like she's hiding something.
.....

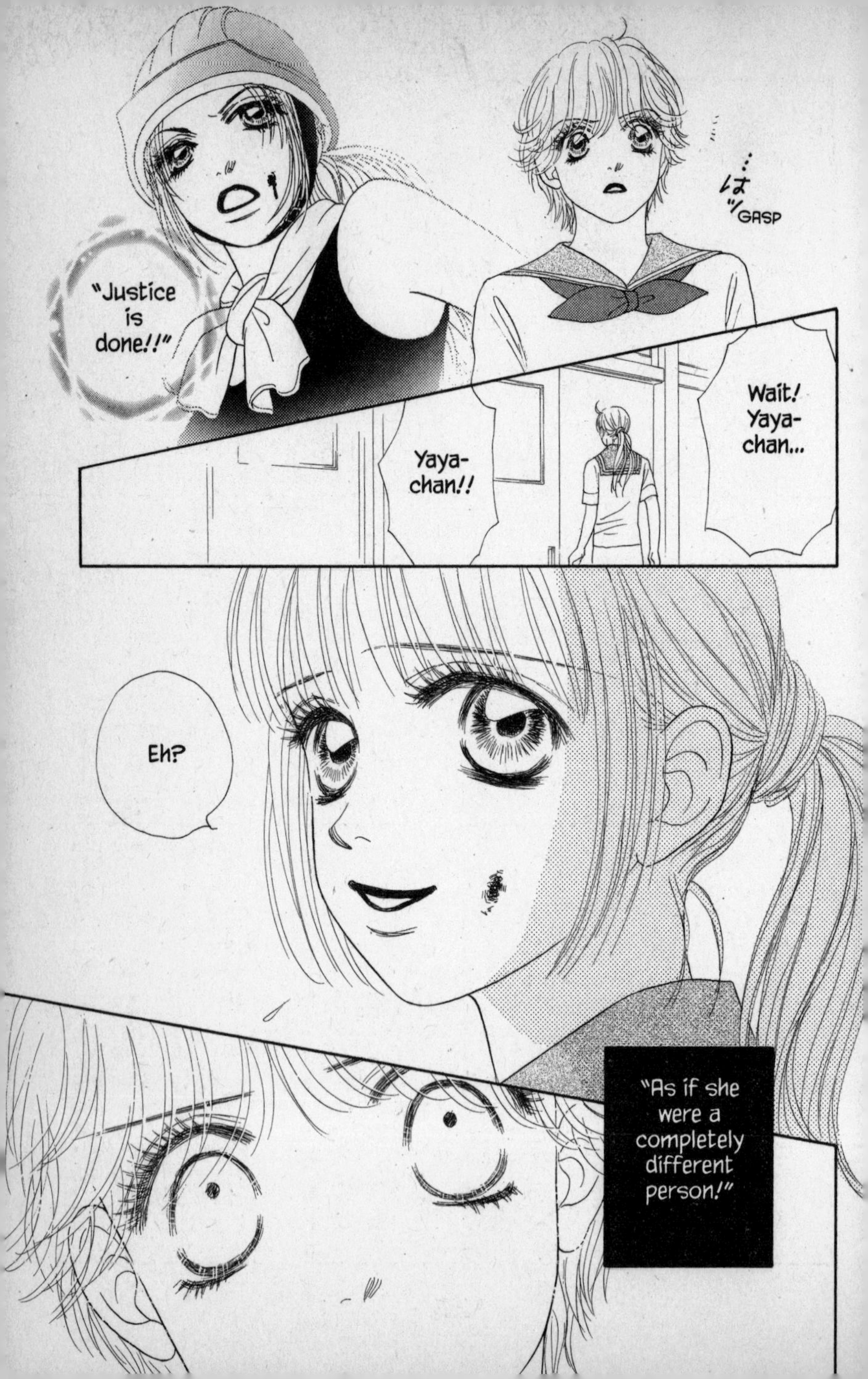
…はッ
GASP
"Justice is done!!"
Wait! Yaya-chan...
Yaya-chan!!
Eh?
"As if she were a completely different person!"

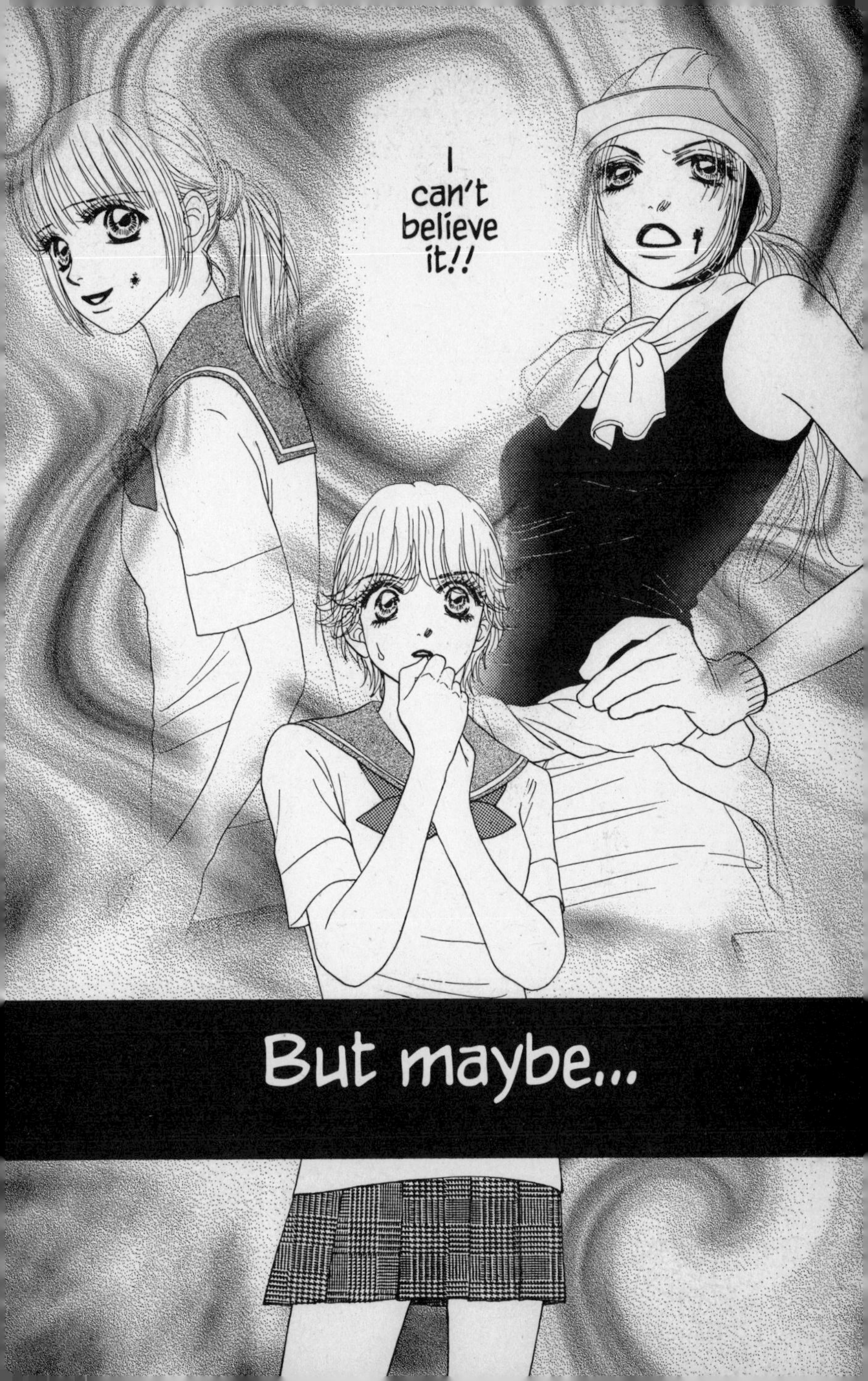
I can't believe it!!
But maybe...

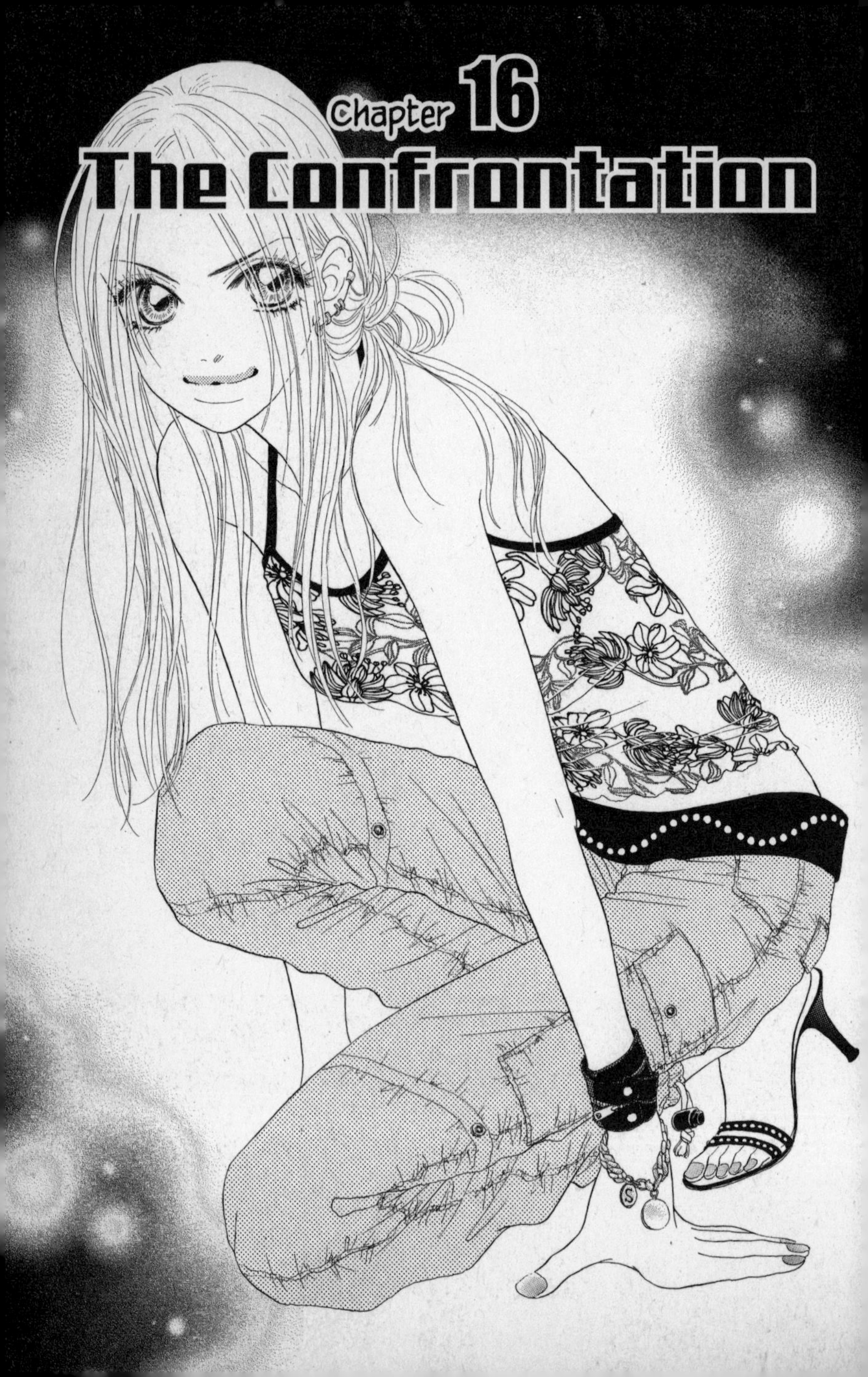
Chapter 16
The Confrontation

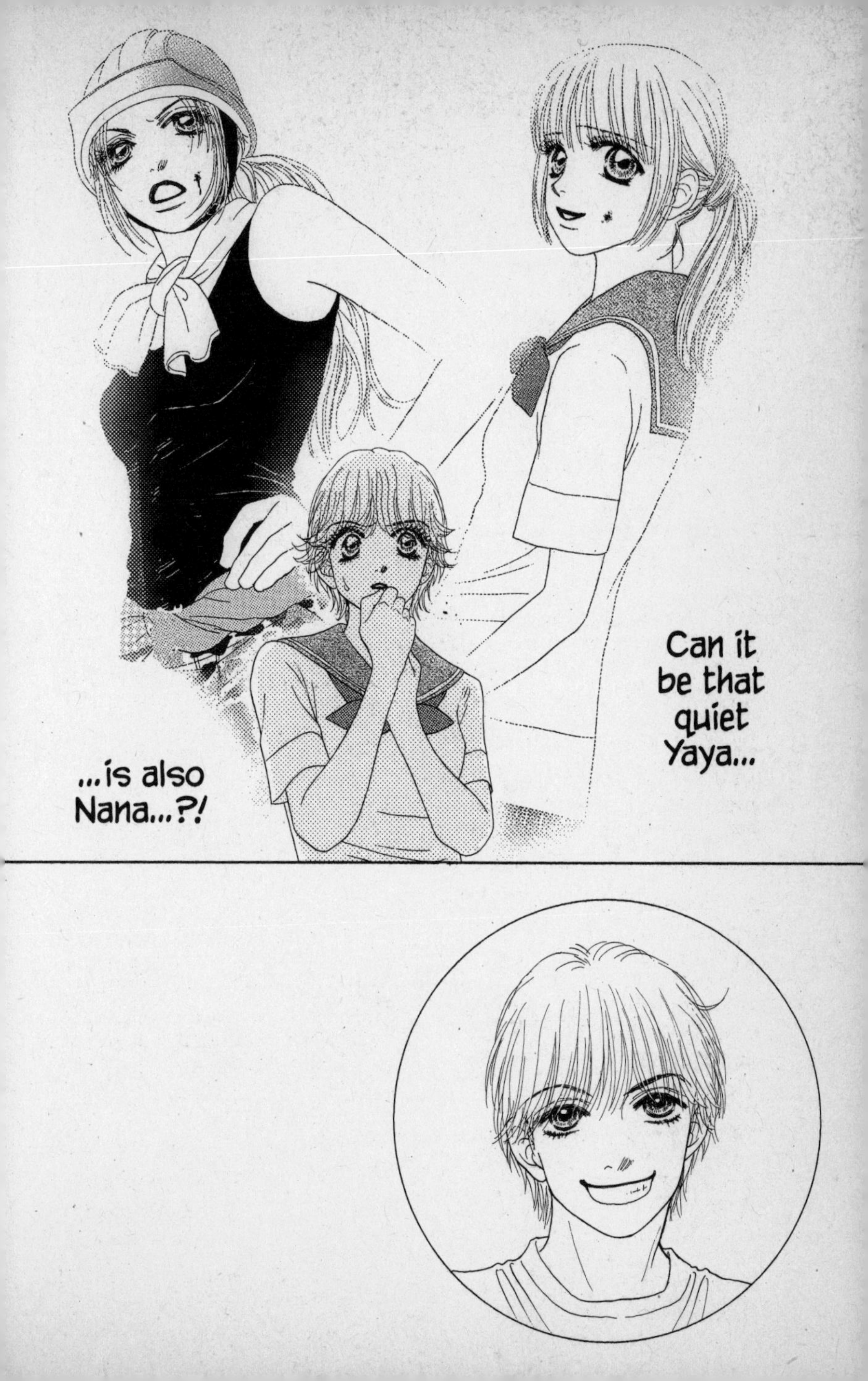
Can it be that quiet Yaya...
...is also Nana...?!

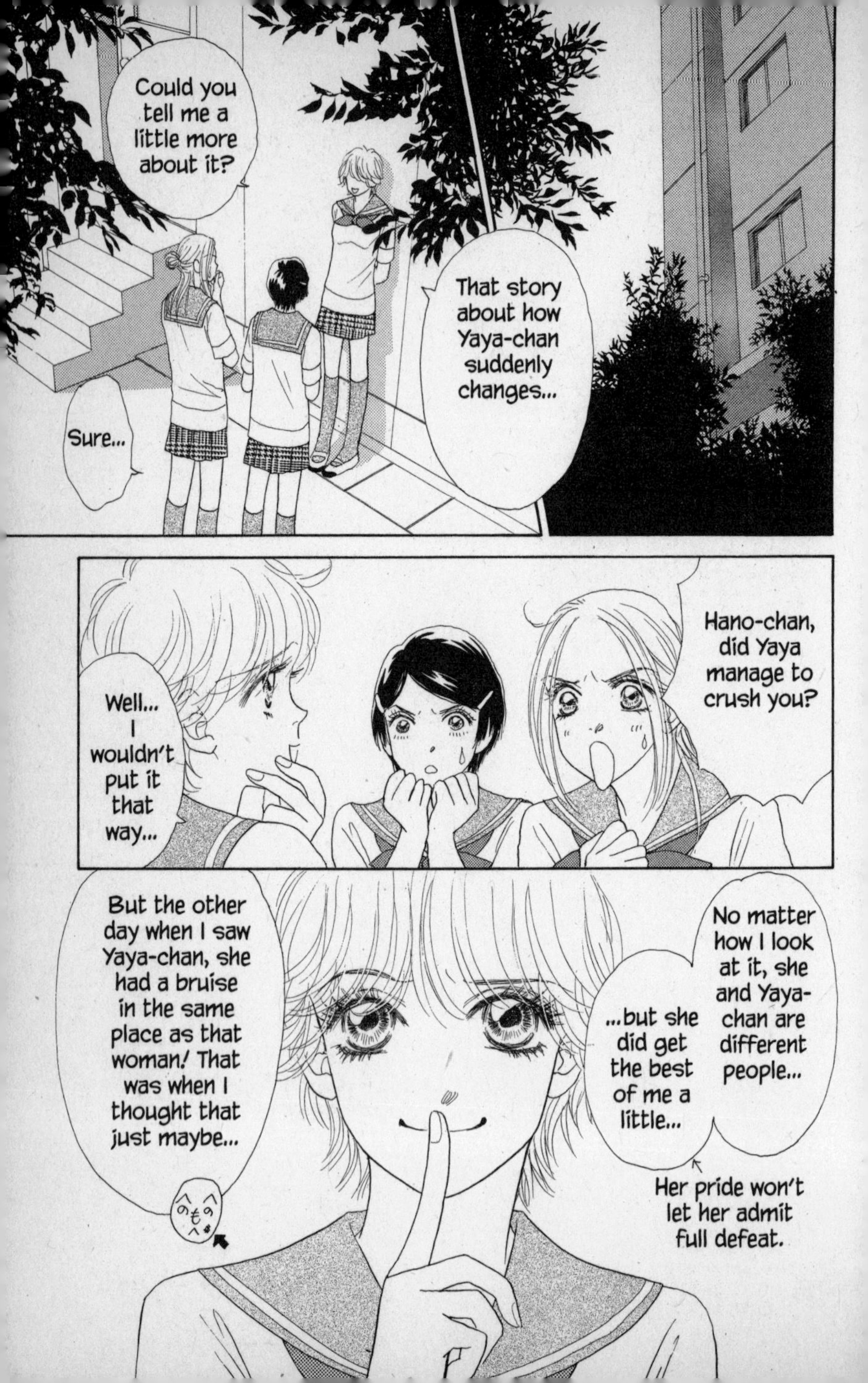
Could you tell me a little more about it?
That story about how Yaya-chan suddenly changes...
Sure...
Hano-chan, did Yaya manage to crush you?
Well... I wouldn't put it that way...
No matter how I look at it, she and Yaya-chan are different people...
...but she did get the best of me a little...
Her pride won't let her admit full defeat.
But the other day when I saw Yaya-chan, she had a bruise in the same place as that woman! That was when I thought that just maybe...

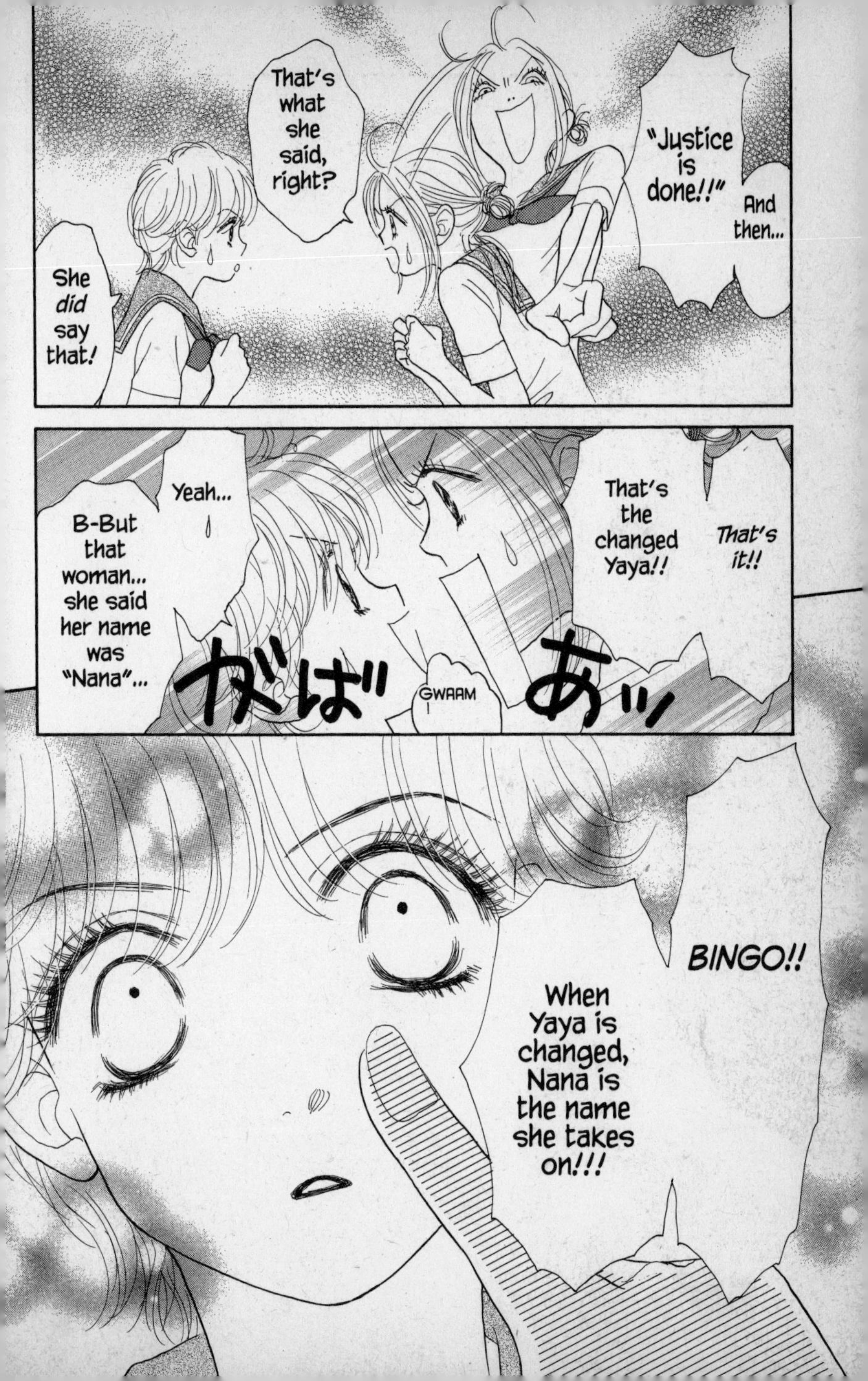
And then...
"Justice is done!!"
That's what she said, right?
She *did* say that!
That's it!!
That's the changed Yaya!!
がばあッ
GWAAM
Yeah...
B-But that woman... she said her name was "Nana"...
BINGO!!
When Yaya is changed, Nana is the name she takes on!!!

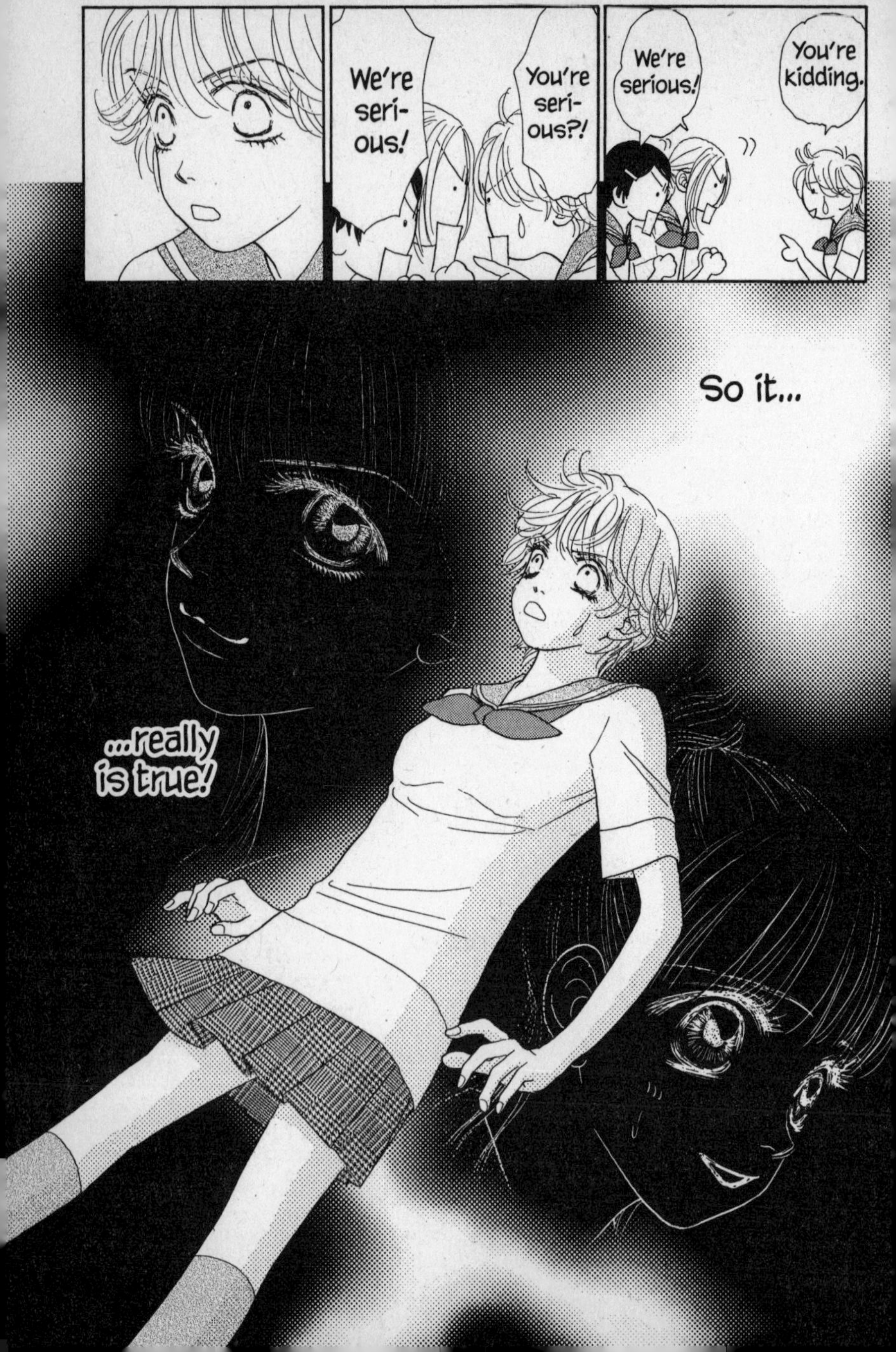
You're kidding.
We're serious!
You're seri-ous?!
We're seri-ous!
So it...
...really is true!

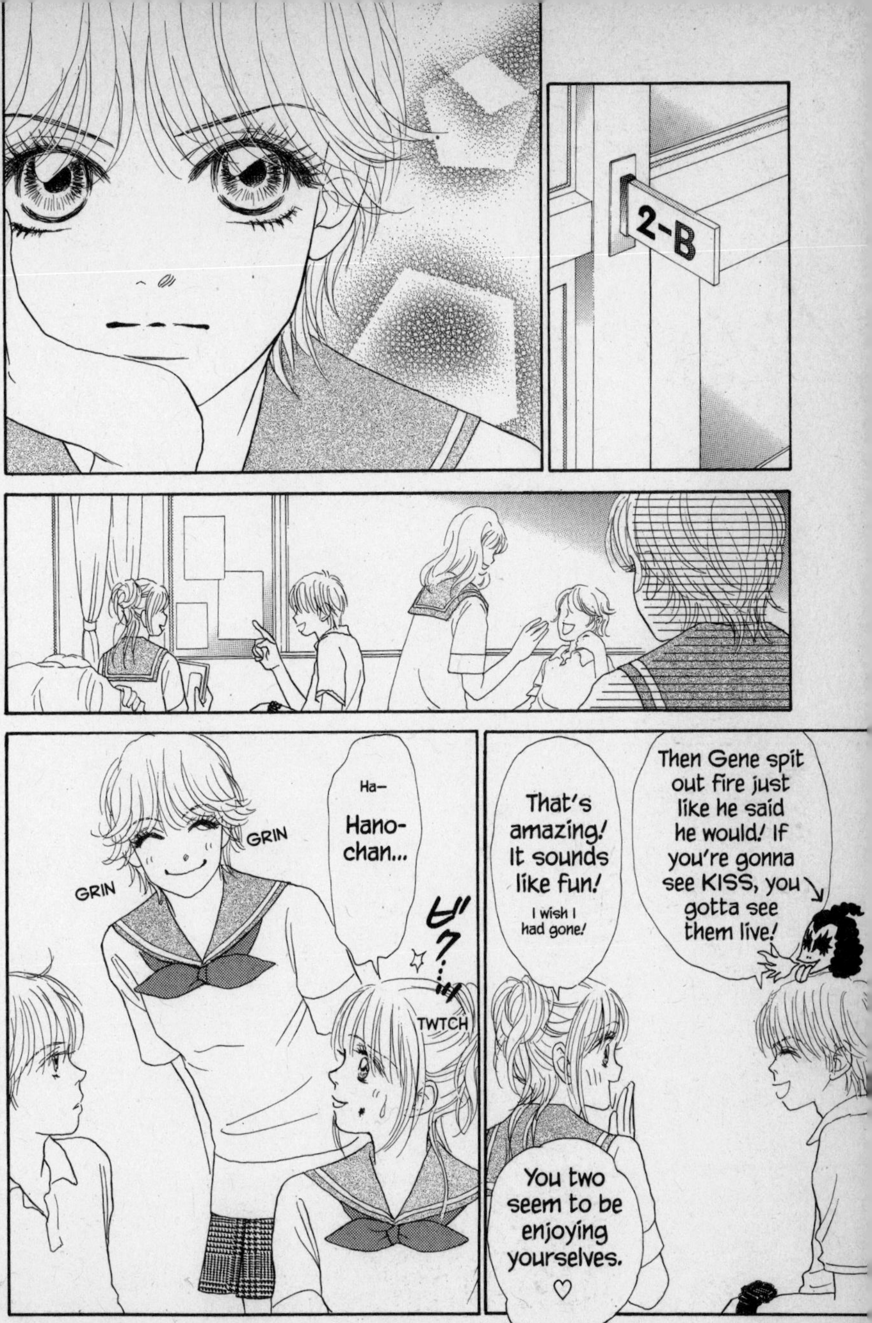
2-B
Then Gene spit out fire just like he said he would! If you're gonna see KISS, you gotta see them live!
That's amazing! It sounds like fun!
I wish I had gone!
You two seem to be enjoying yourselves. ♡
Ha– Hano-chan...
GRIN
GRIN
ビク…
TWTCH

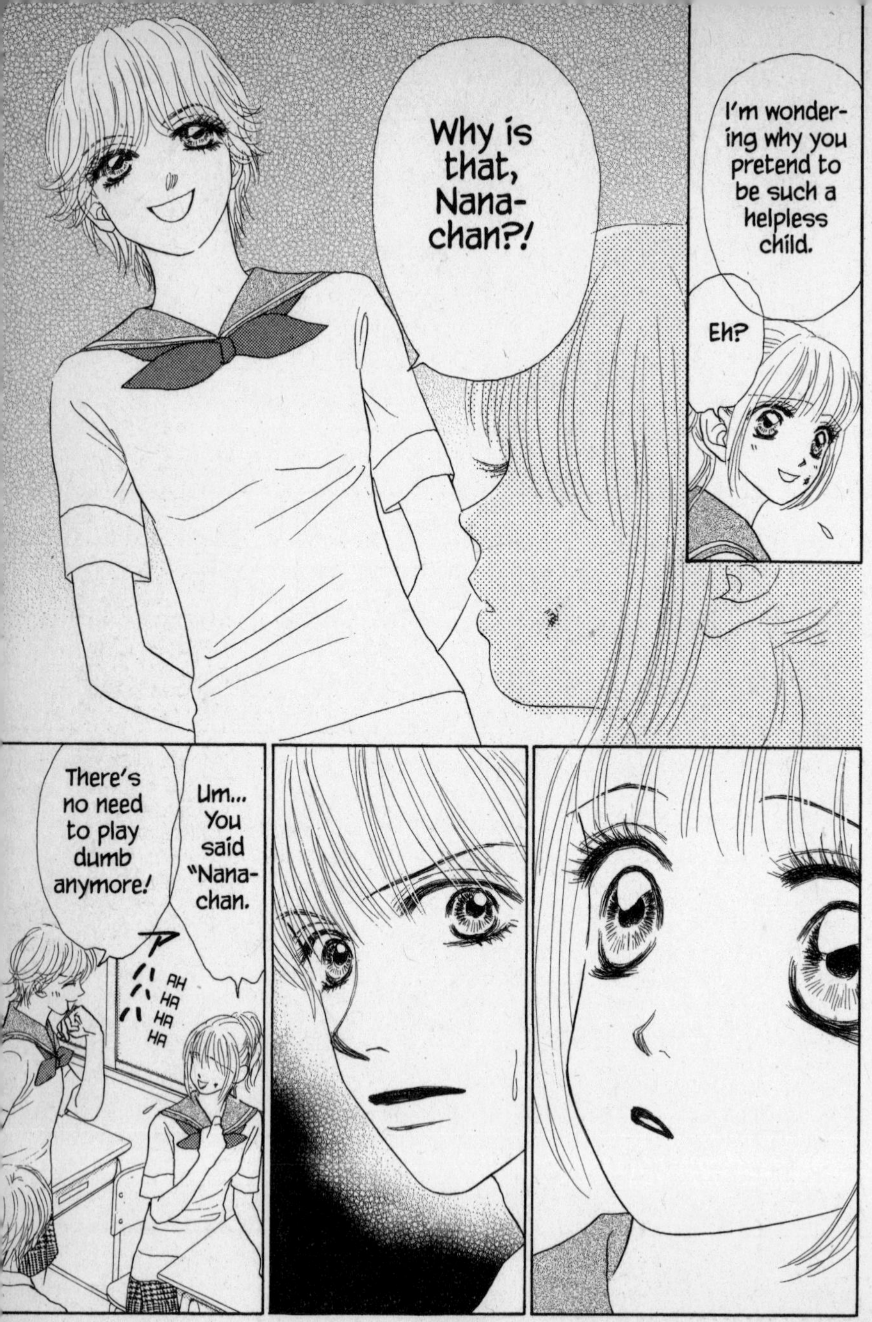
I'm wondering why you pretend to be such a helpless child.
Eh?
Why is that, Nana-chan?!
Um... You said "Nana-chan.
There's no need to play dumb anymore!
アハハハ
AH HA HA HA

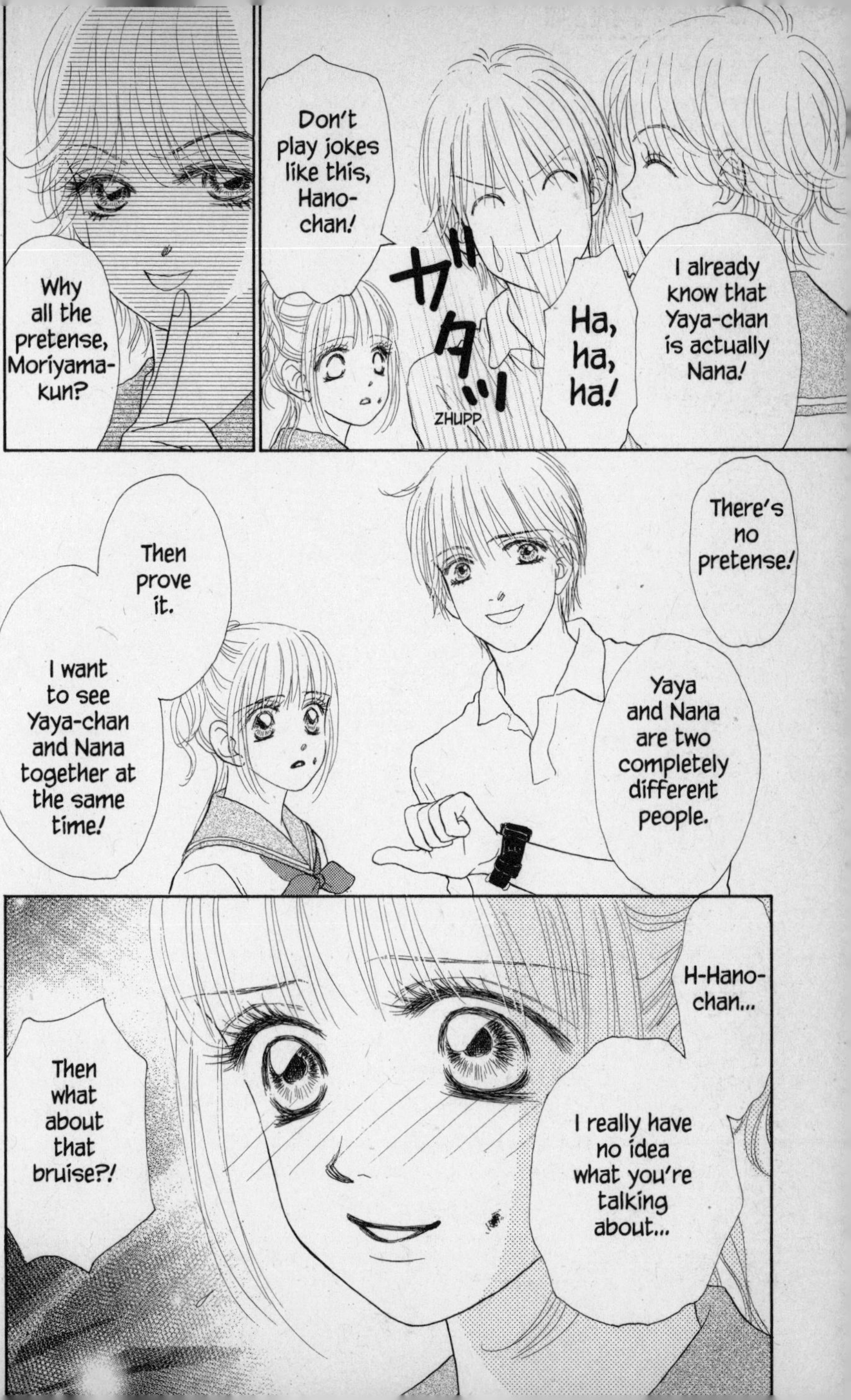
I already know that Yaya-chan is actually Nana!
Ha, ha, ha!
ガタッ
ZHUPP
Don't play jokes like this, Hano-chan!
Why all the pretense, Moriyama-kun?
There's no pretense!
Yaya and Nana are two completely different people.
Then prove it.
I want to see Yaya-chan and Nana together at the same time!
H-Hano-chan...
I really have no idea what you're talking about...
Then what about that bruise?!

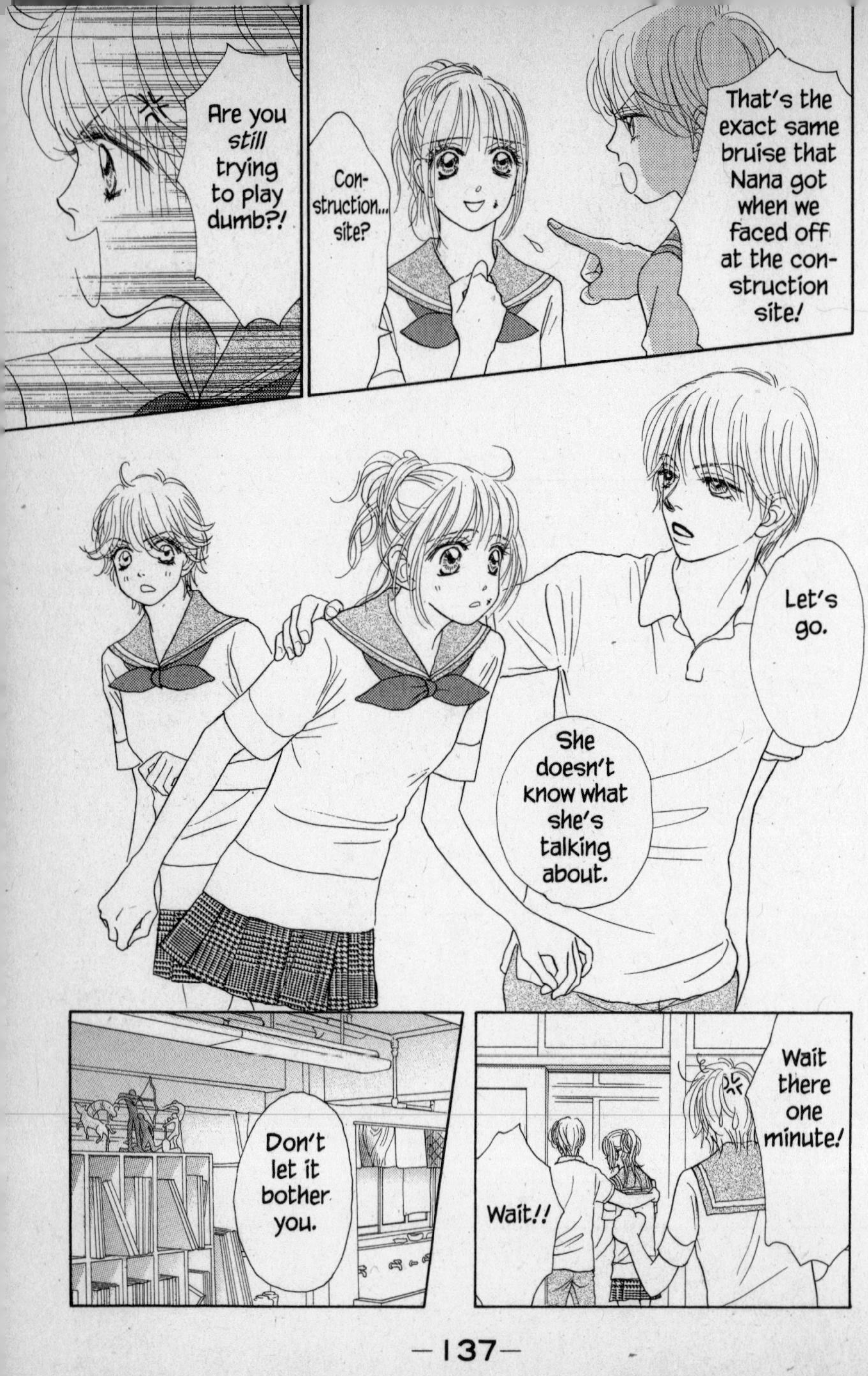
That's the exact same bruise that Nana got when we faced off at the construction site!
Con-struction... site?
Are you *still* trying to play dumb?!
Let's go.
She doesn't know what she's talking about.
Wait there one minute!
Wait!!
Don't let it bother you.

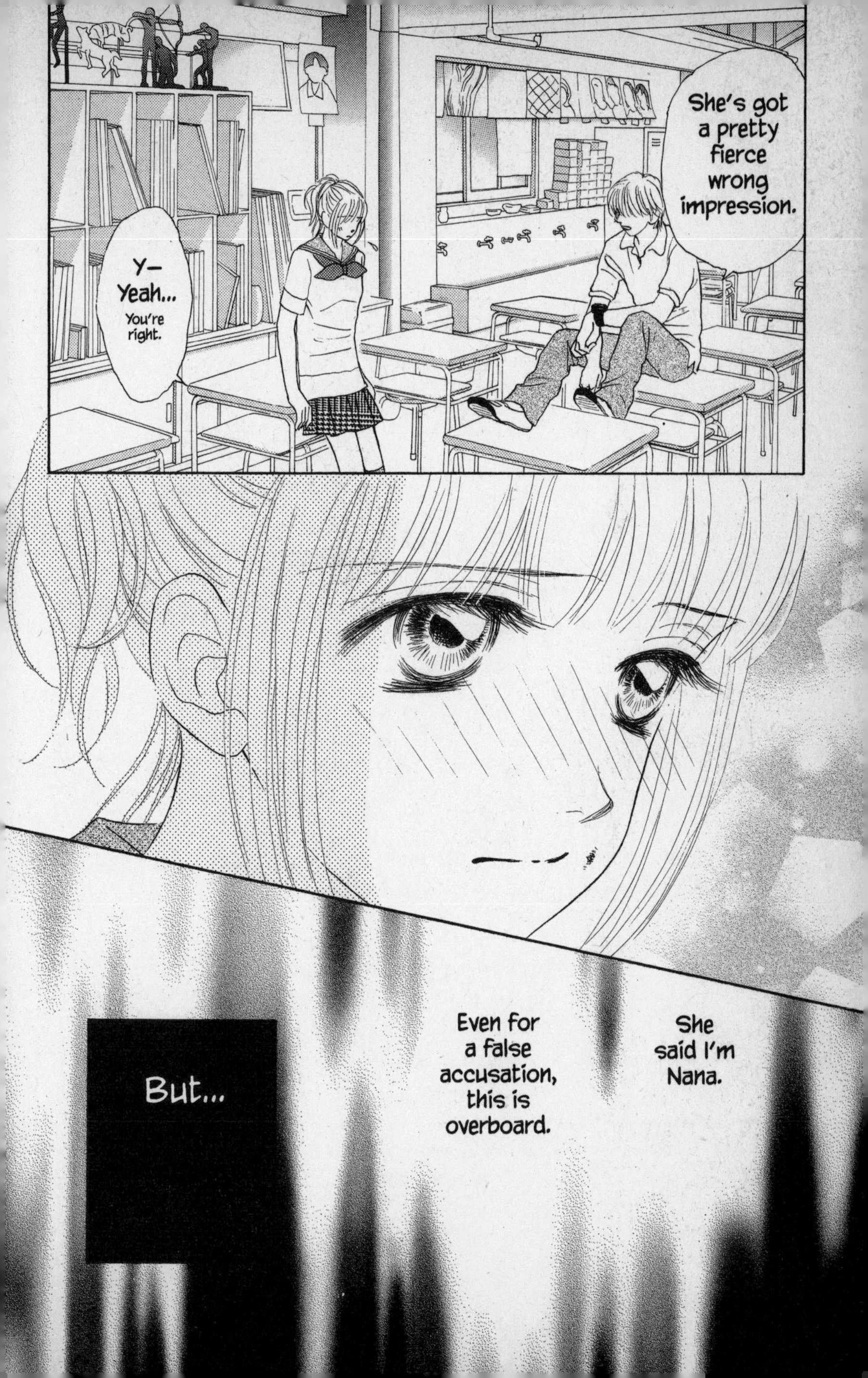
She's got a pretty fierce wrong impression.
Y— Yeah... You're right.
She said I'm Nana.
Even for a false accusation, this is overboard.
But...

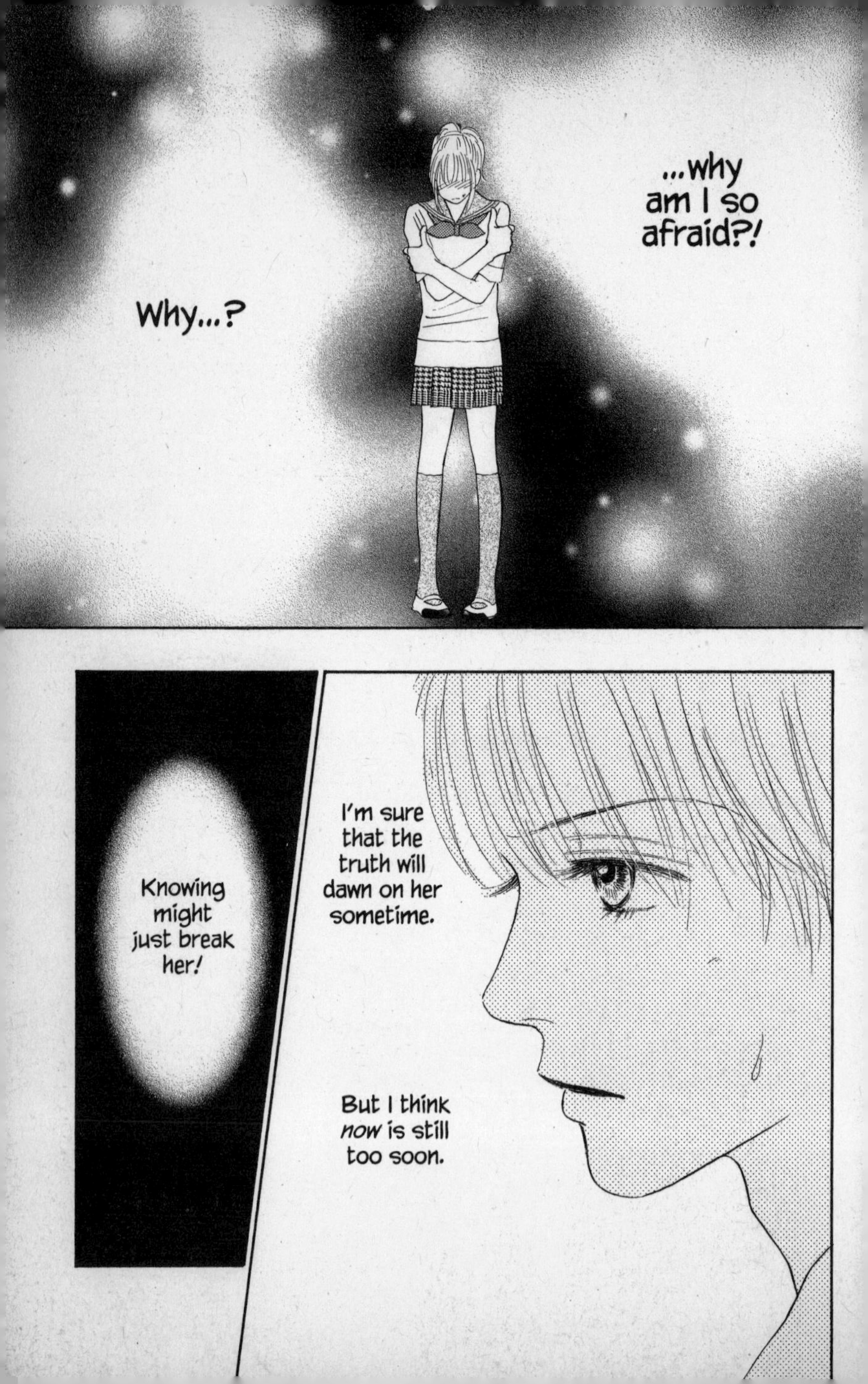
...why am I so afraid?!
Why...?
I'm sure that the truth will dawn on her sometime.
But I think *now* is still too soon.
Knowing might just break her!

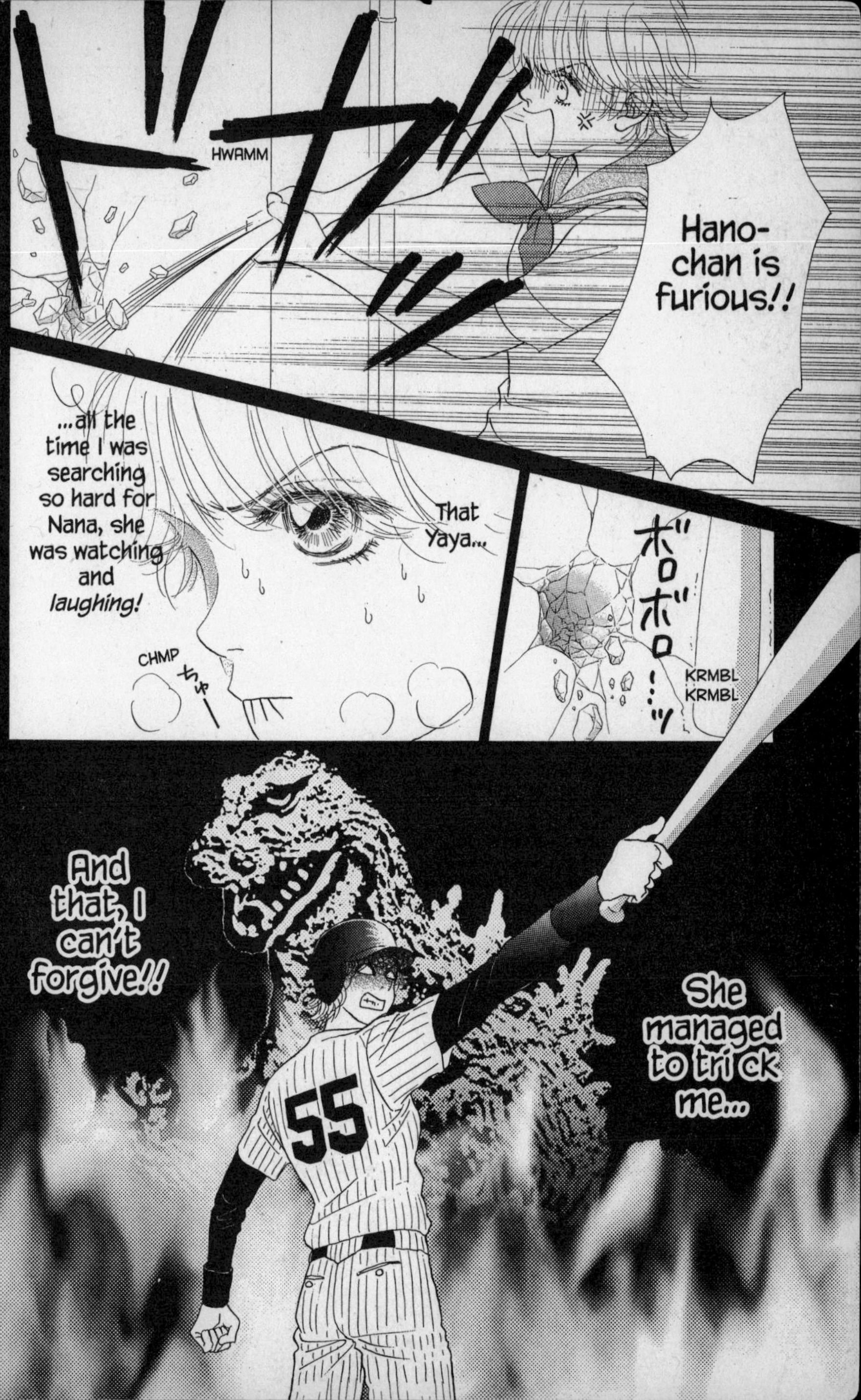
Hano-chan is furious!!
HWAMM
ボロボロ…ッ
KRMBL KRMBL
That Yaya...
...all the time I was searching so hard for Nana, she was watching and *laughing!*
CHMP
ちゅー
She managed to tri ck me...
And that, I can't forgive!!
55

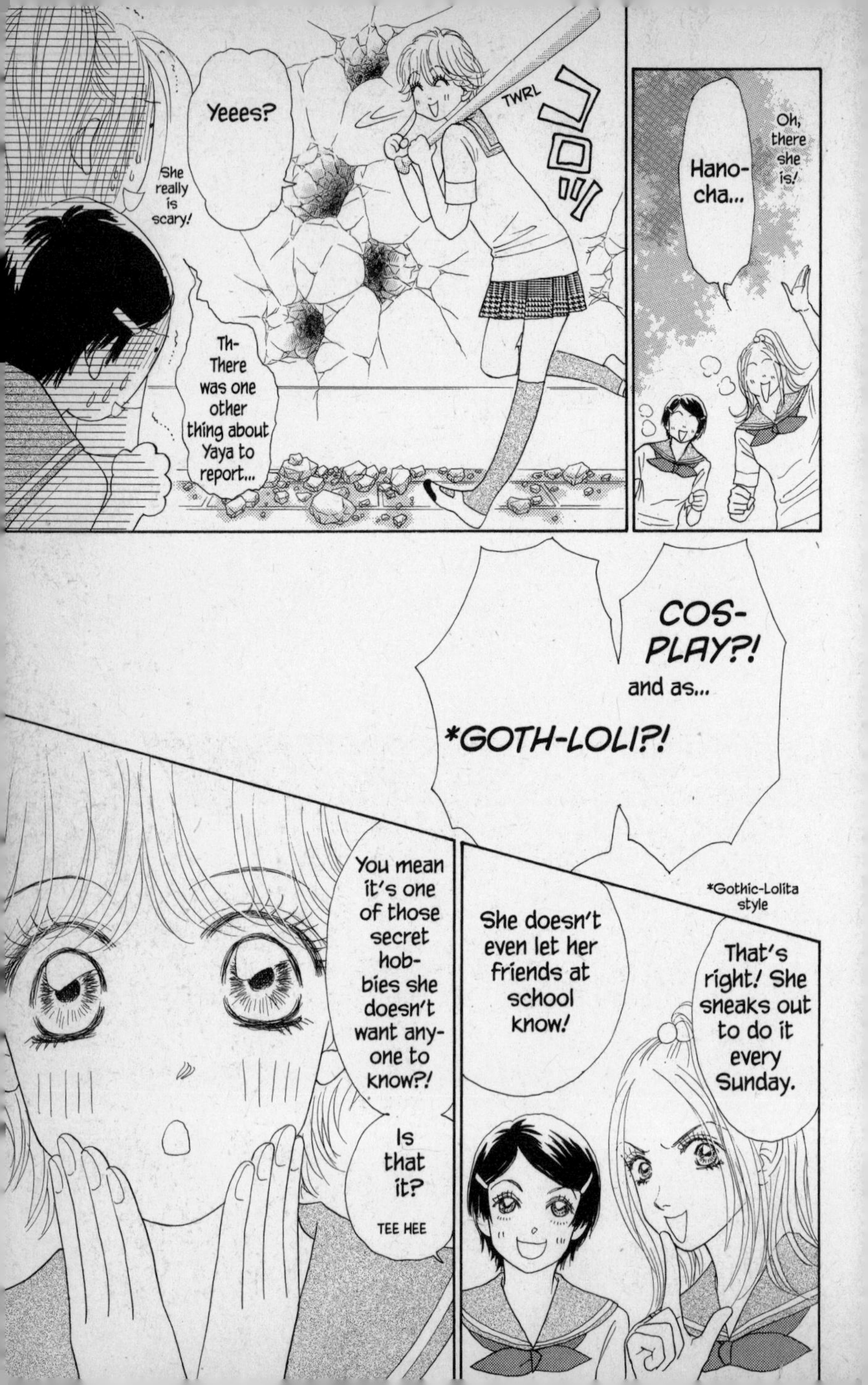
Hano-cha...
Oh, there she is!
TWRL
Yeees?
She really is scary!
Th- There was one other thing about Yaya to report...
COS-PLAY?!
and as...
*GOTH-LOLI?!
That's right! She sneaks out to do it every Sunday.
She doesn't even let her friends at school know!
*Gothic-Lolita style
You mean it's one of those secret hob-bies she doesn't want any-one to know?!
Is that it?
TEE HEE

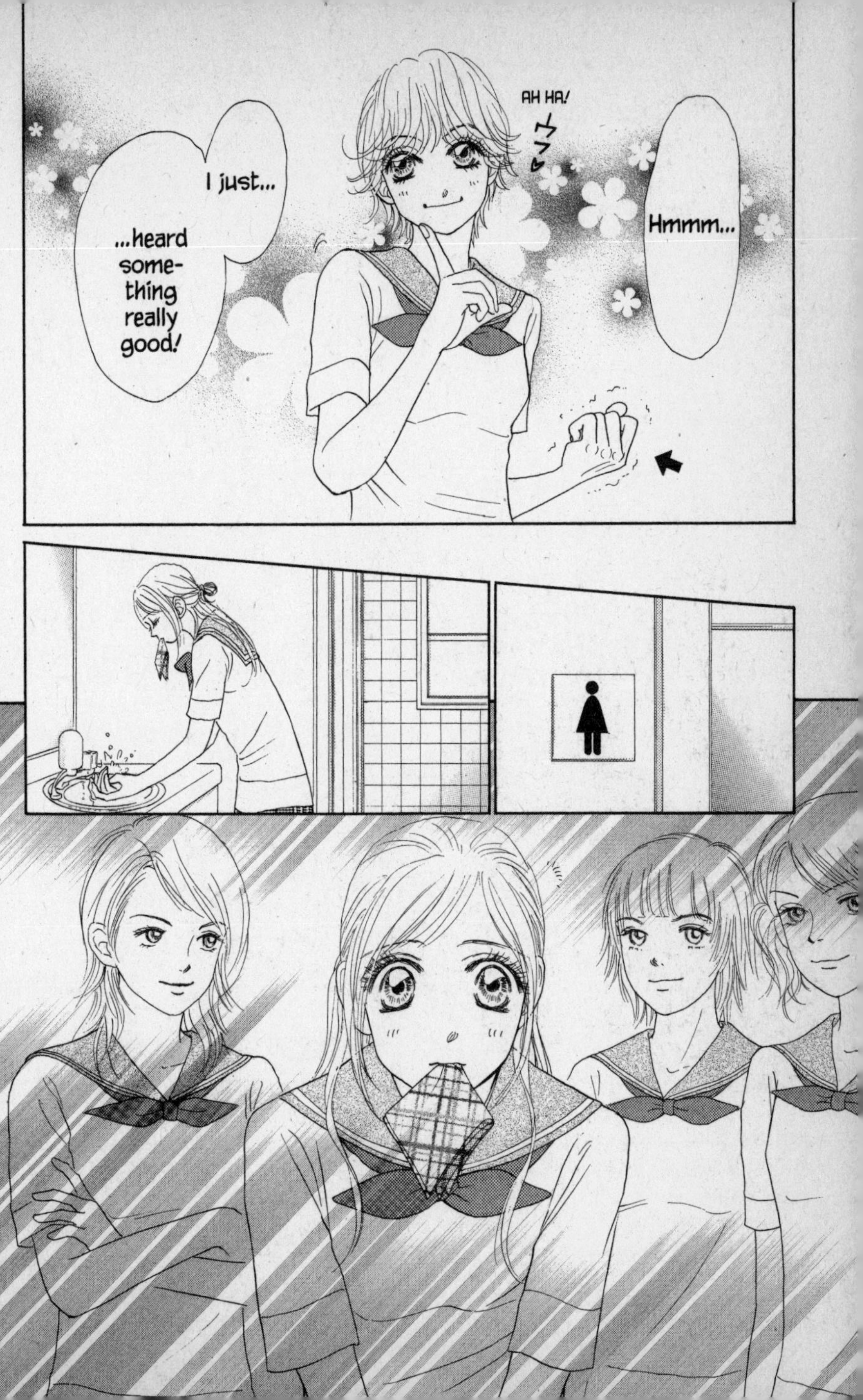
Hmmm...
AH HA!
I just...
...heard some-thing really good!

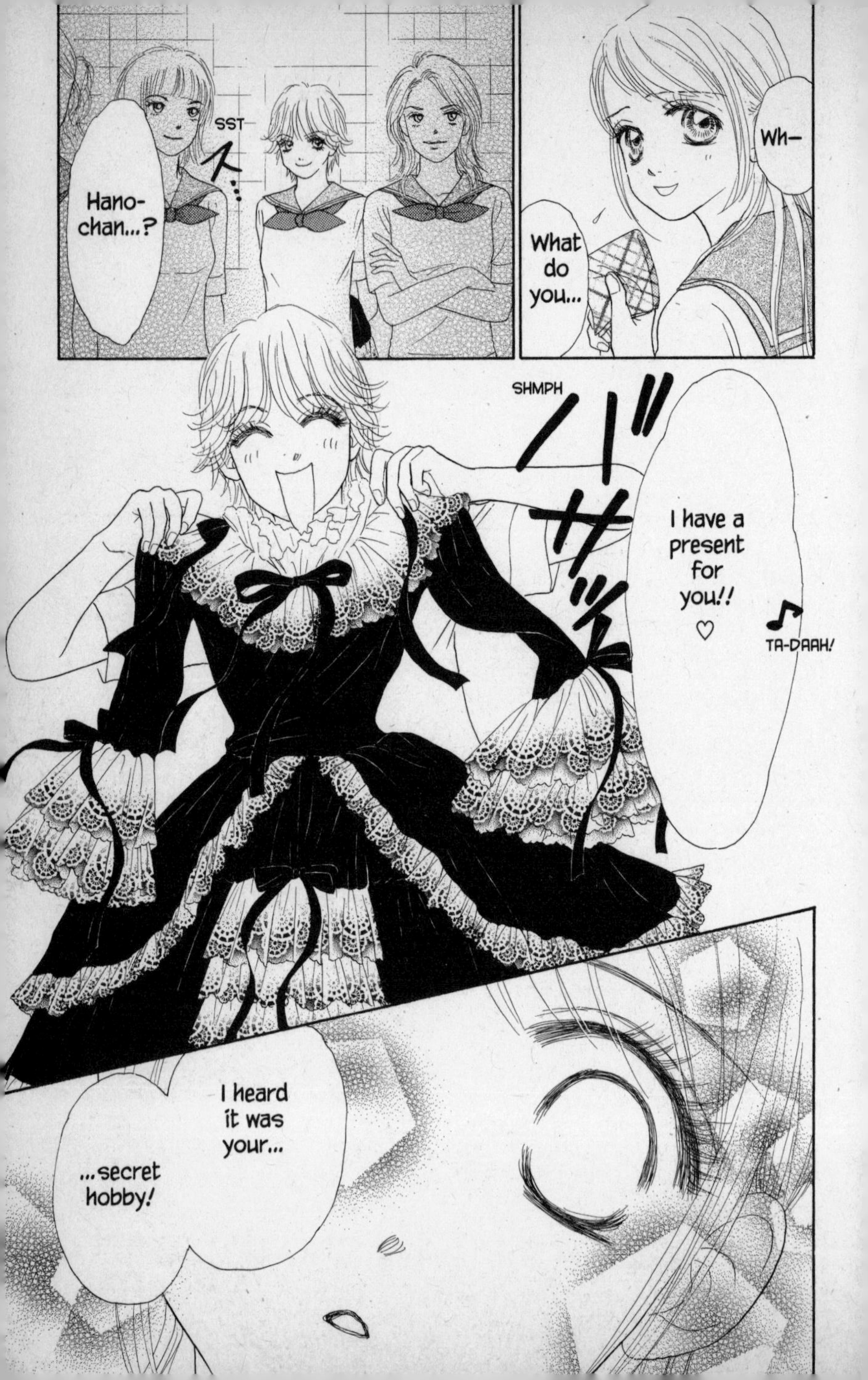
Wh-
What do you...
SST
Hano-chan...?
SHMPH
I have a present for you!! ♡
TA-DAAH!
I heard it was your...
...secret hobby!

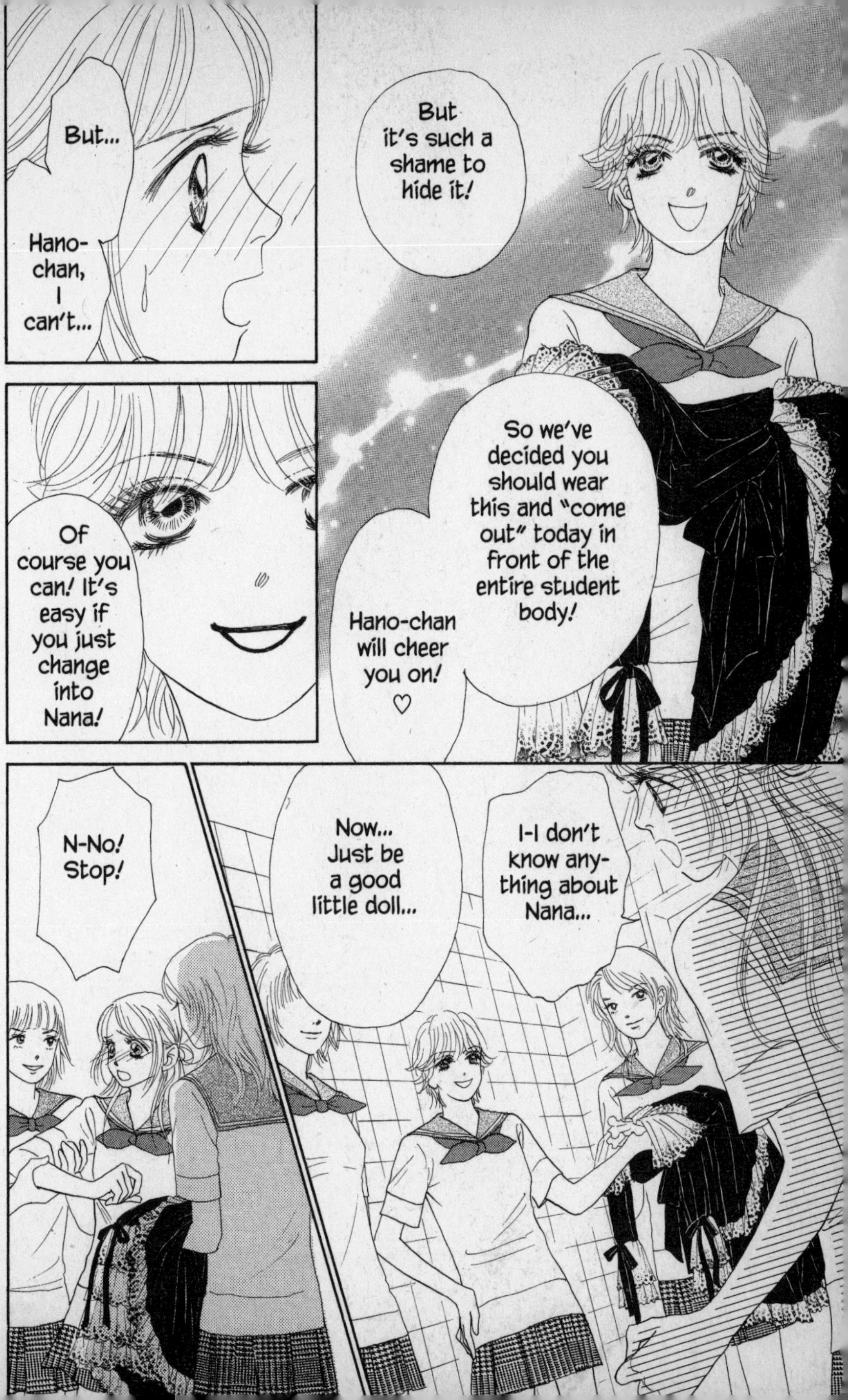
But it's such a shame to hide it!
So we've decided you should wear this and "come out" today in front of the entire student body!
Hano-chan will cheer you on! ♡
But...
Hano-chan, I can't...
Of course you can! It's easy if you just change into Nana!
I-I don't know any-thing about Nana...
Now... Just be a good little doll...
N-No! Stop!

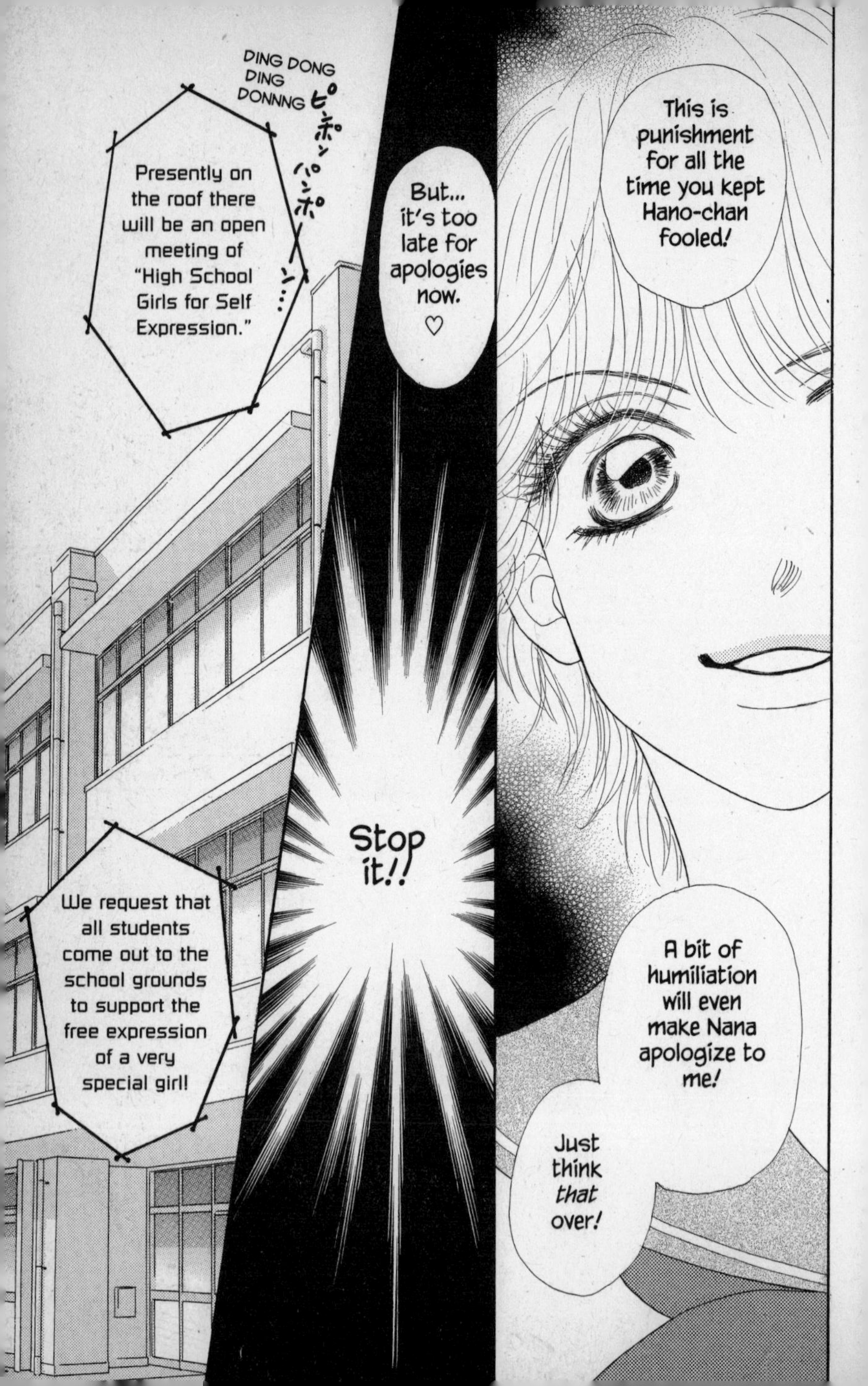
This is punishment for all the time you kept Hano-chan fooled!
A bit of humiliation will even make Nana apologize to me!
Just think *that* over!
But... it's too late for apologies now. ♡
Stop it!!
DING DONG DING DONNNG
ピンポンパンポーン…
Presently on the roof there will be an open meeting of "High School Girls for Self Expression."
We request that all students come out to the school grounds to support the free expression of a very special girl!

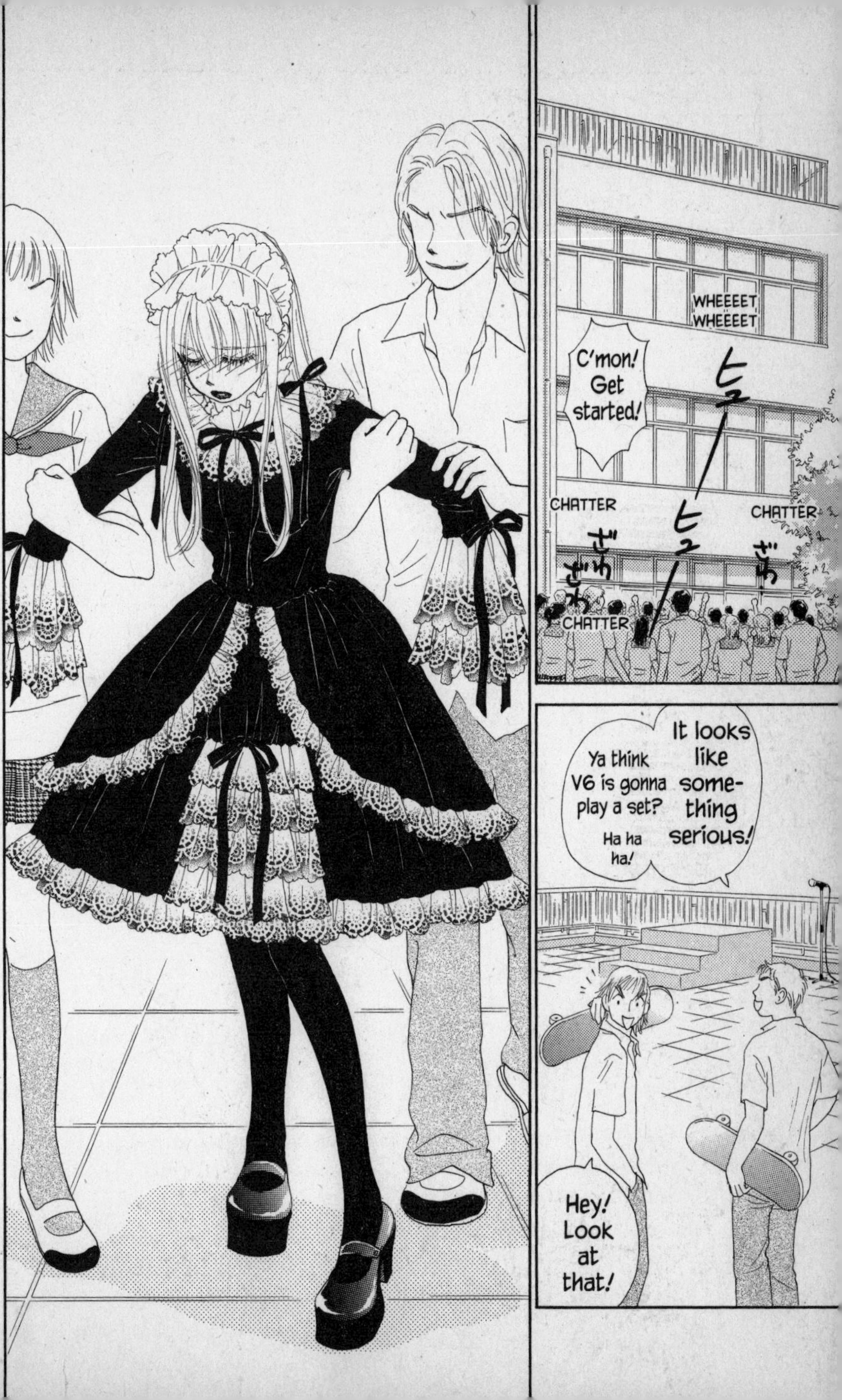
WHEEEET WHEEEET
ヒュー
ヒュー
C'mon! Get started!
CHATTER
ざわ
CHATTER
ざわ ざわ
CHATTER
It looks like some-thing serious!
Ya think V6 is gonna play a set?
Ha ha ha!
Hey! Look at that!

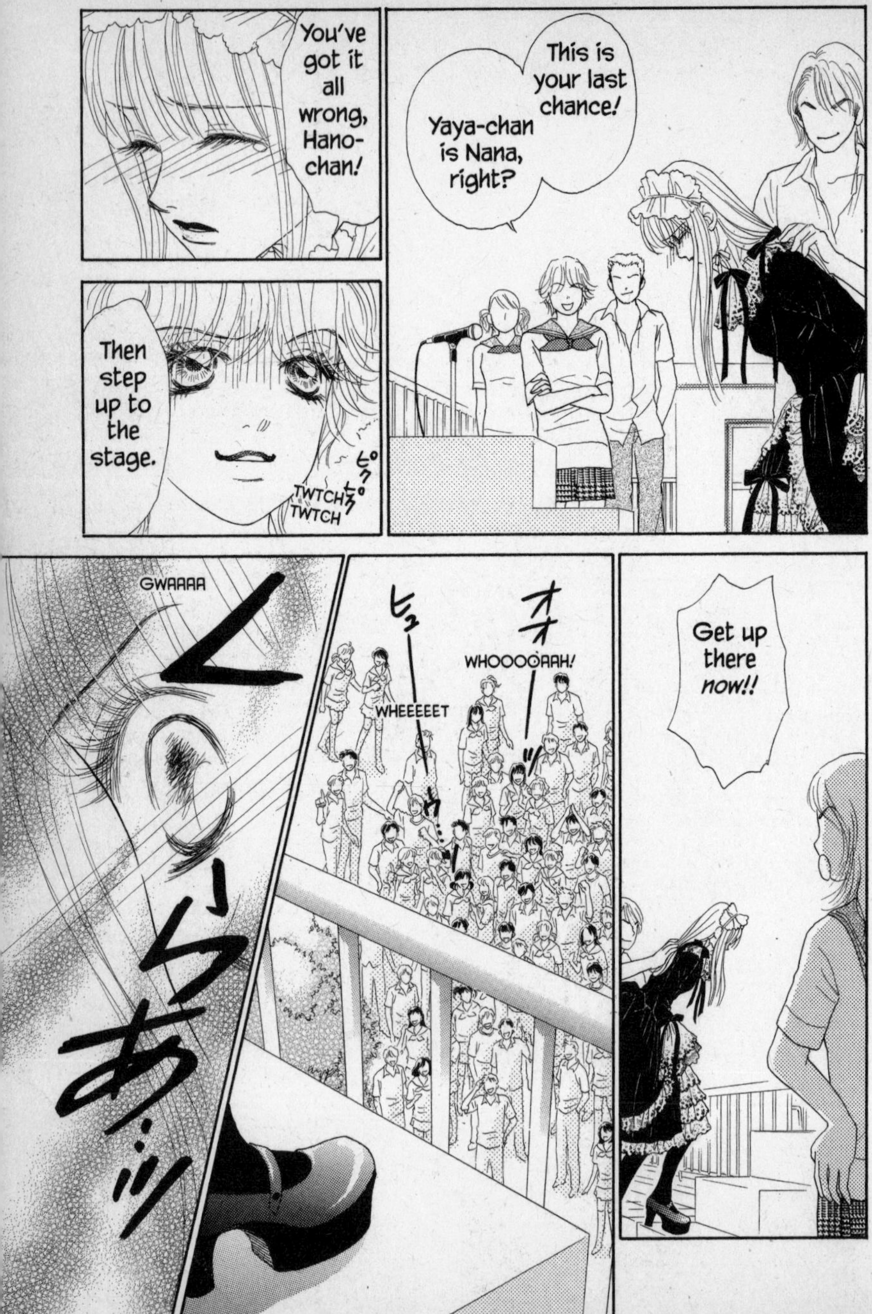
This is your last chance!
Yaya-chan is Nana, right?
You've got it all wrong, Hano-chan!
Then step up to the stage.
TWTCH TWTCH
Get up there *now!!*
WHOOOOAAH!
WHEEEEET
GWAAAA

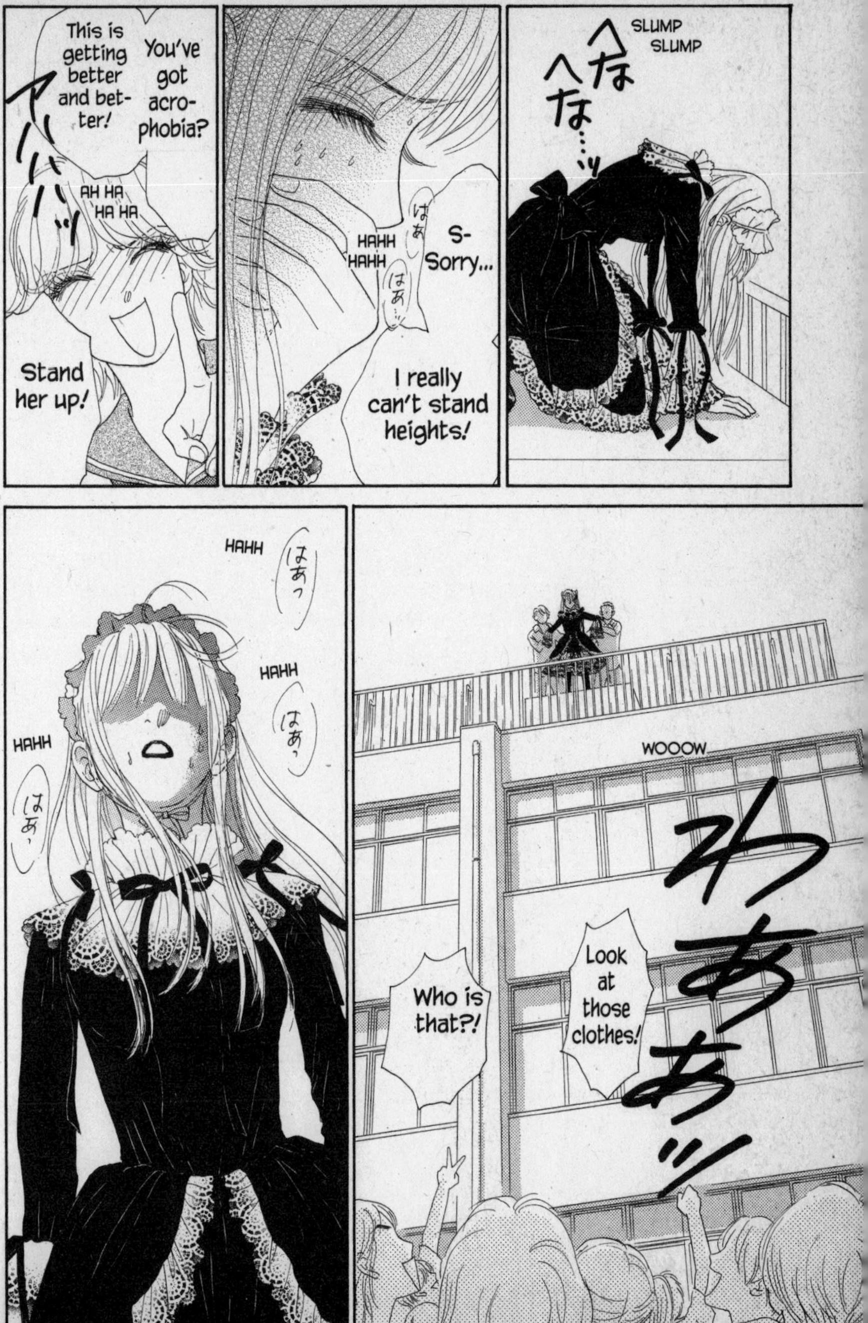
SLUMP SLUMP
へなへな…ッ
S-Sorry...
HAHH HAHH
はぁ はぁ…
I really can't stand heights!
You've got acrophobia?
This is getting better and better!
AH HA HA HA
アハハッ
Stand her up!
WOOOW
わあああッ
Look at those clothes!
Who is that?!
HAHH
はあっ
HAHH
はあっ
HAHH
はあっ

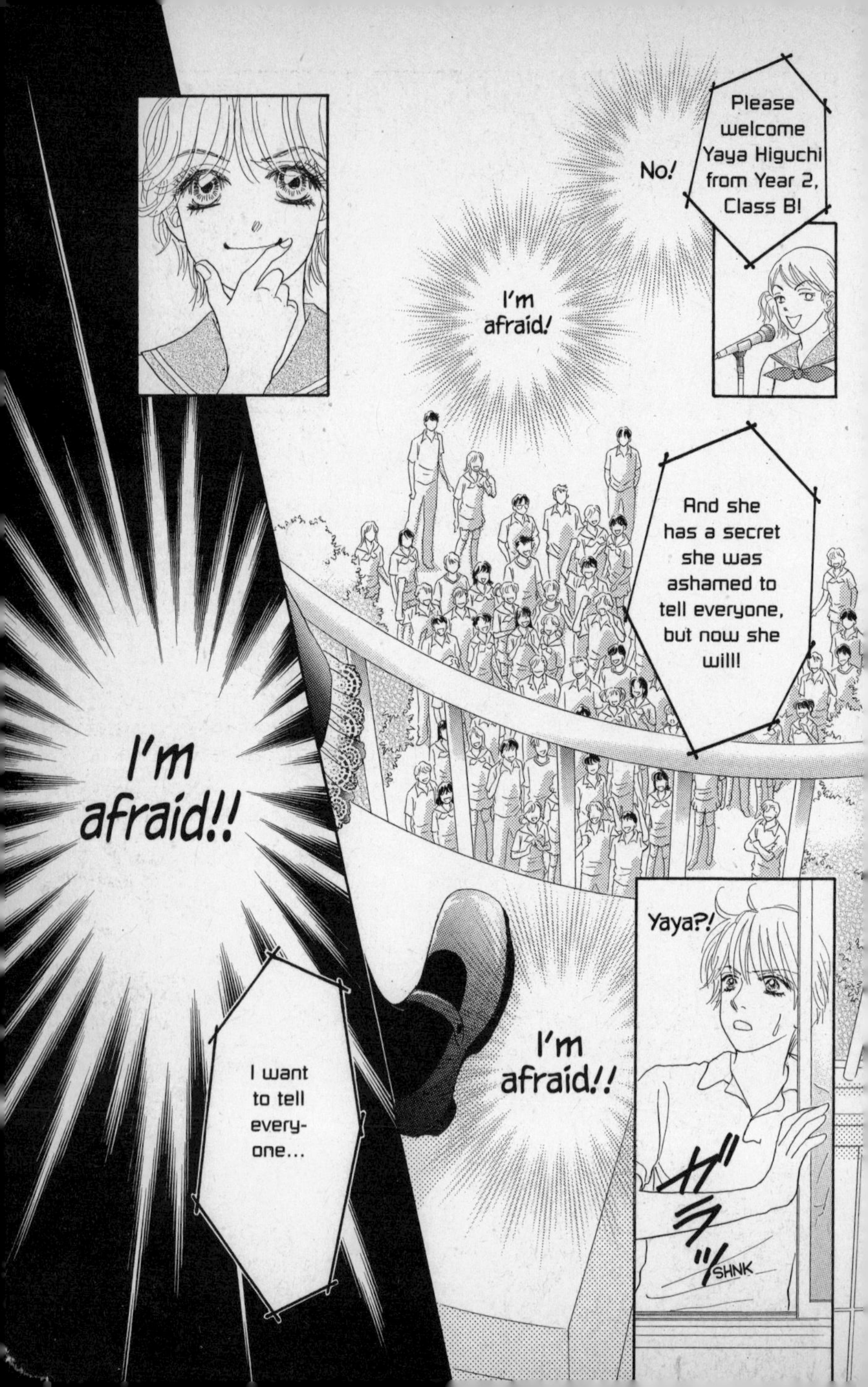
Please welcome Yaya Higuchi from Year 2, Class B!
No!
I'm afraid!
And she has a secret she was ashamed to tell everyone, but now she will!
I'm afraid!!
Yaya?!
ガラッ
SHNK
I'm afraid!!
I want to tell every-one...

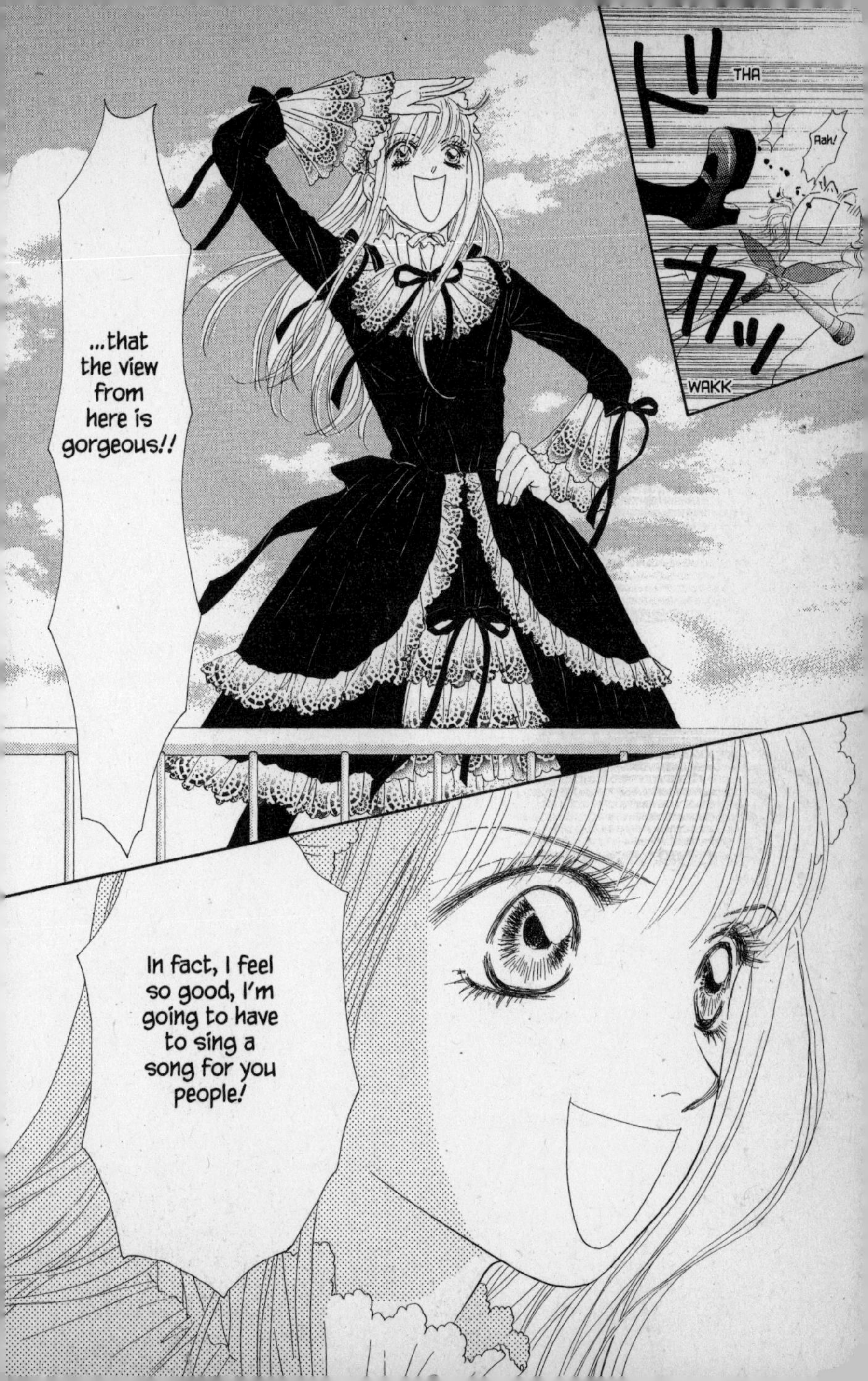
THA
ドカッ
Aah!
WAKK
...that the view from here is gorgeous!!
In fact, I feel so good, I'm going to have to sing a song for you people!

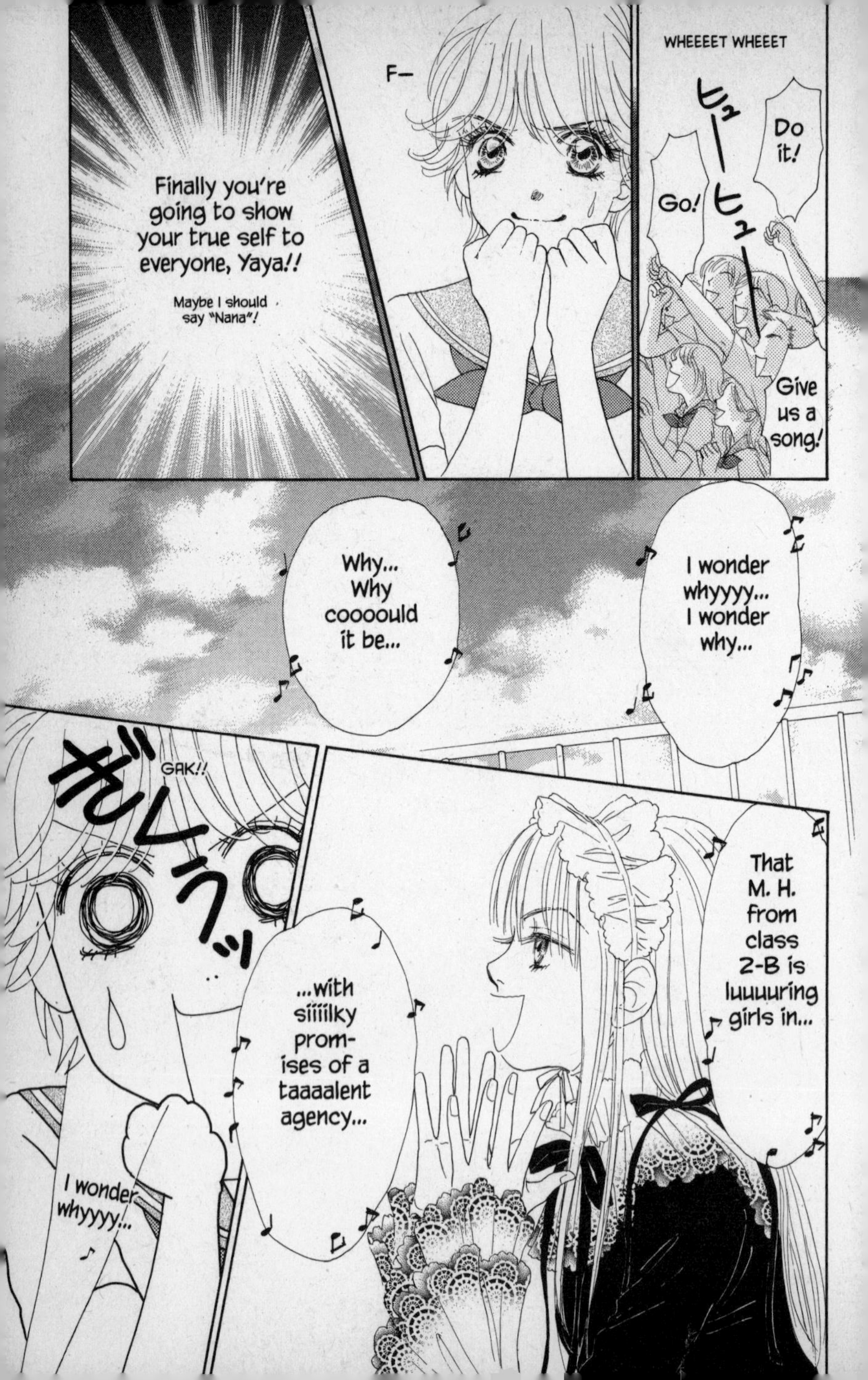

WHEEEET WHEEET
ヒューヒュー
Do it!
Go!
Give us a song!
F—
Finally you're going to show your true self to everyone, Yaya!!
Maybe I should say "Nana"!
I wonder whyyyy... I wonder why...
Why... Why cooooould it be...
That M. H. from class 2-B is luuuuring girls in...
...with siiiilky promises of a taaaalent agency...
GAK!!
I wonder whyyyy...

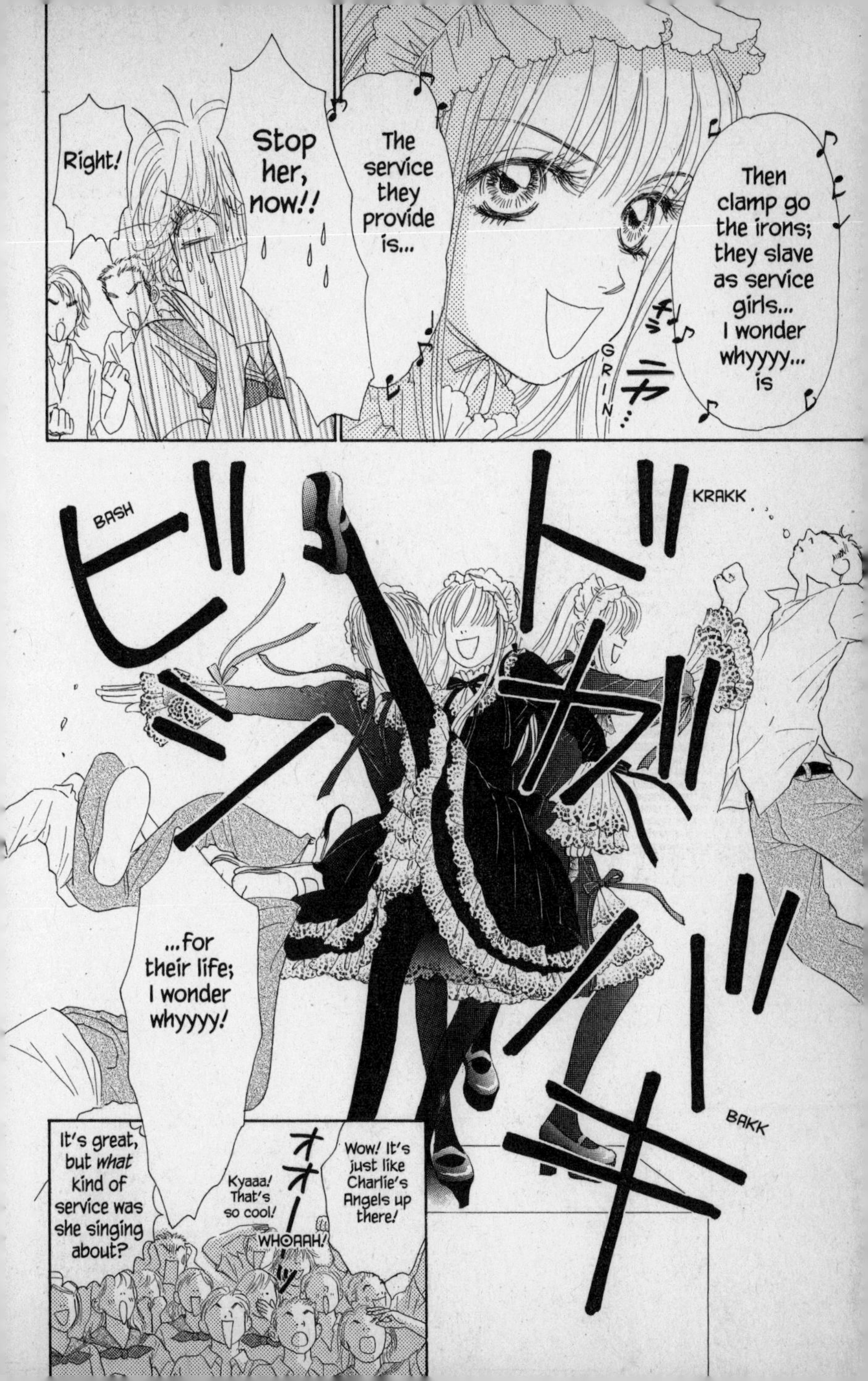
Then clamp go the irons; they slave as service girls... I wonder whyyyy... is
GRIN...
The service they provide is...
Stop her, now!!
Right!
KRAKK
BASH
...for their life; I wonder whyyyy!
BAKK
Wow! It's just like Charlie's Angels up there!
Kyaaa! That's so cool!
WHOAAH!
It's great, but *what* kind of service was she singing about?

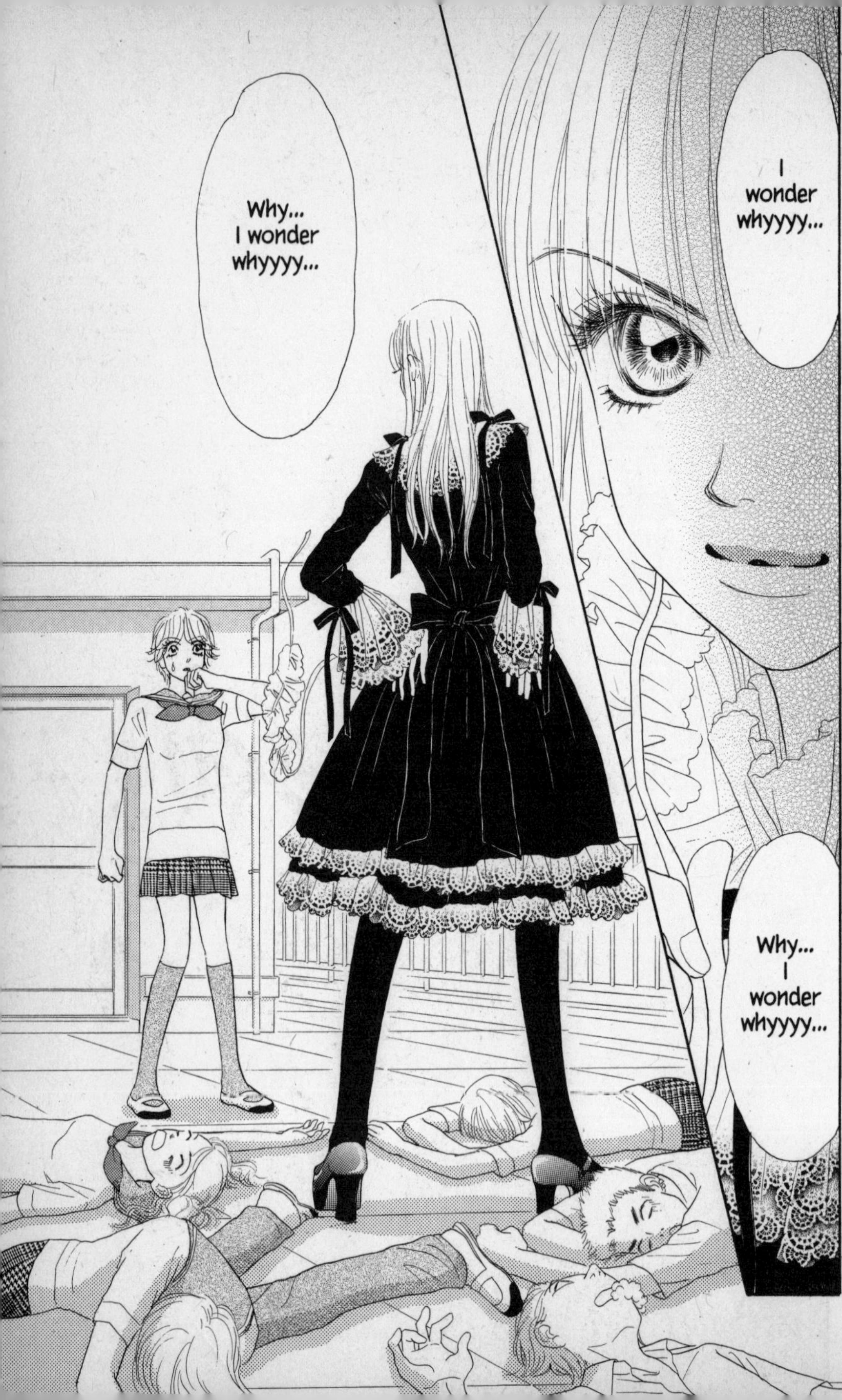
I wonder whyyyy...
Why... I wonder whyyyy...
Why... I wonder whyyyy...

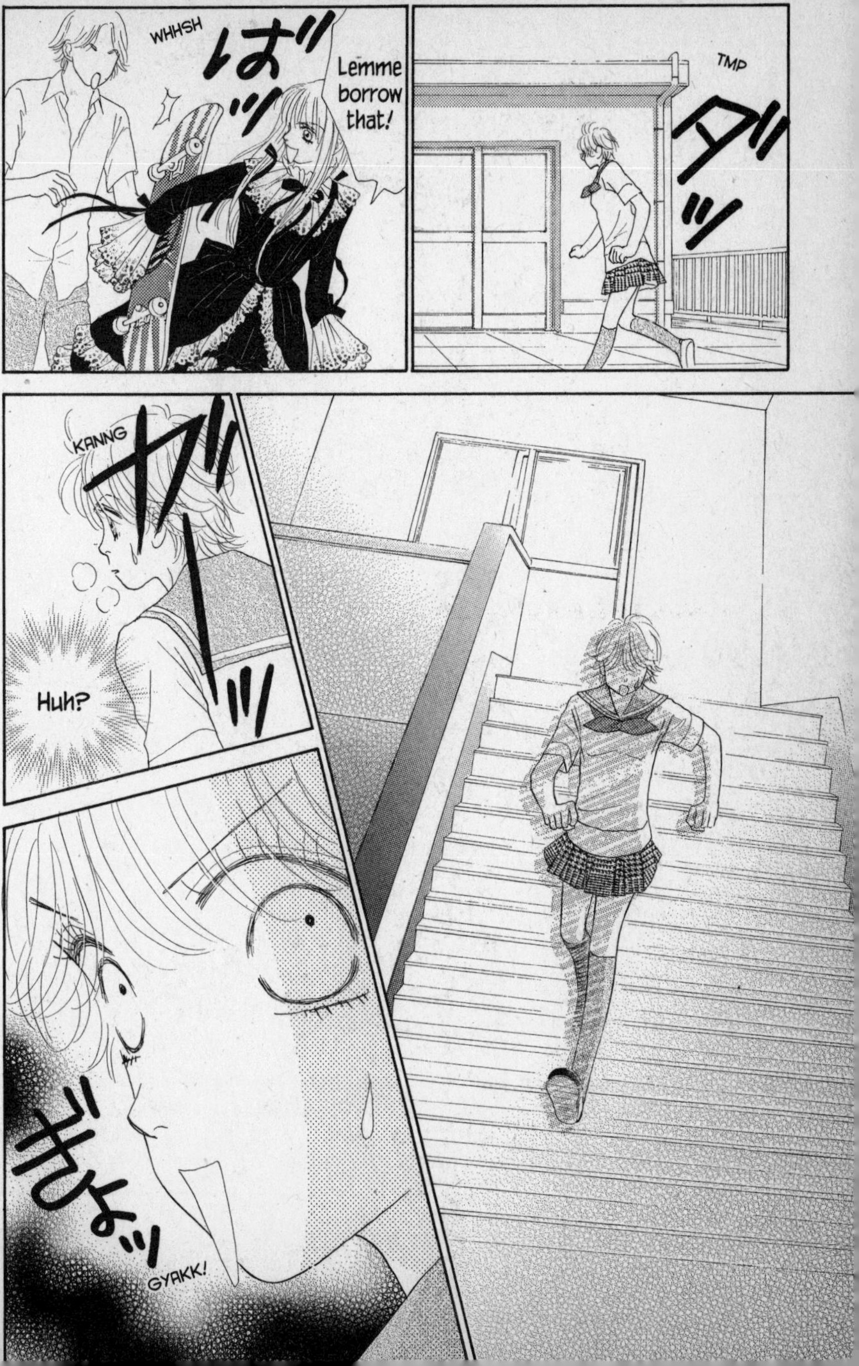
TMP
ダッ
WHHSH
ばッ
Lemme borrow that!
KANNG
ガーッ
Huh?
ぎょッ
GYAKK!

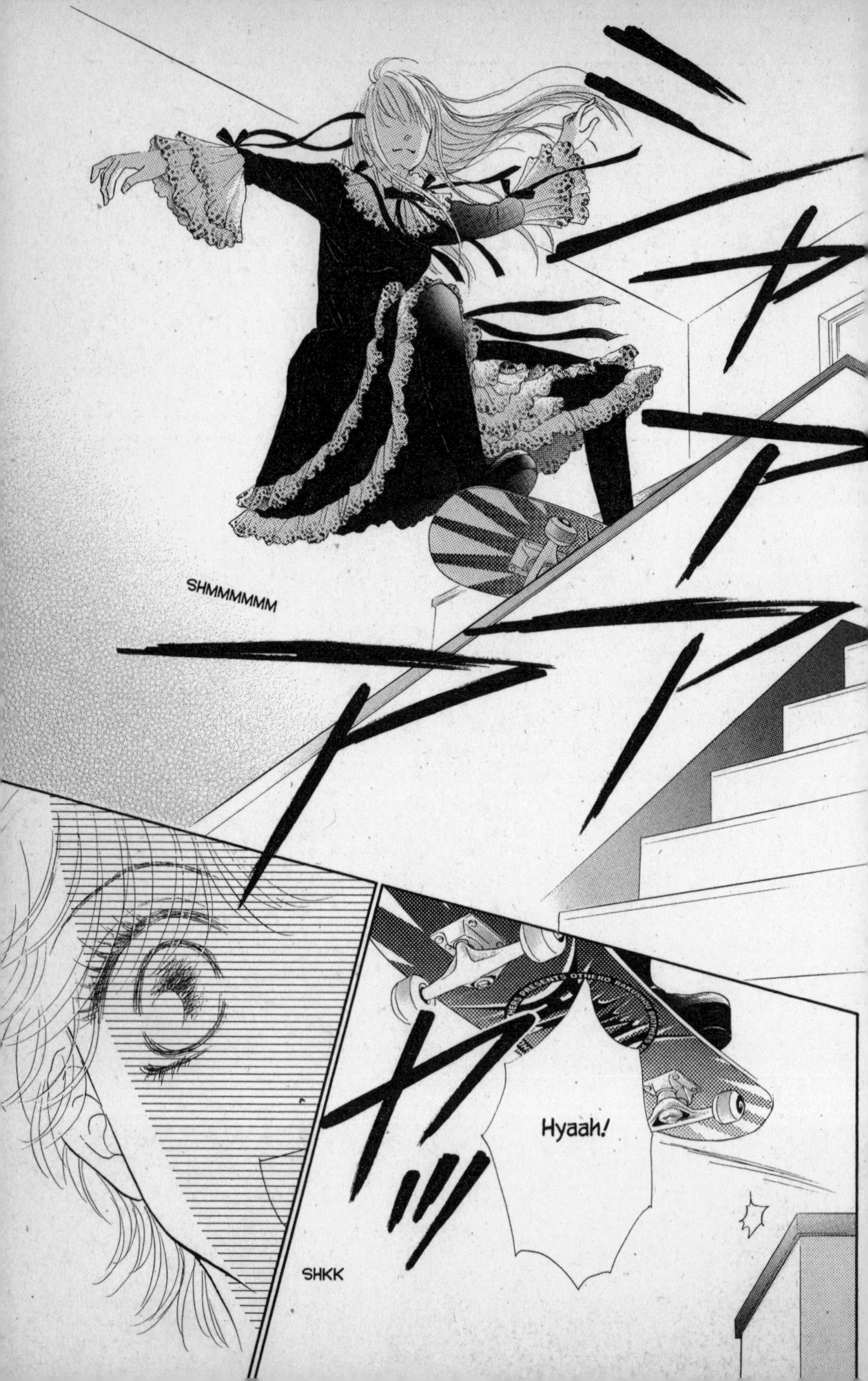
SHMMMMMM
Hyaah!
SHKK

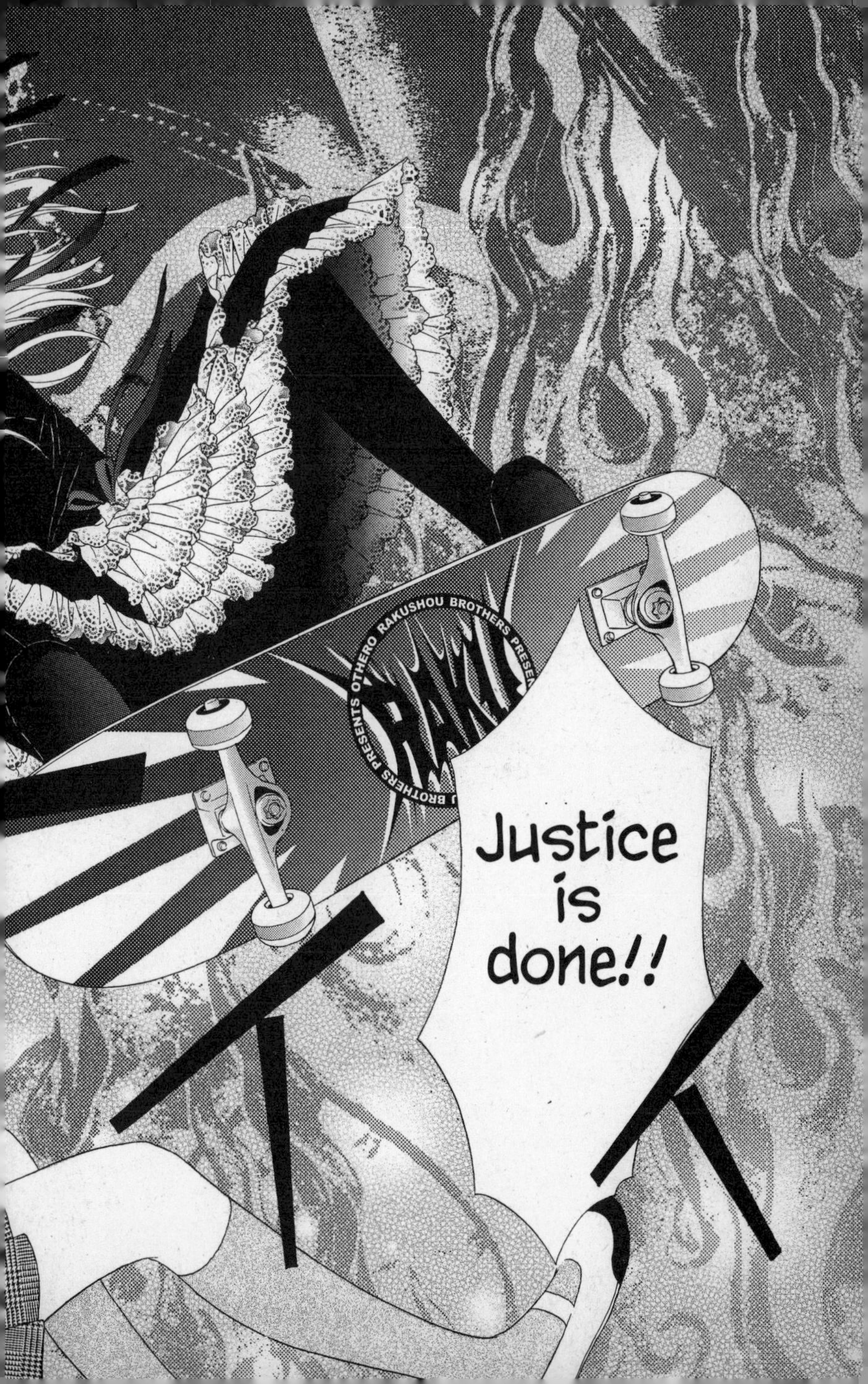
OTHERO RAKUSHOU BROTHERS PRESENTS
Justice is done!!

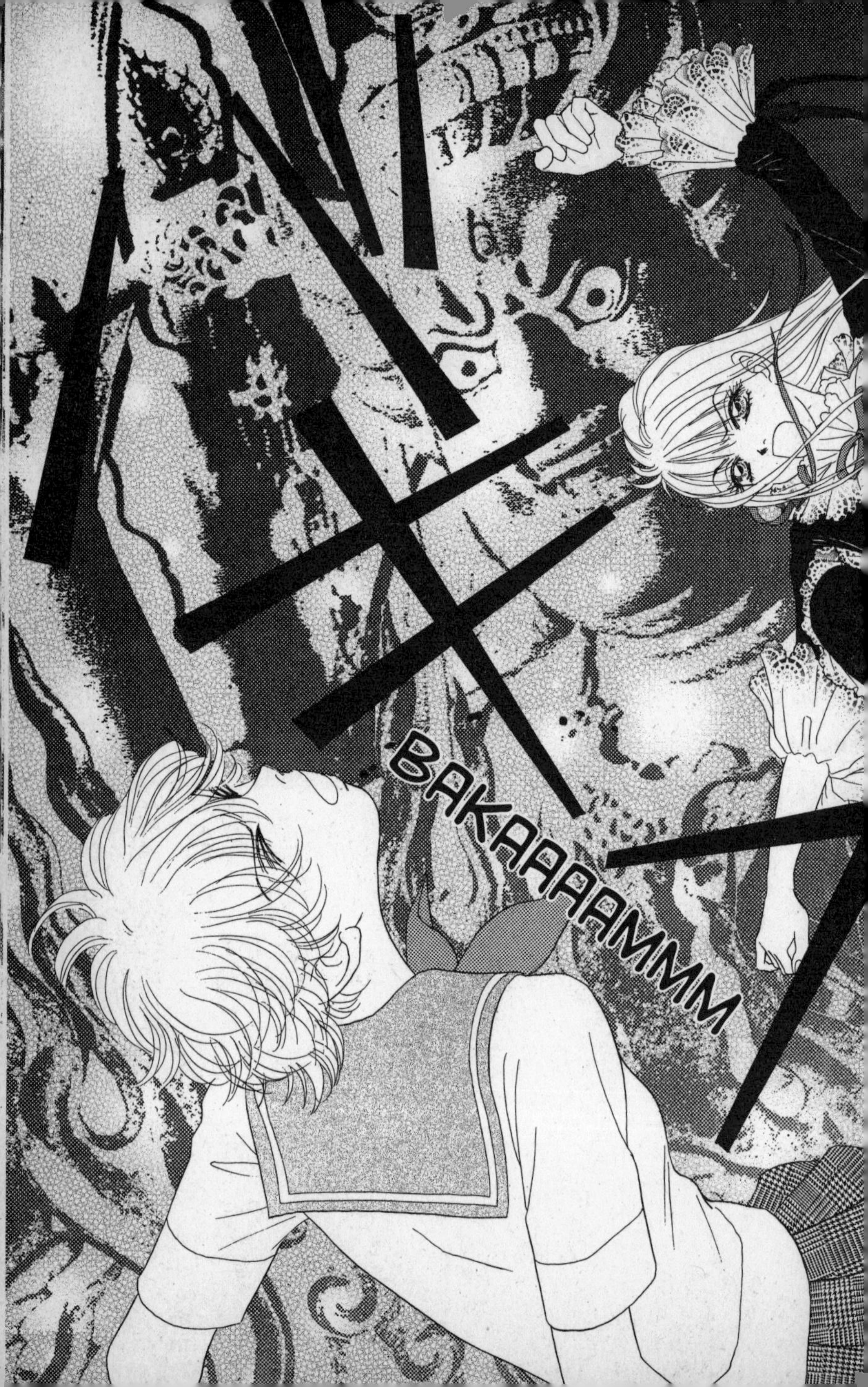
BAKAAAAAMMMM

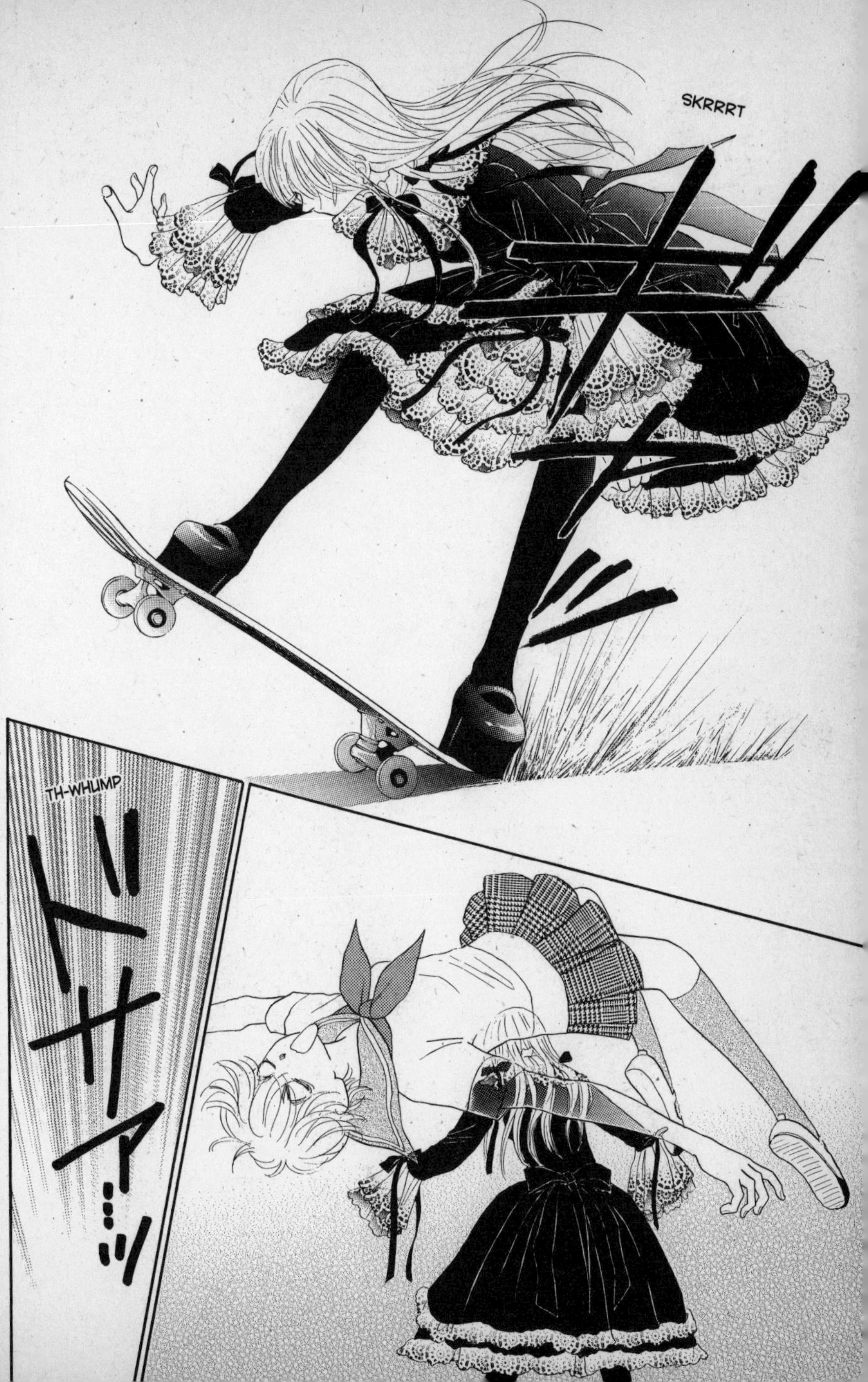
SKRRRT
TH-WHUMP

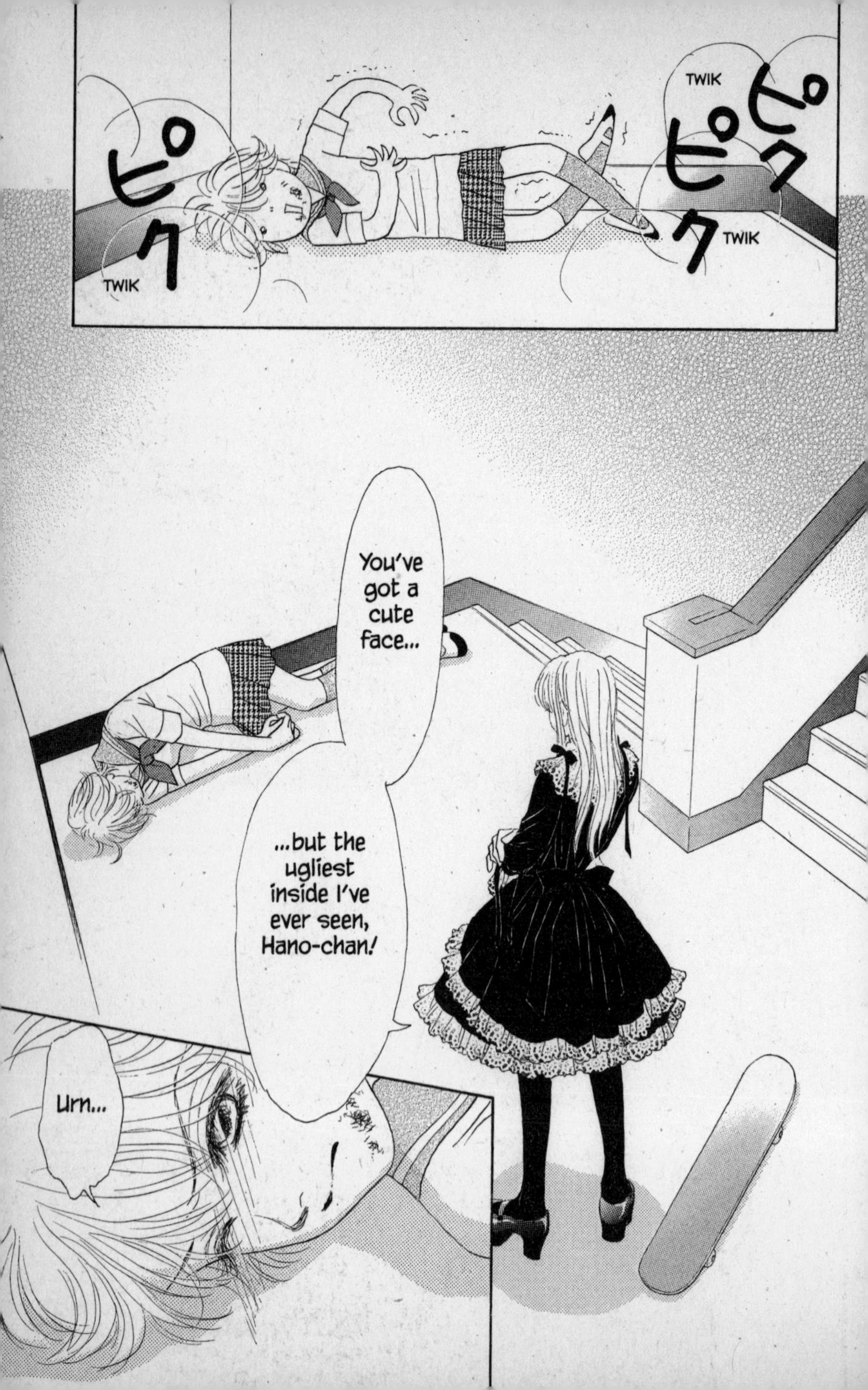
TWIK
ピクピク
TWIK
ピク
TWIK
You've got a cute face...
...but the ugliest inside I've ever seen, Hano-chan!
Urn...

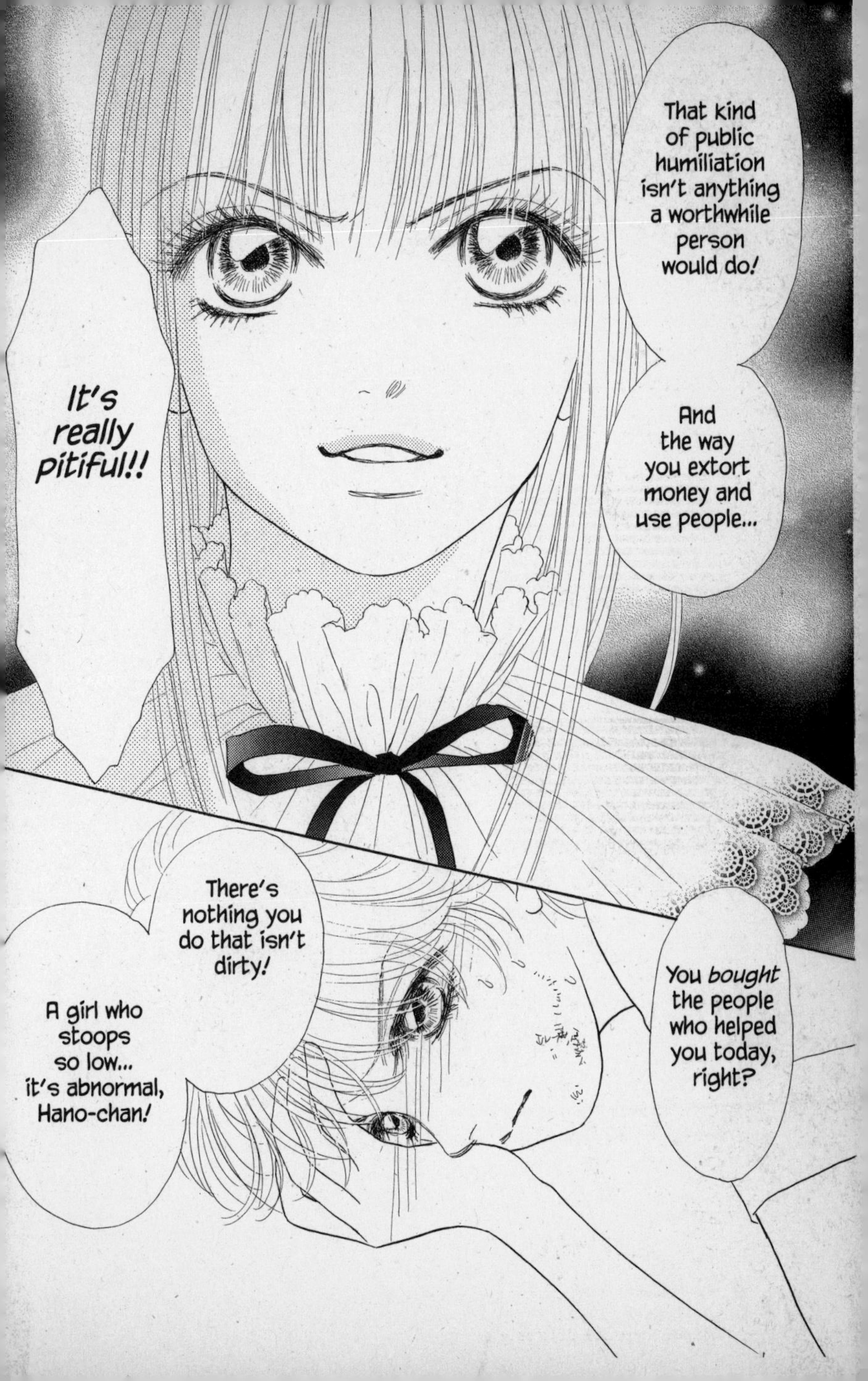
That kind of public humiliation isn't anything a worthwhile person would do!
And the way you extort money and use people...
It's really pitiful!!
You *bought* the people who helped you today, right?
There's nothing you do that isn't dirty!
A girl who stoops so low... it's abnormal, Hano-chan!

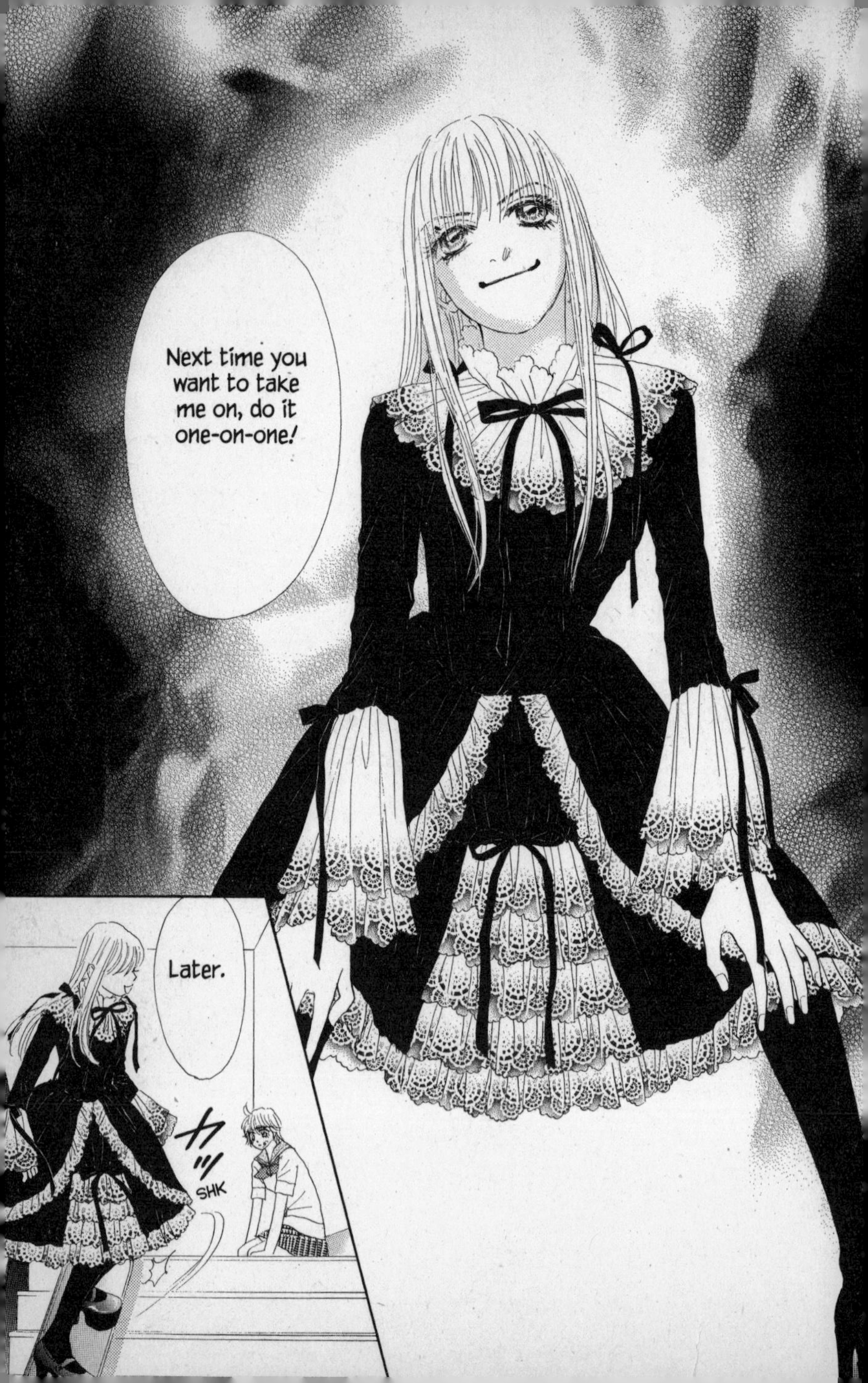
Next time you want to take me on, do it one-on-one!
Later.
カツ
SHK

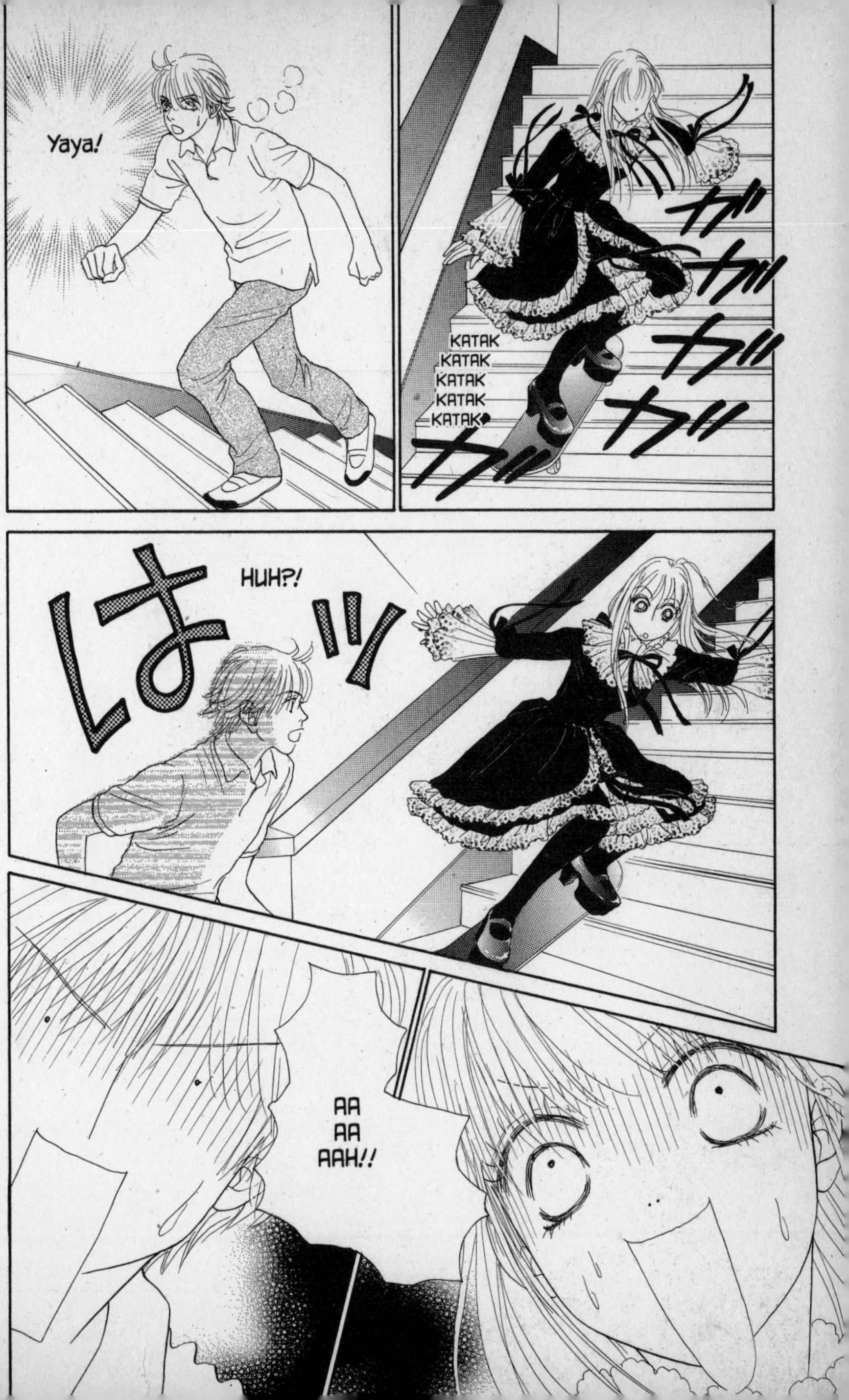
KATAK
KATAK
KATAK
KATAK
KATAK
Yaya!
はッ
HUH?!
AA
AA
AAH!!

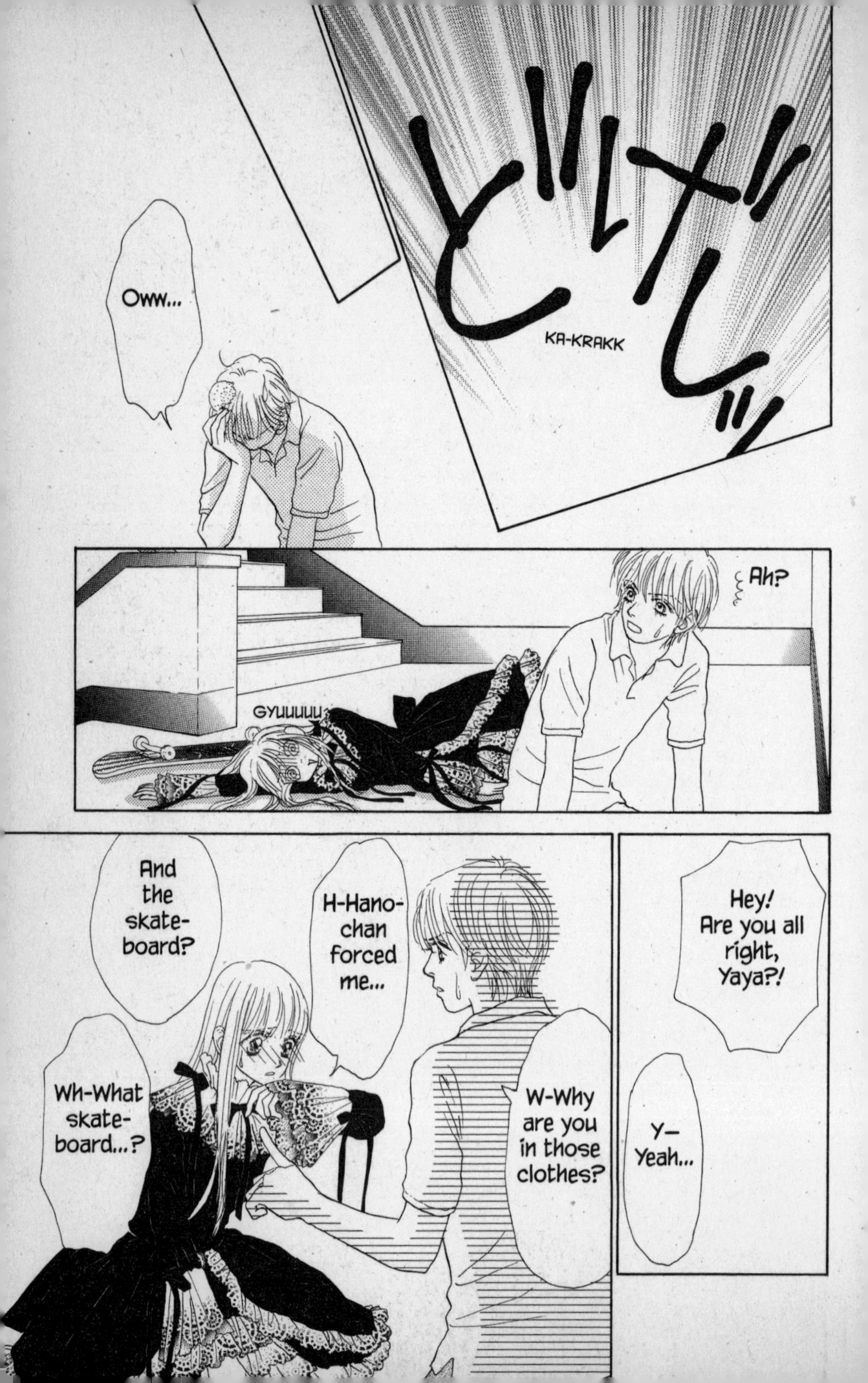

どげしッ
KA-KRAKK
Oww...
Ah?
GYUUUUU
Hey! Are you all right, Yaya?!
Y— Yeah...
W-Why are you in those clothes?
H-Hano-chan forced me...
And the skate-board?
Wh-What skate-board...?

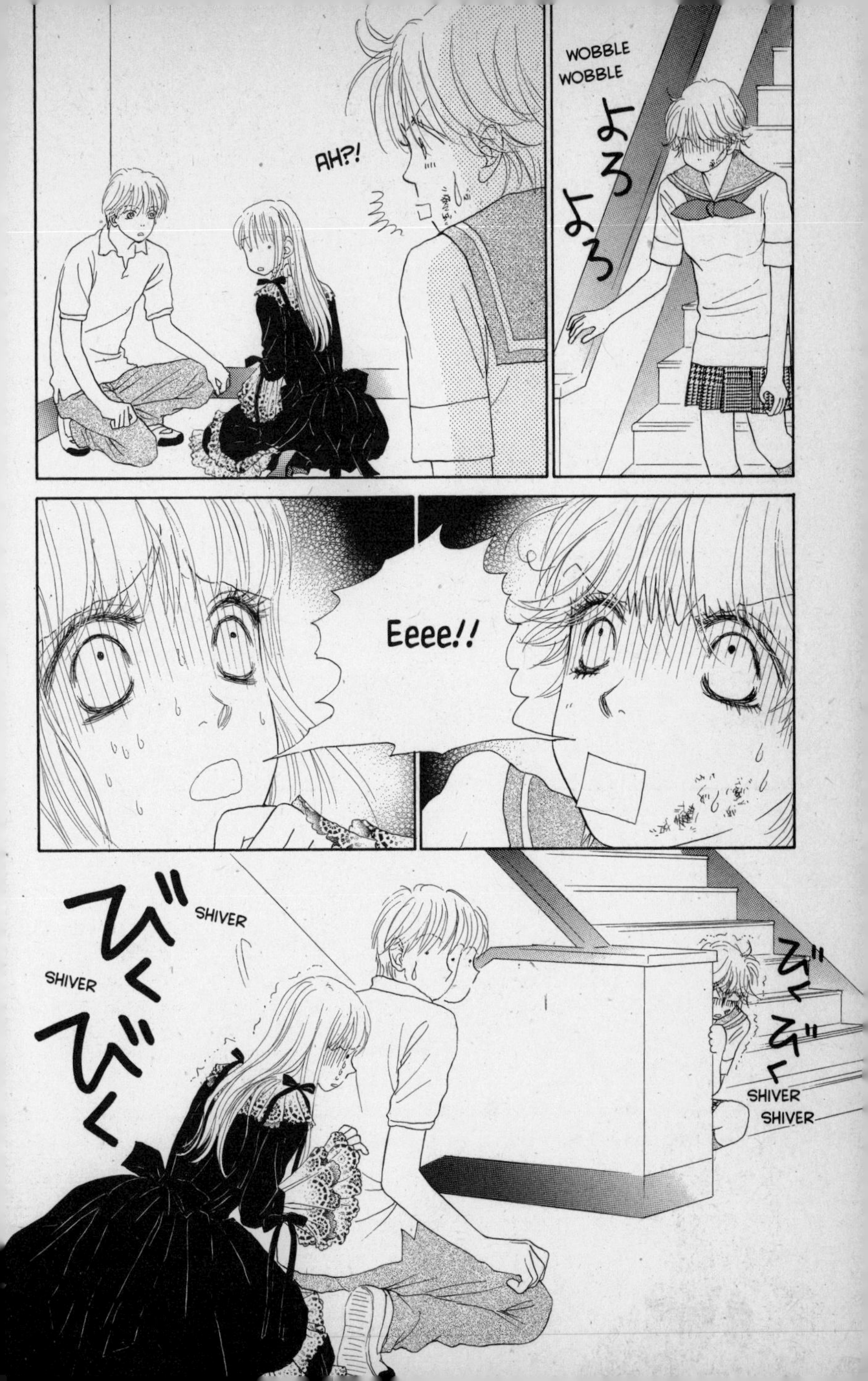
WOBBLE WOBBLE
よろよろ
AH?!
Eeee!!
びくびく
SHIVER SHIVER
びくびく
SHIVER
SHIVER

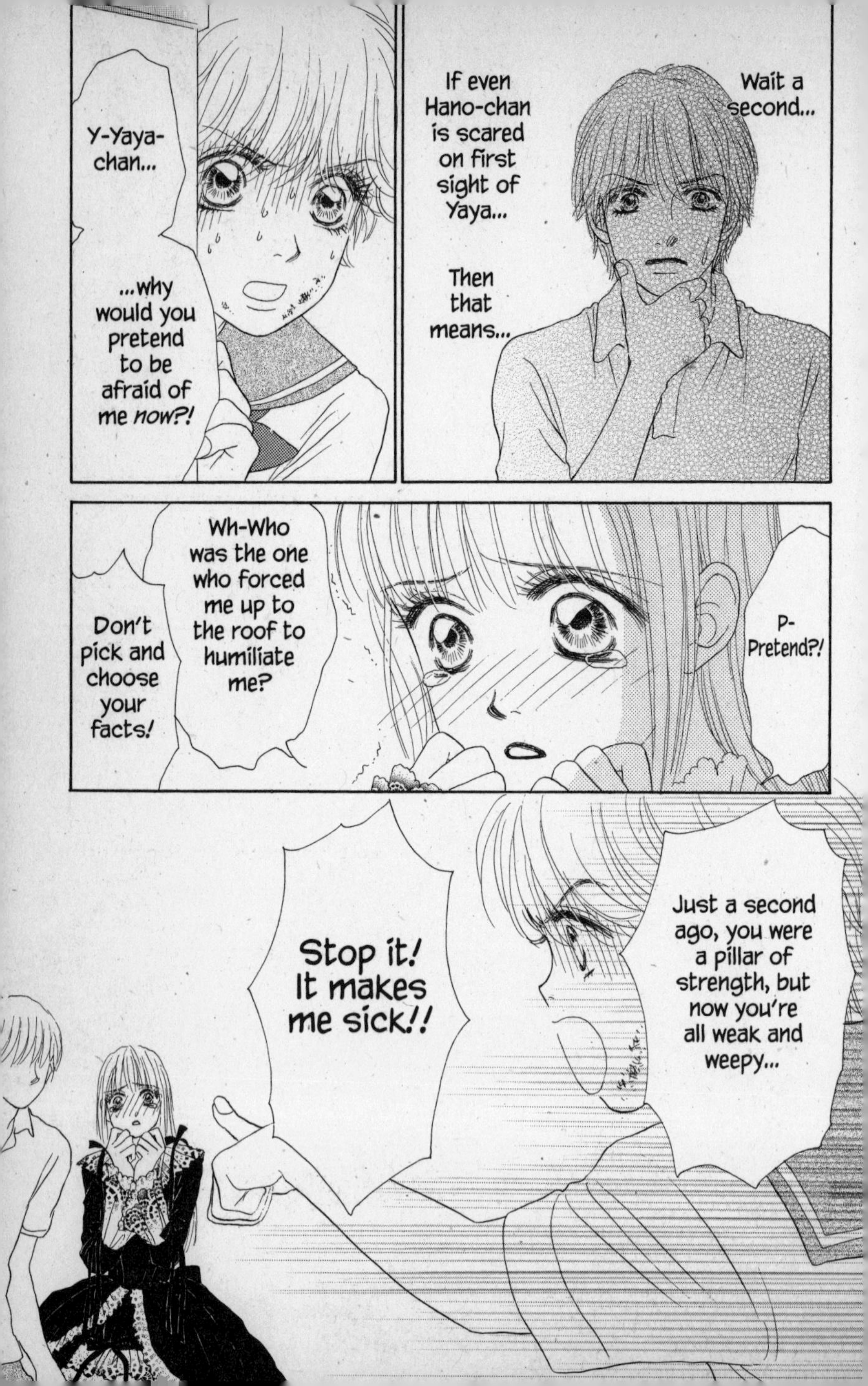
Wait a second...
If even Hano-chan is scared on first sight of Yaya...
Then that means...
Y-Yaya-chan...
...why would you pretend to be afraid of me *now*?!
P-Pretend?!
Wh-Who was the one who forced me up to the roof to humiliate me?
Don't pick and choose your facts!
Just a second ago, you were a pillar of strength, but now you're all weak and weepy...
Stop it! It makes me sick!!

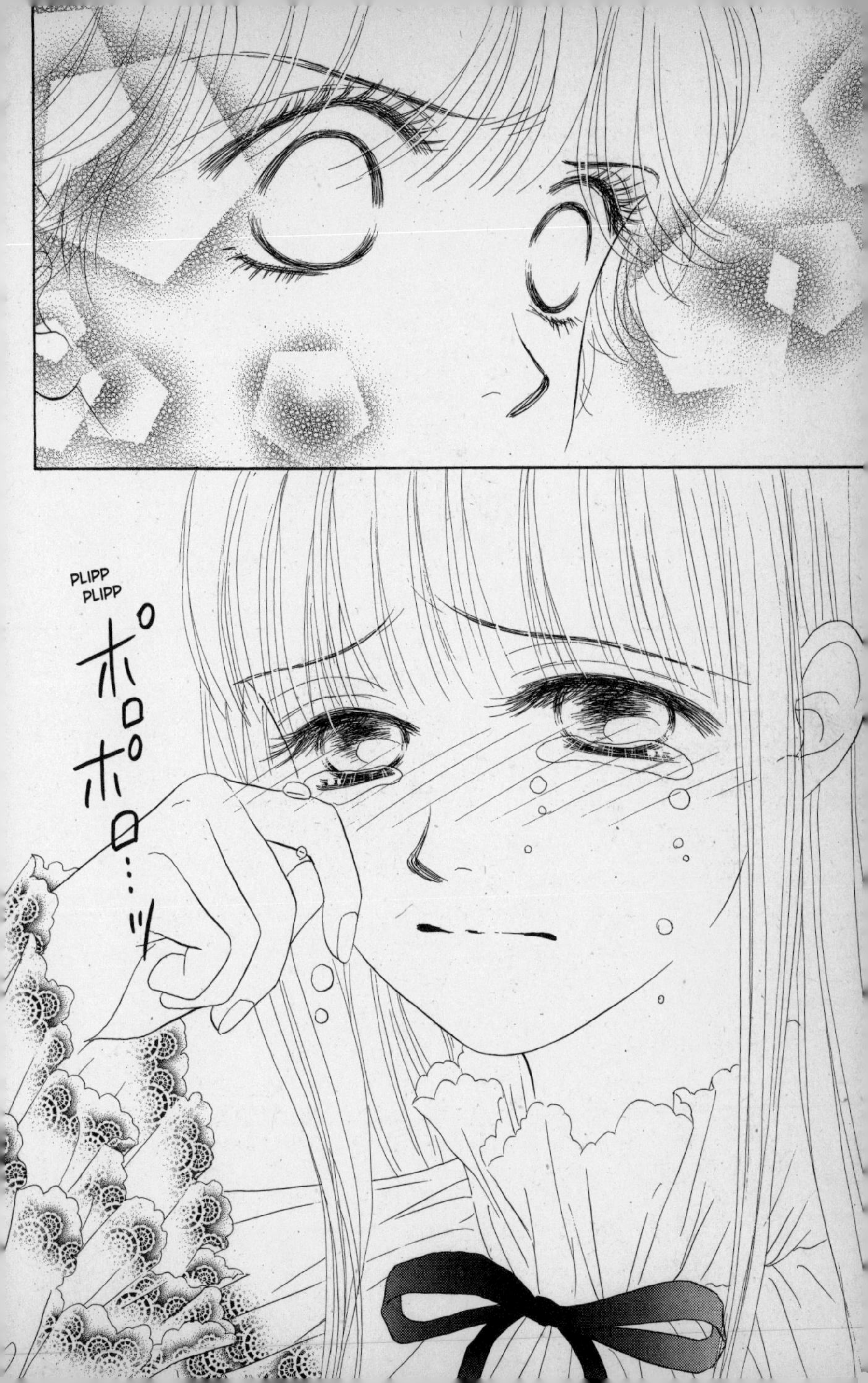
PLIPP
PLIPP
ポロポロ…ッ

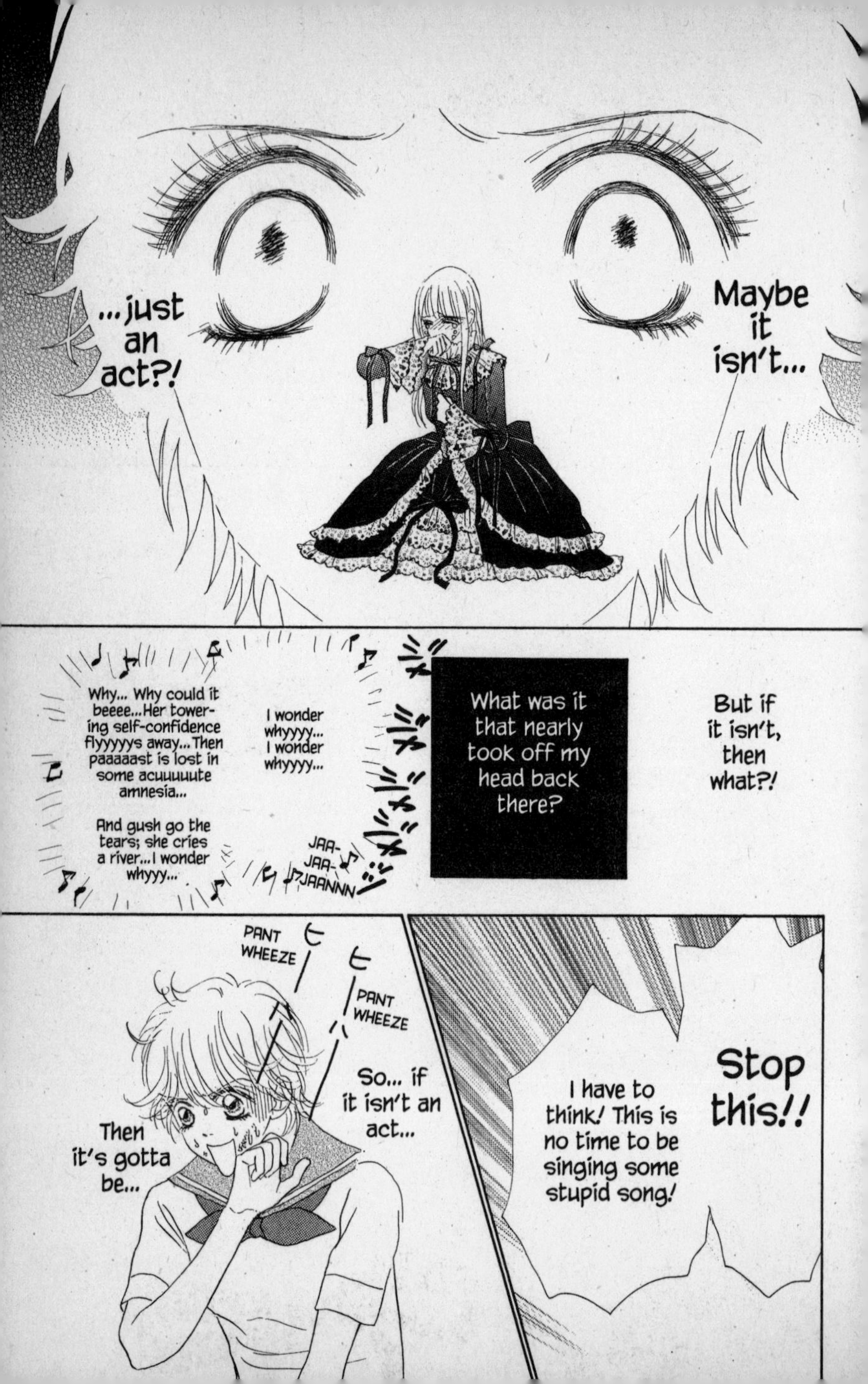
Maybe it isn't...
...just an act?!
But if it isn't, then what?!
What was it that nearly took off my head back there?
JAA-JAA-JAANNN
I wonder whyyyy... I wonder whyyyy...
Why... Why could it beeee...Her towering self-confidence flyyyyys away...Then paaaaast is lost in some acuuuuute amnesia...
And gush go the tears; she cries a river...I wonder whyyy...
Stop this!!
I have to think! This is no time to be singing some stupid song!
PANT WHEEZE
PANT WHEEZE
So... if it isn't an act...
Then it's gotta be...

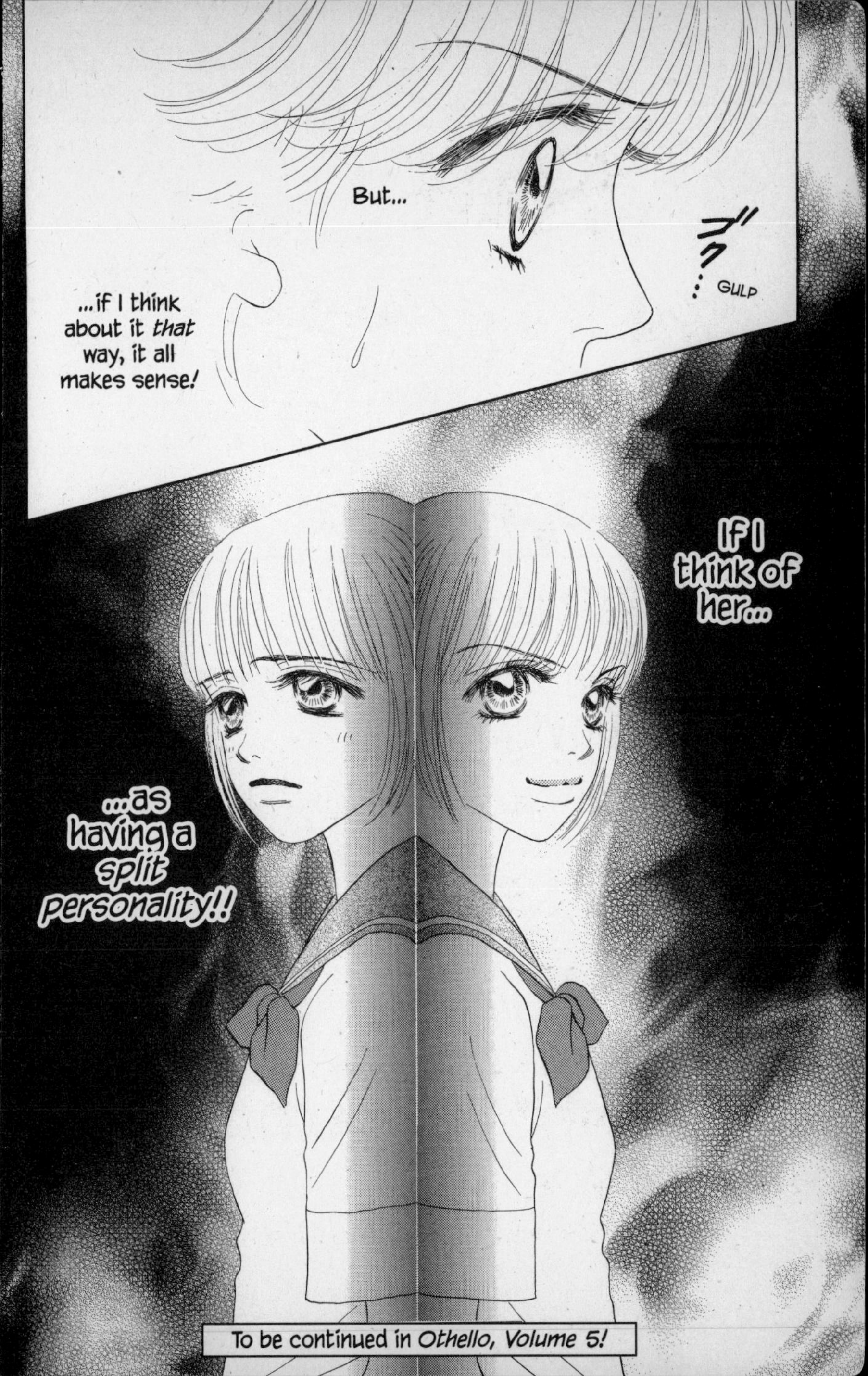
ゴク…
GULP
But...
...if I think about it *that* way, it all makes sense!
If I think of her...
...as having a split personality!!
To be continued in *Othello*, Volume 5!

Staff

THANK YOU ALL!!

vol. 9~16 (~2003.4)

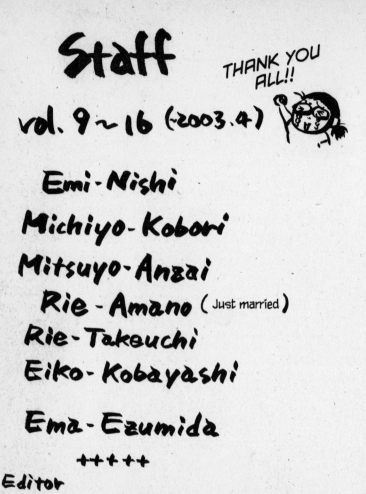

Emi-Nishi

Michiyo-Kobori

Mitsuyo-Anzai

Rie-Amano (Just married)

Rie-Takeuchi

Eiko-Kobayashi

Ema-Ezumida

+ + + + +

Editor

Satoru-Matsumoto (New Editor in Chief)

Izumi-Morisada (New Editor)

+Home Page+

http://home.f02.itscom.net/ikezawa/

About the Author

Satomi Ikezawa's previous work before *Othello* is *Guru Guru Pon-chan*. She currently continues to work on *Othello*, which is being serialized in the Kodansha weekly manga magazine, *Bessatsu Friend*.

Ikezawa won the 24th Kodansha Manga Prize in 2000 for *Guru Guru Pon-chan*.

She has two Labradors, named Guts and Ponta.

Translation Notes

Japanese is a tricky language for most Westerners, and translation is often more art than science. For your edification and reading pleasure, here are notes on some of the places where we could have gone in a different direction in our translation of the work, or where a Japanese cultural reference is used.

"H" Manga, Page 17

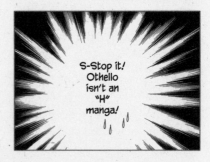

S-Stop it! Othello isn't an "H" manga!

"H" is short for "hentai," which means lecher or pervert, and "H" manga, anime, or other productions can be as innocent as sex-farce or as disturbing as some of the worst fetishist illegal pornographic material. But usually when someone says "H" (pronounced "eichi"), they are referring to people with a greater than normal interest in sex or sexually charged material.

Aru-Aru (Hakkutsu! Aru-Aru Daijiten), Page 40

Aru-Aru was a game show that seemed doomed to be just another standard Japanese quiz show where several minor celebrities guess at foreign or domestic trivia. However, after its first set of shows, Aru-Aru shifted its focus to health issues and advice on proper behavior, and that's when the show's popularity truly took off.

"For 7", Page 54

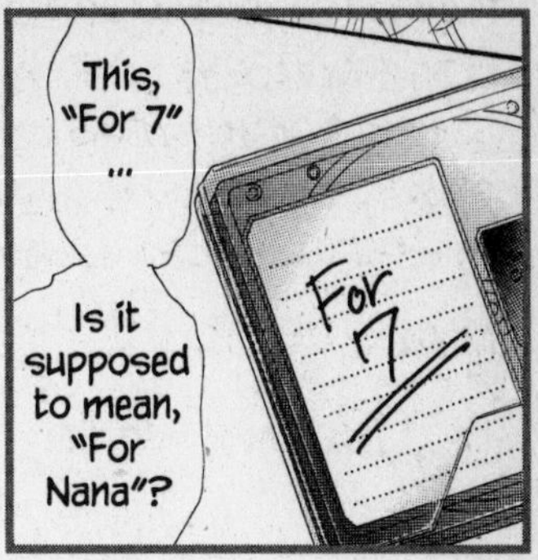
This, "For 7" ...
Is it supposed to mean, "For Nana"?
For 7

In the same way the words "first" and "second" mean pretty much the same thing as the words "one" and "two" (without sounding the same any way), the numbers in Japanese also have various ways of being pronounced. The number 7, for example, can be pronounced "shichi," but it can also be pronounced "nana."

Becoming "Talent", Page 61

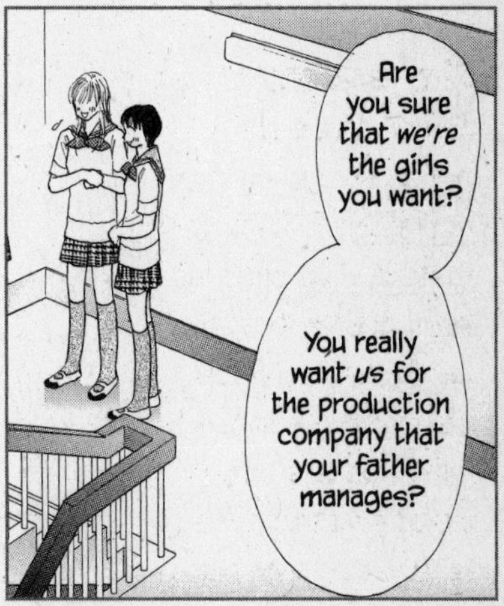
Are you sure that *we're* the girls you want?
You really want *us* for the production company that your father manages?

Japan has a pervasive "Idol" system for generating new stars out of pretty-but-talentless teenage girls. The debut of the ironically named "Talent" is usually accompanied by a pop-single, a small part on a nighttime TV drama, endorsements and commercials, and other marketing-hype techniques. The shelf life of these idols can be counted in weeks, and then they are quickly forgotten. Rumors fly about what can happen to new idols ranging from, at best, exhaustive schedules to, at worst, sexual and physical abuse. The agency run by Hano-chan's father seems to be one of the idol factories that produce these disposable stars.

Costs of the agency, Page 62

A good rule of thumb for approximating yen costs to dollars is to divide the yen cost by 100. So Hano-chan's stated costs come out to approximately $1000.00 admission fee and $250.00 per month tuition, which Hano-chan "bargains down" to a $500.00 admission fee and $200.00 per month.

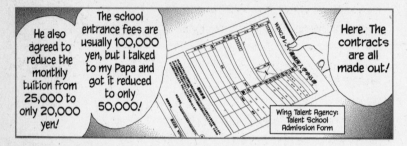

Here. The contracts are all made out!
Wing Talent Agency: Talent School Admission Form
The school entrance fees are usually 100,000 yen, but I talked to my Papa and got it reduced to only 50,000!
He also agreed to reduce the monthly tuition from 25,000 to only 20,000 yen!

The stamp (hanko), Page 72

Wing Talent Agency: Talent School Admission Form
WINGタレント養成所入学申込書
All it needs is your signa-ture and stamp.
I'll fill in all of the boring contract details! I even brought our

If non-Japanese people go to Japan, their signature is all that is needed to endorse legal documents. But Japanese nationals also have a wooden, hand-made stamp called a hanko, which is registered at the local city hall, to affix their seal to contracts and other legal work. Sharp-eyed fans of Japanese cinema will remember the climax of *A Taxing Woman* when hundreds of hanko are discovered in the criminal's house. Each of these stamps represented a different bank account.

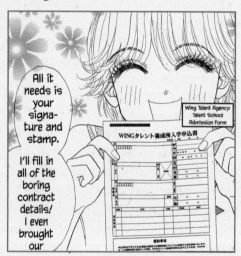

Bob Sapp, Page 92

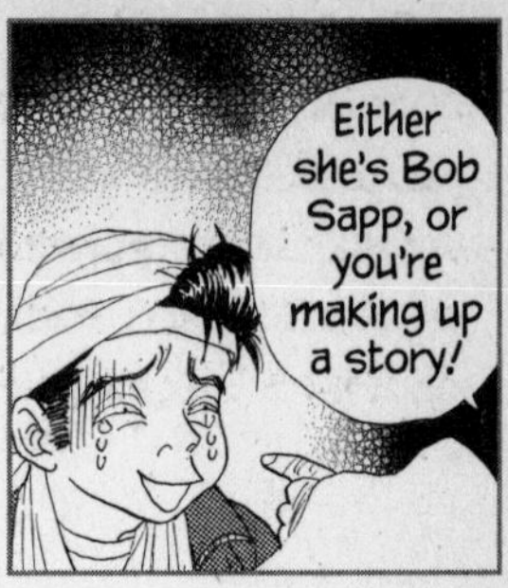
Either she's Bob Sapp, or you're making up a story!

One of the stars of the mixed martial-arts tournament league, K-1, and the IWGP Heavyweight Champion for 2004 is Bob "The Beast" Sapp, a 342 lb. hulk of muscle, bone, and not an ounce of fat. Reported to bench-press more than 650 lbs., lifting Detchan and a sofa would be a breeze for him.

Ayaya, Page 99

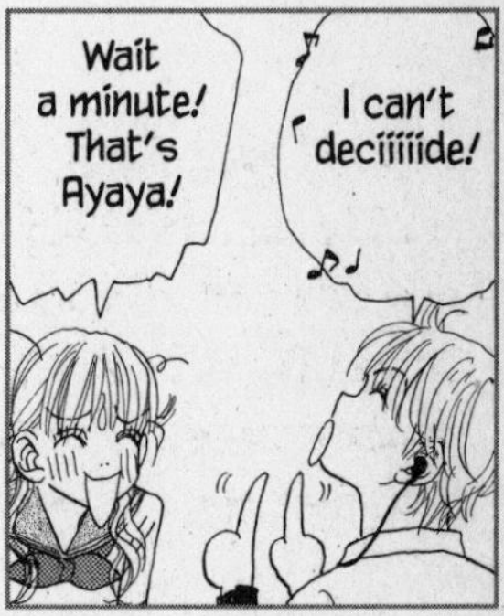
I can't deciiiiide!
Wait a minute! That's Ayaya!

Because it was a popular commercial on television, the song "Ne~e" by Aya Matsuura (nicknamed Ayaya) became a tune (and lyrics) that nearly the entire nation of Japan could sing in 2002.

Image Club, Page 116

One of the darker sides of Japan is the thriving sex trade. This can range from hostess bars where pretty girls will talk and flirt with male customers, to peep shows, to soapland and massage parlors, and finally to unabashed prostitution. These flesh markets go by such names as Play Spots, Image Clubs, Fashion Health, and Pink Salons.

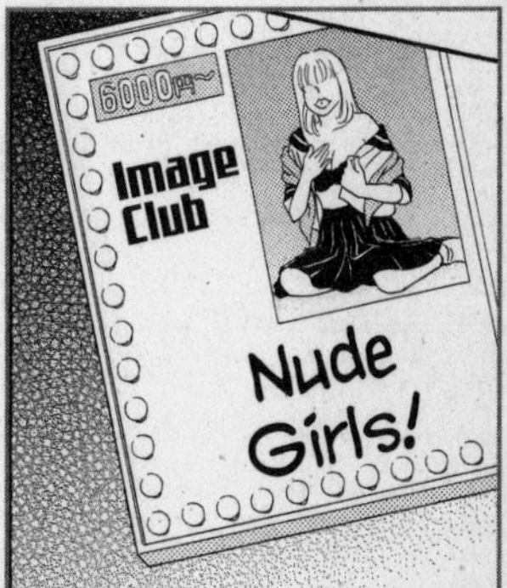
6000円~
Image Club
Nude Girls!

Payment, Page 123

Jobs in Japan can pay daily, weekly, every two weeks or monthly, but since checks are unusual in Japan, the pay is distributed either by direct bank transfer, or, more commonly, by cash in an envelope.

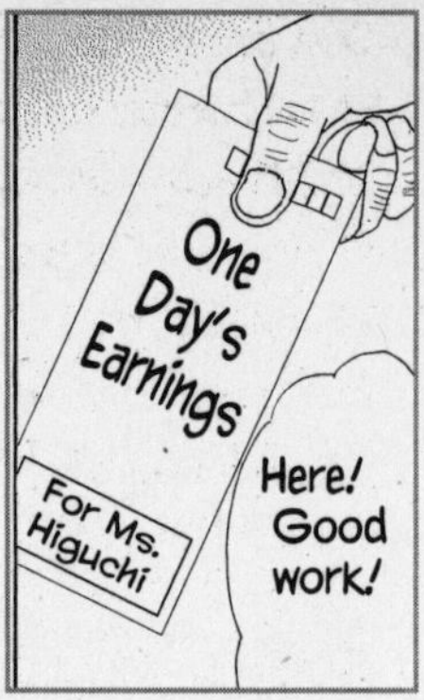
One Day's Earnings
For Ms. Higuchi
Here! Good work!

V6, Page 146

After a decade of popularity and more than fifteen albums, V6 has broken from its boy-band roots to become an established part of the Japanese popular music scene.

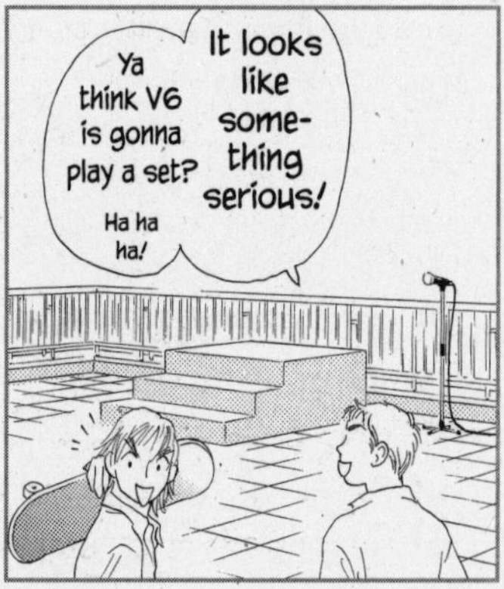
It looks like some-thing serious!
Ya think V6 is gonna play a set?
Ha ha ha!

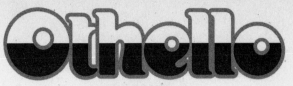

VOLUME 5

BY SATOMI IKEZAWA

TAKING MATTERS TO NEW HEIGHTS

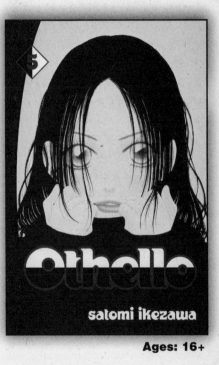

Master manipulator Megumi Hano—Hano-chan—is enraged by her failure to bring down timid Yaya Higuchi and her alter ego, the confident and boisterous Nana. So Hano-chan decides to take the ultimate revenge. Using the singing contract that Yaya desperately wishes to null and void as a means to her mean-spirited ends, Hano-chan makes her an offer. She will rip it up . . . if Yaya agrees to play a little game with her. If Yaya can catch Hano-chan and steal the contract, Hano will cancel the agreement and return the application fee. Sounds simple, yes? But there's a little hitch. Yaya must chase Hano while skydiving!

Ages: 16+

Includes special extras after the story!

VOLUME 5: On sale September 27, 2005

For more information and to sign up for Del Rey's manga e-newsletter, visit www.delreymanga.com

Dear Readers,

   We are delighted to present you with a preview of our newest Del Ray manga series, GURU GURU PON-CHAN by OTHELLO creator Satomi Ikezawa!

   Ponta is an energetic, mischievous Labrador retriever puppy, the Koizumi family's pet. When Grandpa Koizumi, an amateur inventor, creates the Chit-chat Bone, Ponta's craving causes trouble. She eats the bone—and turns into a human girl!

   Surprised but undaunted, Ponta ventures out of the house and meets Mirai Iwaki, the most popular boy at school. Soon, she's in love! Using the power of the Chit-chat Bone, Ponta switches back and forth from dog to girl—but can she win Mirai's affections?

   This is a re-bark-ably original manga full of fun and romance. We hope this preview will make you drool for the first volume! Look for in stores on July 27, 2005!

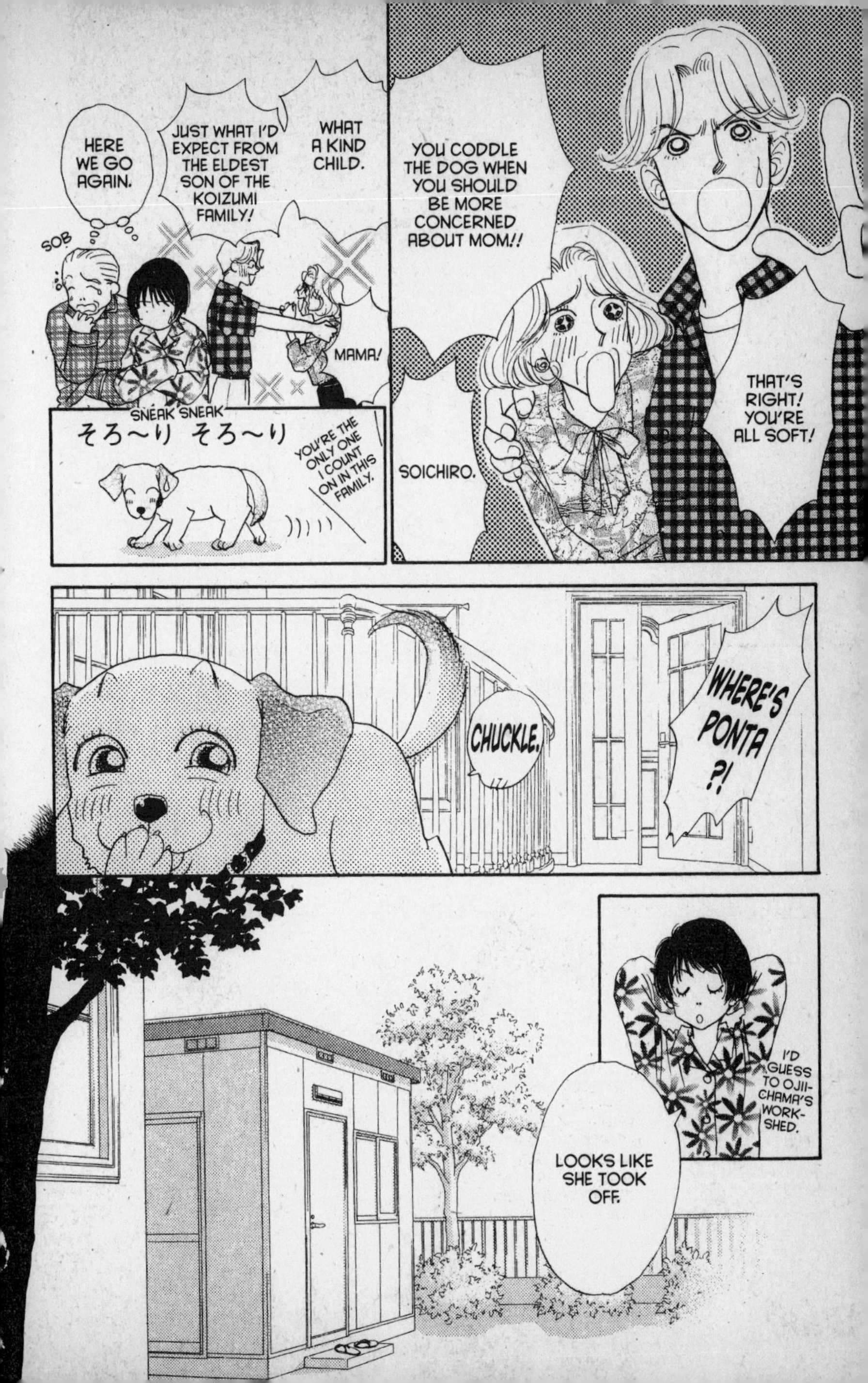
YOU CODDLE THE DOG WHEN YOU SHOULD BE MORE CONCERNED ABOUT MOM!!
THAT'S RIGHT! YOU'RE ALL SOFT!
SOICHIRO.
WHAT A KIND CHILD.
JUST WHAT I'D EXPECT FROM THE ELDEST SON OF THE KOIZUMI FAMILY!
HERE WE GO AGAIN.
SOB
MAMA!
YOU'RE THE ONLY ONE I COUNT ON IN THIS FAMILY.
SNEAK SNEAK
そろ～り そろ～り
WHERE'S PONTA ?!
CHUCKLE.
I'D GUESS TO OJII-CHAMA'S WORK-SHED.
LOOKS LIKE SHE TOOK OFF.

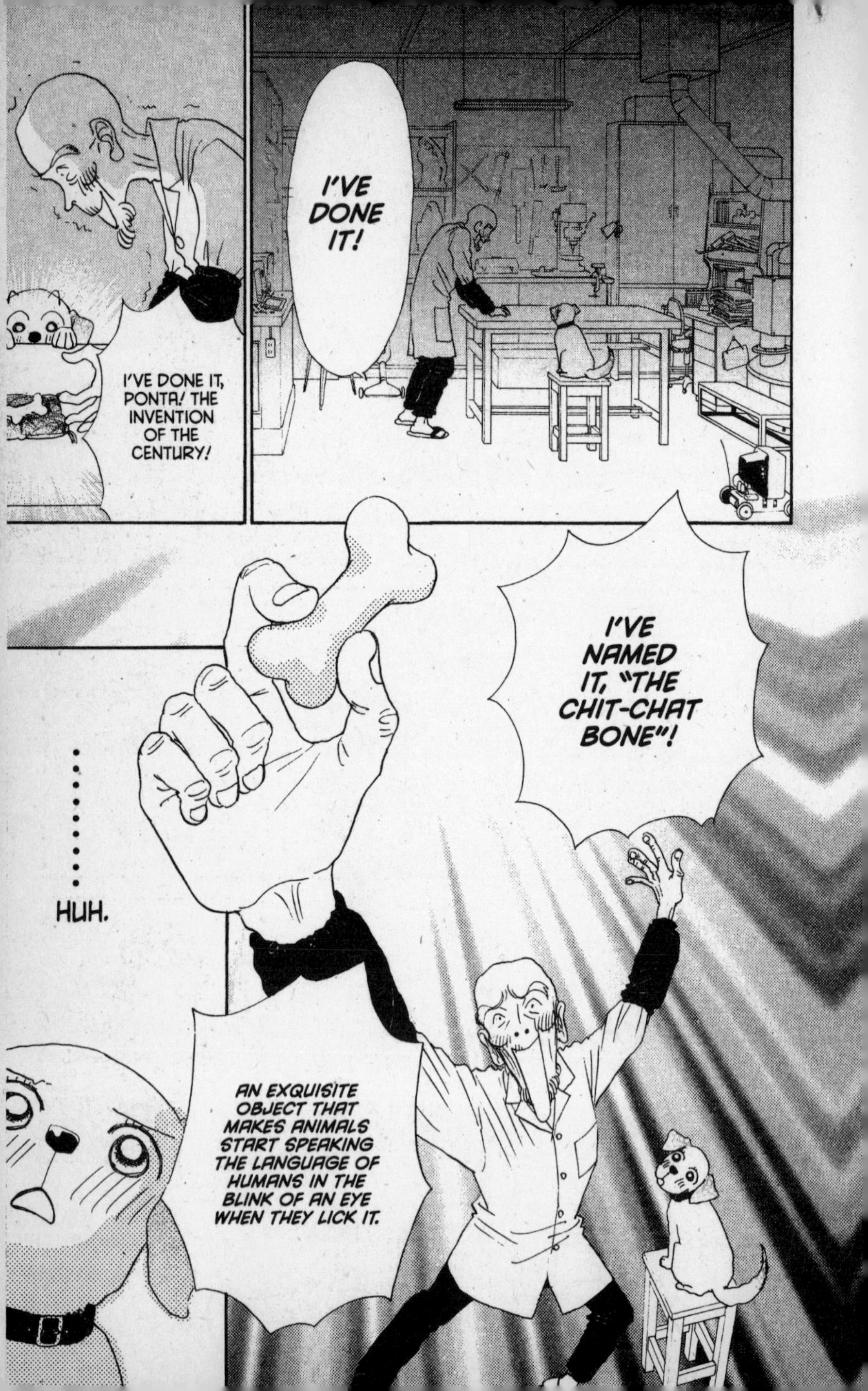
I'VE DONE IT!
I'VE DONE IT, PONTA! THE INVENTION OF THE CENTURY!
I'VE NAMED IT, "THE CHIT-CHAT BONE"!
AN EXQUISITE OBJECT THAT MAKES ANIMALS START SPEAKING THE LANGUAGE OF HUMANS IN THE BLINK OF AN EYE WHEN THEY LICK IT.
....
HUH.

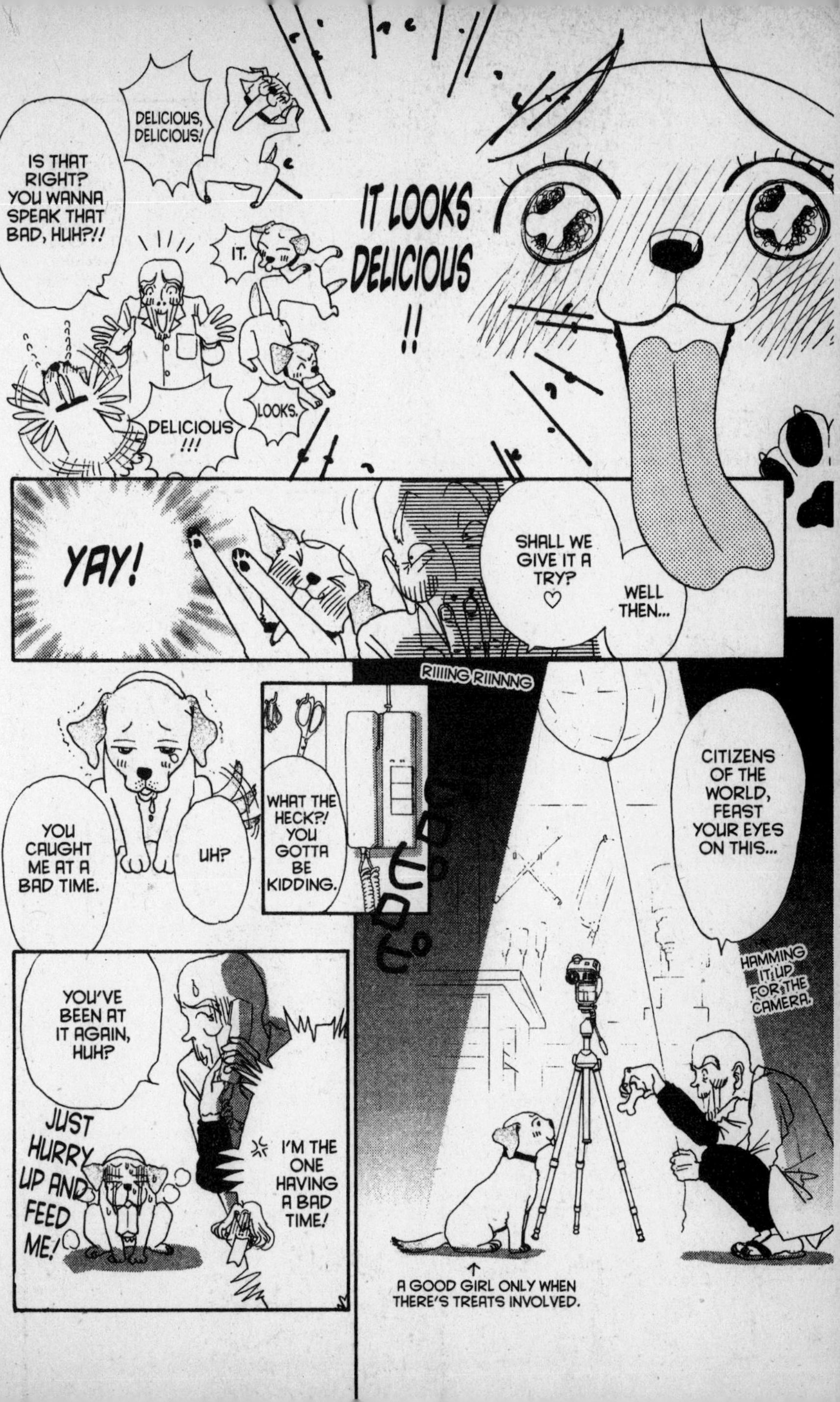
IT LOOKS DELICIOUS !!
DELICIOUS, DELICIOUS!
IS THAT RIGHT? YOU WANNA SPEAK THAT BAD, HUH?!!
IT.
LOOKS.
DELICIOUS !!!
WELL THEN...
SHALL WE GIVE IT A TRY? ♡
YAY!
CITIZENS OF THE WORLD, FEAST YOUR EYES ON THIS...
HAMMING IT UP FOR THE CAMERA.
A GOOD GIRL ONLY WHEN THERE'S TREATS INVOLVED.
RIIIING RIINNNG
WHAT THE HECK?! YOU GOTTA BE KIDDING.
UH?
YOU CAUGHT ME AT A BAD TIME.
YOU'VE BEEN AT IT AGAIN, HUH?
I'M THE ONE HAVING A BAD TIME!
JUST HURRY UP AND FEED ME!

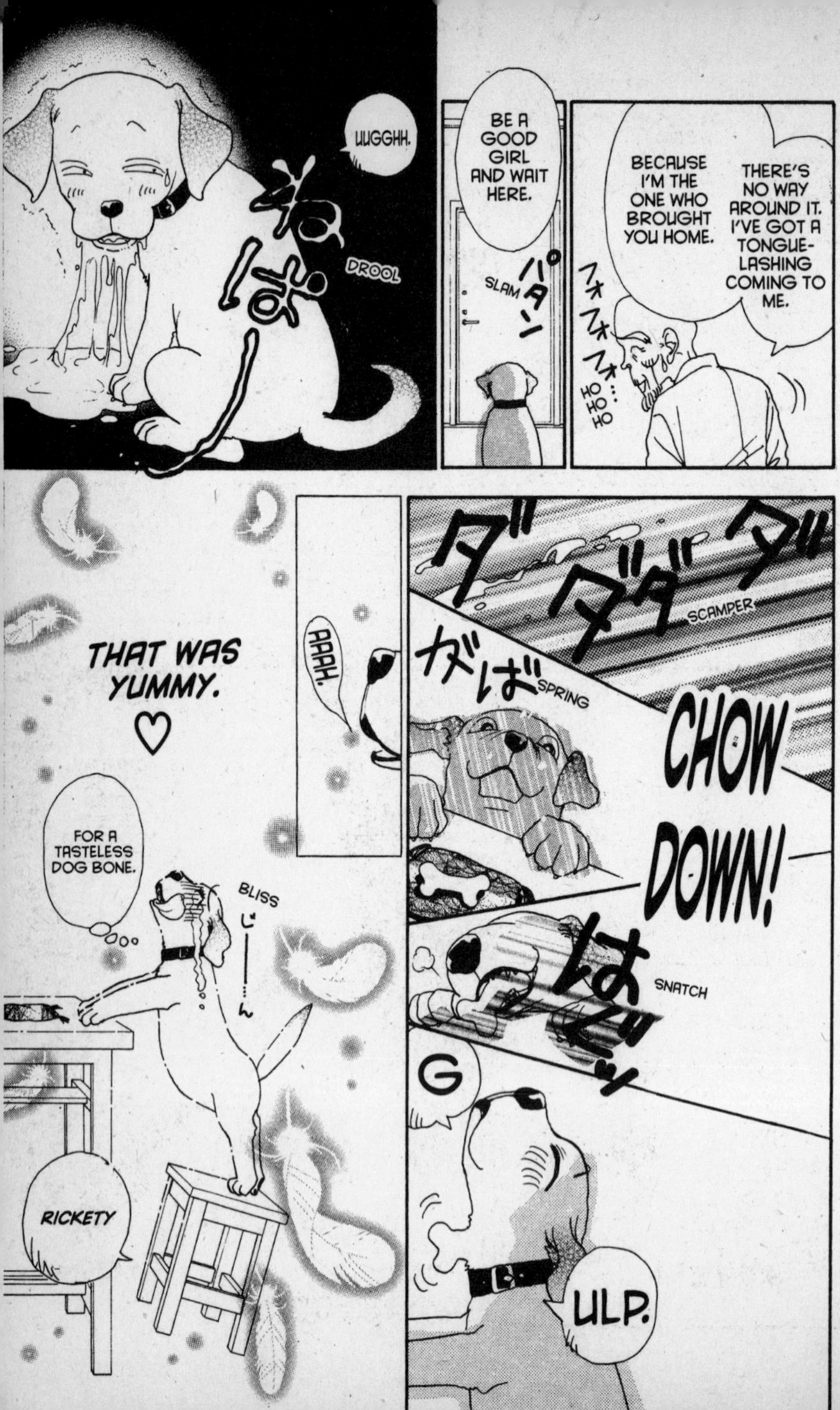

THERE'S NO WAY AROUND IT. I'VE GOT A TONGUE-LASHING COMING TO ME.
BECAUSE I'M THE ONE WHO BROUGHT YOU HOME.
フォフォフォ… HO HO HO
BE A GOOD GIRL AND WAIT HERE.
パタン SLAM
UUGGHH.
DROOL
ダダダダ SCAMPER
がば SPRING
CHOW DOWN!
SNATCH
G
ULP.
AAAH.
THAT WAS YUMMY. ♡
FOR A TASTELESS DOG BONE.
BLISS
RICKETY

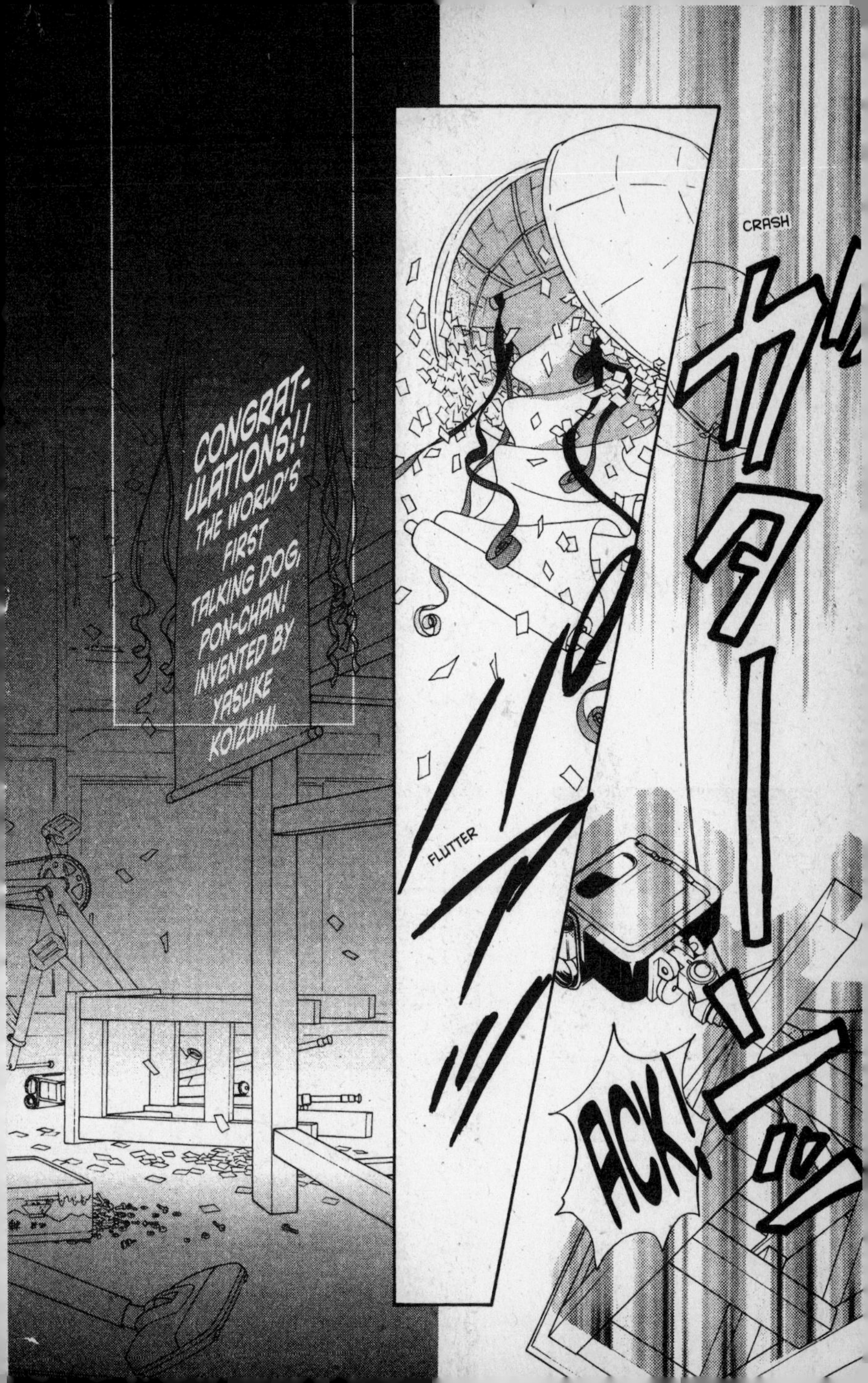
CRASH
ACK!
FLUTTER
CONGRATULATIONS!! THE WORLD'S FIRST TALKING DOG, PON-CHAN! INVENTED BY YASUKE KOIZUMI.

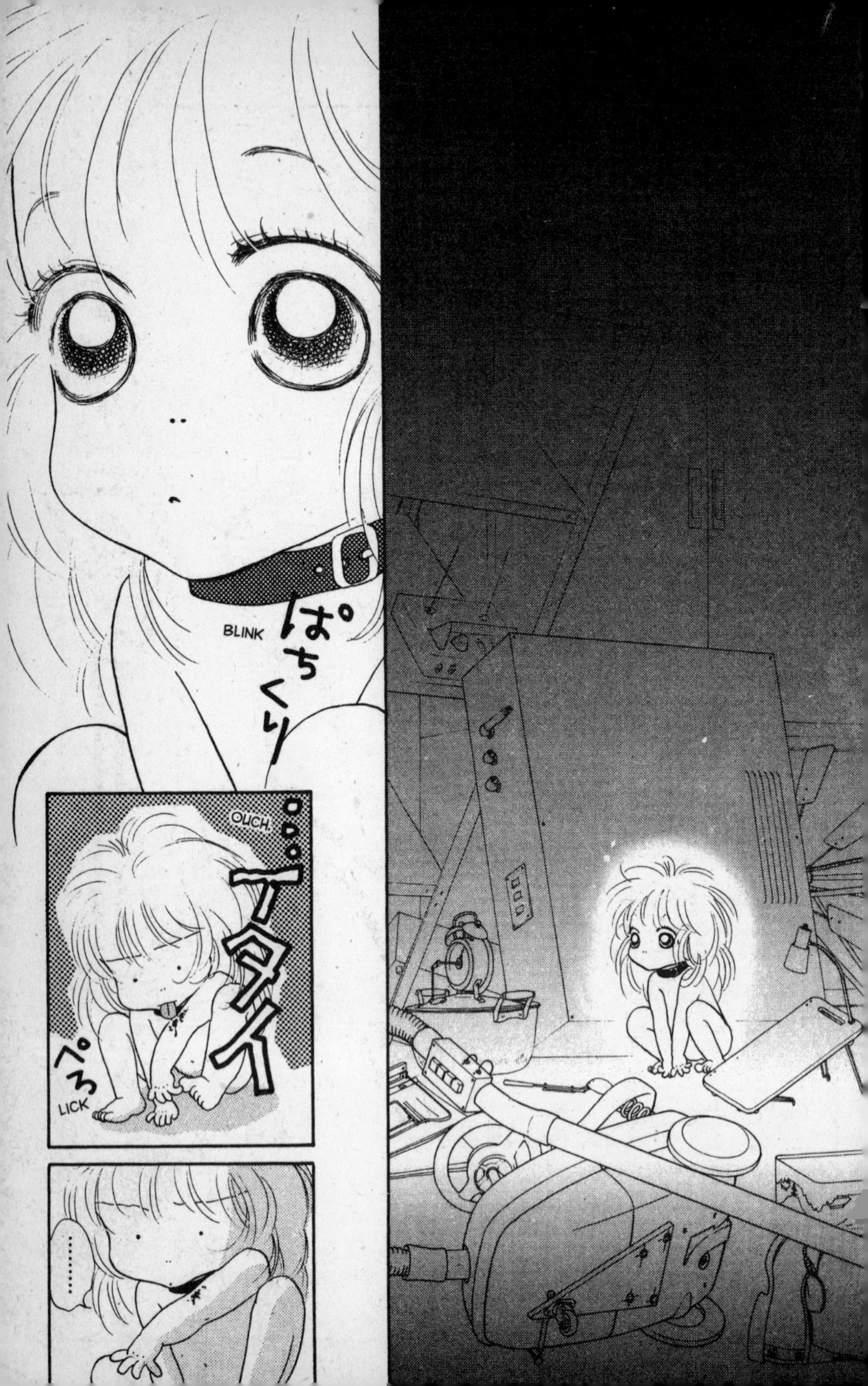
ぱちくり
BLINK
。。。イタイ
OUCH.
ぺろ
LICK
......

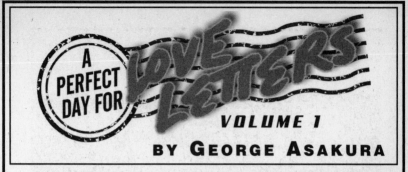

A PERFECT DAY FOR LOVE LETTERS
VOLUME 1
BY GEORGE ASAKURA

FIVE LETTERS, FIVE STORIES . . . FIVE CHANCES AT LOVE

What would you do if someone you didn't know sent you a letter that said they'd been watching you? Would it creep you out? Would you write back? In "Love Letters in the Library," two very different people find common ground through their love of books.

If someone spoke to your heart in a letter but had a bad reputation... would you take a chance in getting to know him? "To One Who Doesn't Know Me" reminds us not to judge a book by its cover.

"Flowers Blooming in the Snow" is a beautiful story about a lost young girl who learns to leave her troubled past behind, with the help of a caring boy.

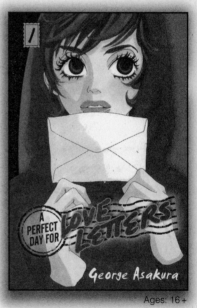

Ages: 16 +

George Asakura leads us through these and other stories with humor, wit, and enough mystery to keep us guessing with each new delivery. You've got mail!

Includes special extras after the story!

VOLUME 1: On sale June 28, 2005

For more information and to sign up for Del Rey's manga e-newsletter, visit www.delreymanga.com

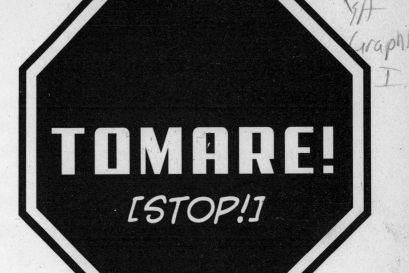

You are going the wrong way!

Manga is a completely different
type of reading experience.

To start at the *beginning*, go to the *end!*

That's right! Authentic manga is read the traditional Japanese
way—from right to left. Exactly the *opposite* of how American
books are read. It's easy to follow: Just go to the other end of
the book, and read each page—and each panel—from right side
to left side, starting at the top right. Now you're experiencing
manga as it was meant to be.

FR

OCT '02